1960

"Mrs. Joe Mehal
1831 S. Harr

This book may be kept

FOURTEEN DAYS

A fine will be charged for each day the book is kept overtime.

GAYLORD 142			PRINTED IN U.S.A.

A CENTURY OF
THE CATHOLIC ESSAY

A CENTURY OF
THE CATHOLIC ESSAY

Edited with Biographical Notes by

RAPHAEL H. GROSS, C.PP.S.
DEPARTMENT OF ENGLISH, ST. JOSEPH'S COLLEGE,
COLLEGEVILLE, INDIANA

J. B. LIPPINCOTT COMPANY
PHILADELPHIA   *NEW YORK*

Imprimi Potest

JOSEPH M. MARLING, C.PP.S.
Provincial

Imprimatur

✠ JOHN G. BENNETT, D.D.
Bishop of Lafayette in Indiana

Feast of the Patronage of St. Joseph
Lafayette, 1946

TO MY FATHER AND MOTHER

PREFACE

ONE hundred years ago, on October 9, 1845, John Henry Newman returned to the Faith of his fathers; one hundred years ago, on that day, began the resurgence of English Catholic life and culture. Younger, more vital, and more articulate than she had been for centuries, the Church in England (and in all English-speaking countries, for that matter) survived what Wilfrid Ward called a "state of siege." Today Newman's glowing prophecy of the Church's resurrection, so masterfully set forth in his sermon, "The Second Spring," is clothed in reality; today, likewise, Newman's other, despairing vision of materialism and irreligion rising like a tide "until only the tops of the mountains would be seen like islands in the waste of waters" is a menace to all Christian civilization.

But out of the Second Spring have come leaders, thinkers, and writers who, "like islands in the waste of waters," bring hope to a world deluged. Inspired by their rich Catholic heritage, they have brought forth a remarkable literature that may yet stem the rising tide. They have heeded the advice of Alice Meynell, "Let us be of the center, not of the province"; many of them have taken literally Louise Imogen Guiney's plea, "Let us crucify ourselves upon our pens."

Happily, the work of these Catholic writers is being each day more widely disseminated, appreciated, and studied. The story of the Revival has been well told by Thureau-Dangin, Maisie Ward, and others. In his *The Catholic Literary Revival,* Calvert Alexander wrote an enthusiastic study of the literature. Thomas William Walsh, Joyce Kilmer, Shane Leslie, Theodore Maynard and, latest, Alfred Noyes, have in their anthologies made accessible the best poetry of the Revival. The short story was recently popularized by Mary Curtin and Sister Mariella. Catholic prose has been given place by Theodore Maynard and by Carver and Geyer's thin volume, *Representative Catholic Essays*. Both of these collections, unfortunately, have been out of print for some years.

The Catholic essay, as a distinct literary genre, is too important a contribution to present-day literature ever to be neglected. For out of the Second Spring have appeared some of the most accomplished essayists of English literature. Few will deny that Newman, Chesterton, and Belloc stand in the front rank of the English masters. So also Alice Meynell, Louise Guiney, and Agnes Repplier. Of Mrs. Meynell it has been said, "No woman has ever written an essay to compare with *The Rhythm of Life*." Christopher Morley has pronounced Miss Guiney "one of the rarest poets and most delicately poised essayists" America has produced. And Miss Repplier is still the recognized dean of American essayists.

To bring the work of these and of other Catholic essayists into focus for the general reader is the aim of this new collection. Catholics and non-Catholics alike, who are concerned with true cultural values, will (I trust) find here a point of view, at once eternally old and eternally new, together with freshness and artistic excellence. The book should prove valuable, too, as supplementary reading in any course on the essay or on Catholic literature. In so far as possible I have tried to assemble representative pieces of the authors included. I have given consideration, moreover, to variety of type and of theme. Part One is largely devoted to the informal essay, and Part Two to the more learned, formal essay. Within these main divisions are such examples of the short-story type of essay as Talbot's "A Date for Saturday Night" and Eden's "The Pensioner of the Pied Brothers"; such biographical essays as Daly's "Charles Waterton: Naturalist" and Martindale's "Hermann the Cripple." The book review essay is represented

by Windle's "The Everlasting Man," and the scholarly essay
by Sister Madeleva's "Chaucer's Nuns."

Not all the essays here gathered tend to indoctrinate or
to increase one's sense of world crisis. For the Catholic writer
frequently steps down from his high purpose to chat familiarly
with his friends on any and all subjects. Yet even in his "good
talk" he is in harmony with Catholic teaching: all that he
writes or speaks is governed, however indirectly, by his Catholic spirit and outlook.

Putting this book together has been something of a burden
light. My sorest disappointment is that I had necessarily to omit
many a choice piece—of men like Newman, Chesterton, and
Belloc, who rightfully have their own anthologies. Such essays
as Heywood Broun's "The Fifty-first Dragon," Agnes Repplier's "A Point of History," and Compton Mackenzie's "Adventures in Food" strongly sought admission. The work of
Shane Leslie, Maurice Francis Egan, Christopher Hollis,
Theodore Maynard, Michael Williams, and others seek an ad-
ditional series. Reviewers, no less than readers, may be
tempted to score the anthologist for his omissions, but be sure,
I have tried genuinely to be a good host. To give here a general study of modern Catholic prose could only be, at best,
inadequate and, in view of the excellent chapters in Alexander's
book, perhaps superfluous. The essays speak for themselves.

The gladdest portion of my task remains—to thank all who
in any way contributed to the making of this book. First, there
are, besides the original authors, the publishers and the copyright holders, who have generously granted me permission to
reprint. There are, second, my fellow-members in the Society
of the Precious Blood, my colleagues on the faculty of St.
Joseph's of Indiana, and my friends—all of whom by their
interest made a greater contribution to this book than they
know. To some I owe a special debt of gratitude: to my former co-worker in the Department of English, the late Father
Paul F. Speckbaugh, a true scholar and a Christ-like priest, by
whose inspiration this book was first begun; to Father Clar-

ence Schuerman, Librarian of St. Joseph's of Indiana, and his assistant, Brother Philip, for their help in obtaining necessary books and references; to Fathers Edwin Kaiser, Rufus Esser, and Edward Maziarz, my associates on the faculty, for their gracious advice and suggestions; to Father Norman Koller, pastor of St. Augustine's Church, Youngstown, Ohio, and Father Marcellus Dreiling, of the St. Joseph's faculty, for their invaluable aid in preparing the manuscript; to Mr. Vincent Starrett, of The Chicago *Tribune,* for tracing a particular essay; to Mrs. Carl Caston, for typing portions of the copy; and to Miss Grace Guiney, Oxford, England, for sending me the emendated versions of Louise Imogen Guiney's "On the Delights of an Incognito" and "The Puppy: A Portrait."

R. H. G.

CONTENTS

PART ONE

The Texture of Life

Fellow-travelers

Length and Breadth

Amenities

PART TWO

Culture and Education

Literature and Art

Biography and Criticism

The Church and the Modern World

PART ONE

1

THE TEXTURE OF LIFE

The Rhythm of Life

BY

ALICE MEYNELL

IF LIFE IS not always poetical, it is at least metrical. Periodicity rules over the mental experience of man, according to the path of the orbit of his thoughts. Distances are not gauged, ellipses not measured, velocities not ascertained, times not known. Nevertheless, the recurrence is sure. What the mind suffered last week, or last year, it does not suffer now; but it will suffer again next week or next year. Happiness is not a matter of events; it depends upon the tides of the mind. Disease is metrical, closing in at shorter and shorter periods towards death, sweeping abroad at longer and longer intervals towards recovery. Sorrow for one cause was intolerable yesterday, and will be intolerable to-morrow; to-day it is easy to bear, but the cause has not passed. Even the burden of a spiritual distress unsolved is bound to leave the heart to a temporary peace; and remorse itself does not remain—it returns. Gaiety takes us by a dear surprise. If we had made a course of notes of its visits, we might have been on the watch, and would have had an expectation instead of a discovery. No one makes such observations; in all the diaries of students of the interior

From *Essays,* by Alice Meynell. Reprinted by permission of the copyright owner, Mr. Wilfrid Meynell.

world, there have never come to light the records of the Kepler of such cycles. But Thomas à Kempis knew of the recurrences, if he did not measure them. In his cell alone with the elements—"What wouldst thou more than these? for out of these were all things made"—he learnt the stay to be found in the depth of the hour of bitterness, and the remembrance that restrains the soul at the coming of the moment of delight, giving it a more conscious welcome, but presaging for it an inexorable flight. And "rarely, rarely comest thou," sighed Shelley, not to Delight merely, but to the Spirit of Delight. Delight can be compelled beforehand, called, and constrained to our service—Ariel can be bound to a daily task; but such artificial violence throws life out of metre, and it is not the spirit that is thus compelled. *That* flits upon an orbit elliptically or parabolically or hyperbolically curved, keeping no man knows what trysts with Time.

It seems fit that Shelley and the author of the "Imitation" should both have been keen and simple enough to perceive these flights, and to guess at the order of this periodicity. Both souls were in close touch with the spirits of their several worlds, and no deliberate human rules, no infractions of the liberty and law of the universal movement, kept from them the knowledge of recurrences. *Eppur si muove.* They knew that presence does not exist without absence; they knew that what is just upon its flight of farewell is already on its long path of return. They knew that what is approaching to the very touch is hastening towards departure. "O wind," cried Shelley, in autumn,

> *O wind,*
> *If winter comes can spring be far behind?*

They knew that the flux is equal to the reflux; that to interrupt with unlawful recurrences, out of time, is to weaken the impulse of onset and retreat; the sweep and impetus of movement. To live in constant efforts after an equal life, whether the equality be sought in mental production, or in spiritual

sweetness, or in the joy of the senses, is to live without either
rest or full activity. The souls of certain of the saints, being
singularly simple and single, have been in the most complete
subjection to the law of periodicity. Ecstasy and desolation
visited them by seasons. They endured, during spaces of
vacant time, the interior loss of all for which they had sacrificed the world. They rejoiced in the uncovenanted beatitude
of sweetness alighting in their hearts. Like them are the
poets whom, three times or ten times in the course of a long
life, the Muse has approached, touched, and forsaken. And
yet hardly like them; not always so docile, nor so wholly prepared for the departure, the brevity, of the golden and irrev-
ocable hour. Few poets have fully recognized the metrical
absence of their Muse. For full recognition is expressed in
one only way—silence.

It has been found that several tribes in Africa and in
America worship the moon, and not the sun; a great number
worship both; but no tribes are known to adore the sun, and
not the moon. On her depend the tides; and she is Selene,
mother of Herse, bringer of the dews that recurrently irri-
gate lands where rain is rare. More than any other companion of earth is she the Measurer. Early Indo-Germanic
languages knew her by that name. Her metrical phases are
the symbol of the order of recurrence. Constancy in approach
and in departure is the reason of her inconstancies. Juliet
will not receive a vow spoken in invocation of the moon; but
Juliet did not live to know that love itself has tidal times—
lapses and ebbs which are due to the metrical rule of the
interior heart, but which the lover vainly and unkindly attributes to some outward alteration in the beloved. For man
—except those elect already named—is hardly aware of periodicity. The individual man either never learns it fully, or
learns it late. And he learns it so late, because it is a matter
of cumulative experience upon which cumulative evidence is
long lacking. It is in the after-part of each life that the law
is learnt so definitely as to do away with the hope or fear of

continuance. That young sorrow comes so near to despair is a result of this young ignorance. So is the early hope of great achievement. Life seems so long, and its capacity so great, to one who knows nothing of all the intervals it needs must hold—intervals between aspirations, between actions, pauses as inevitable as the pauses of sleep. And life looks impossible to the young unfortunate, unaware of the inevitable and unfailing refreshment. It would be for their peace to learn that there is a tide in the affairs of men, in a sense more subtle— if it is not too audacious to add a meaning to Shakespeare— than the phrase was meant to contain. Their joy is flying away from them on its way home; their life will wax and wane; and if they would be wise, they must wake and rest in its phases, knowing that they are ruled by the law that commands all things—a sun's revolutions and the rhythmic pangs of maternity.

Definition of a Gentleman

BY

JOHN HENRY NEWMAN

. . . IT IS ALMOST a definition of a gentleman to say he is one who never inflicts pain. This description is both refined and, as far as it goes, accurate. He is mainly occupied in merely removing the obstacles which hinder the free and unembarrassed action of those about him; and he concurs with their movements rather than takes the initiative himself. His benefits may be considered as parallel to what are called comforts or conveniences in arrangements of a personal nature:

From *The Idea of a University,* by John Henry Newman. Reprinted by permission of the publisher, Longmans, Green & Co., Inc., New York.

like an easy chair or a good fire, which do their part in dispelling cold and fatigue, though nature provides both means of rest and animal heat without them. The true gentleman in like manner carefully avoids whatever may cause a jar or a jolt in the minds of those with whom he is cast;—all clashing of opinion, or collision of feeling, all restraint, or suspicion, or gloom, or resentment, his great concern being to make every one at their ease and at home. He has his eyes on all his company; he is tender towards the bashful, gentle towards the distant, and merciful towards the absurd; he can recollect to whom he is speaking; he guards against unseasonable allusions, or topics which may irritate; he is seldom prominent in conversation, and never wearisome. He makes light of favours while he does them, and seems to be receiving when he is conferring. He never speaks of himself except when compelled, never defends himself by a mere retort, he has no ears for slander or gossip, is scrupulous in imputing motives to those who interfere with him, and interprets every thing for the best. He is never mean or little in his disputes, never takes unfair advantage, never mistakes personalities or sharp sayings for arguments, or insinuates evils which he dare not say out. From a long-sighted prudence, he observes the maxim of the ancient sage, that we should ever conduct ourselves towards our enemy as if he were one day to be our friend. He has too much good sense to be affronted at insults, he is too well employed to remember injuries, and too indolent to bear malice. He is patient, forbearing, and resigned, on philosophical principles; he submits to pain, because it is inevitable, to bereavement, because it is irreparable, and to death, because it is his destiny. If he engages in controversy of any kind, his disciplined intellect preserves him from the blundering discourtesy of better, perhaps, but less educated minds; who, like blunt weapons, tear and hack instead of cutting clean, who mistake the point in argument, waste their strength on trifles, misconceive their adversary, and leave the question more involved than they find it. He may be right or wrong in his opinion, but he is too clear-headed to be unjust; he is as simple as he is forcible, and as brief as he is decisive. Nowhere shall we find greater candour, consideration, indulgence; he throws himself into the minds of his opponents, he accounts for their mistakes. He knows the weakness of human reason as well as its strength, its province and its limits. If he be an unbeliever, he will be too profound and large-minded to ridicule religion or to act against it; he is too wise to be a dogmatist or fanatic in his infidelity. He respects piety and devotion; he even supports institutions as venerable, beautiful, or useful, to which he does not assent; he honours the ministers of religion, and it contents him to decline its mysteries without assailing or denouncing them. He is a friend of religious toleration, and that, not only because his philosophy has taught him to look on all forms of faith with an impartial eye, but also from the gentleness and effeminacy of feeling, which is the attendant on civilization.

Not that he may not hold a religion too, in his own way, even when he is not a Christian. In that case his religion is one of imagination and sentiment; it is the embodiment of those ideas of the sublime, majestic, and beautiful, without which there can be no large philosophy. Sometimes he acknowledges the being of God, sometimes he invests an unknown principle or quality with the attributes of perfection. And this deduction of his reason, or creation of his fancy, he makes the occasion of such excellent thoughts, and the starting-point of so varied and systematic a teaching, that he even seems like a disciple of Christianity itself. From the very accuracy and steadiness of his logical powers, he is able to see what sentiments are consistent in those who hold any religious doctrine at all, and he appears to others to feel and to hold a whole circle of theological truths, which exist in his mind not otherwise than as a number of deductions.

Goodness and Gayety

BY

AGNES REPPLIER

"Can surly Virtue hope to find a friend?"
—Dr. Johnson

SIR LESLIE STEPHEN has recorded his conviction that a sense of humour, being irreconcilable with some of the cardinal virtues, is lacking in most good men. Father Faber asserted, on the contrary, that a sense of humour is a great help in the religious life, and emphasized this somewhat unusual point of view with the decisive statement: "Perhaps nature does not contribute a greater help to grace than this."

Here are conflicting verdicts to be well considered. Sir Leslie Stephen knew more about humour than did Father Faber; Father Faber knew more about "grace" than did Sir Leslie Stephen; and both disputants were widely acquainted with their fellow-men. Sir Leslie Stephen had a pretty wit of his own, but it may have lacked the qualities which make for holiness. There was in it the element of denial. He seldom entered the shrine where we worship our ideals in secret. He stood outside, remarks Mr. Birrell cheerily, "with a pail of cold water." Father Faber also possessed a vein of irony which was the outcome of a priestly experience with the cherished foibles of the world. He entered unbidden into the shrine where we worship our illusions in secret, and chilled us with unwelcome truths. I know of no harder experience than this. It takes time and trouble to persuade ourselves that the things we want to do are the things we ought to do.

From *Americans and Others*, by Agnes Repplier. Reprinted by arrangement with the publisher. Houghton Mifflin Company, Boston.

We balance our spiritual accounts with care. We insert glib phrases about duty into all our reckonings. There is nothing, or next to nothing, which cannot, if adroitly catalogued, be considered a duty; and it is this delicate mental adjustment which is disturbed by Father Faber's ridicule. "Self-deceit," he caustically observes, "seems to thrive on prayer, and to grow fat on contemplation."

If a sense of humour forces us to be candid with ourselves, then it can be reconciled, not only with the cardinal virtues—which are but a chilly quartette—but with the flaming charities which have consumed the souls of saints. The true humorist, objects Sir Leslie Stephen, sees the world as a tragi-comedy, a Vanity Fair, in which enthusiasm is out of place. But if the true humorist also sees himself presiding, in the sacred name of duty, over a booth in Vanity Fair, he may yet reach perfection. What Father Faber opposed so strenuously were, not the vanities of the profane, of the openly and cheerfully unregenerate; but the vanities of a devout and fashionable congregation, making especial terms—by virtue of its exalted station—with Providence. These were the people whom he regarded all his priestly life with whimsical dismay. "Their voluntary social arrangements," he wrote in "Spiritual Conferences," "are the tyranny of circumstance, claiming our tenderest pity, and to be managed like the work of a Xavier, or a Vincent of Paul, which hardly left the saints time to pray. Their sheer worldliness is to be considered as an interior trial, with all manner of cloudy grand things to be said about it. They must avoid uneasiness, for such great graces as theirs can grow only in calmness and tranquillity."

This is irony rather than humour, but it implies a capacity to see the tragi-comedy of the world, without necessarily losing the power of enthusiasm. It also explains why Father Faber regarded an honest sense of the ridiculous as a help to goodness. The man or woman who is impervious to the absurd cannot well be stripped of self-delusion. For him, for her, there is no shaft which wounds. The admirable advice of

Thomas à Kempis to keep away from people whom we desire
to please, and the quiet perfection of his warning to the cen-
sorious, "In judging others, a man toileth in vain; for the
most part he is mistaken, and he easily sinneth; but in judging
and scrutinizing himself, he always labour th with profit,"
can make their just appeal only to the humorous sense. So,
too, the counsel of Saint Francis de Sales to the nuns who
wanted to go barefooted, "Keep your shoes and change your
brains"; the cautious query of Pope Gregory the First, concerning John the Faster, "Does he abstain even from the
truth?" Cardinal Newman's axiom, "It is never worth while
to call whity-brown white, for the sake of avoiding scandal";
and Father Faber's own felicitous comment on religious
"hedgers," "A moderation which consists in taking immod-
erate liberties with God is hardly what the Fathers of the
Desert meant when they preached their crusade in favour
of discretion";—are all spoken to those hardy and humorous
souls who can bear to be honest with themselves.

The ardent reformer, intolerant of the ordinary processes
of life, the ardent philanthropist, intolerant of an imperfect
civilization, the ardent zealot, intolerant of man's unspiritual
nature, are seldom disposed to gayety. A noble impatience
of spirit inclines them to anger or to sadness. John Wesley,
reformer, philanthropist, zealot, and surpassingly great in
all three characters, strangled within his own breast the simple
desire to be gay. He was a young man when he formed the
resolution, "to labour after continual seriousness, not willingly indulging myself in the least levity of behaviour, or in
laughter,—no, not for a moment"; and for more than fifty
years he kept—probably with no great difficulty—this stern
resolve. The mediæval saying, that laughter has sin for a
father and folly for a mother, would have meant to Wesley
more than a figure of speech. Nothing could rob him of a
dry and bitter humour ("They won't let me go to Bedlam,"
he wrote, "because they say I make the inmates mad, nor
into Newgate, because I make them wicked"); but there was

little in his creed or in the scenes of his labours to promote cheerfulness of spirit.

This disciplining of nature, honest, erring human nature, which could, if permitted, make out a fair case for itself, is not an essential element of the evangelist's code. In the hands of men less great than Wesley, it has been known to nullify the work of a lifetime. The Lincolnshire farmer who, after listening to a sermon on Hell, said to his wife, "Noä, Sally, it woänt do. Noä constitootion could stand it," expressed in his own fashion the healthy limit of endurance. Our spiritual constitutions break under a pitiless strain. When we read in the diary of Henry Alline, quoted by Dr. William James in his "Varieties of Religious Experience," "On Wednesday the twelfth I preached at a wedding, and had the happiness thereby to be the means of excluding the carnal mirth," we are not merely sorry for the wedding guests, but beset by doubts as to their moral gain.

Why should Henry Martyn, that fervent young missionary who gave his life for his cause with the straight-forward simplicity of a soldier, have regretted so bitterly an occasional lapse into good spirits? He was inhumanly serious, and he prayed by night and day to be saved from his "besetting sin" of levity. He was consumed by the flame of religious zeal, and he bewailed at grievous length, in his diary, his "light, worldly spirit." He toiled unrestingly, taking no heed of his own physical weakness, and he asked himself (when he had a minute to spare) what would become of his soul, should he be struck dead in a "careless mood." We have Mr. Birrell's word for it that once, in an old book about India, he came across an after-dinner jest of Henry Martyn's; but the idea was so incongruous that the startled essayist was disposed to doubt the evidence of his senses. "There must have been a mistake somewhere."

To such a man the world is not, and never can be, a tragicomedy, and laughter seems forever out of place. When a Madeira negress, a good Christian after her benighted fashion, asked Martyn if the English were ever baptized, he did not think the innocent question funny, he thought it horrible. He found Saint Basil's writings unsatisfactory, as lacking "evangelical truth"; and, could he have heard this great doctor of the Church fling back a witticism in the court of an angry magistrate, he would probably have felt more doubtful than ever concerning the status of the early Fathers. It is a relief to turn from the letters of Martyn, with their aloofness from the cheerful currents of earth, to the letters of Bishop Heber, who, albeit a missionary and a keen one, had always a laugh for the absurdities which beset his wandering life. He could even tell with relish the story of the drunken pedlar whom he met in Wales, and who confided to him that, having sold all his wares, he was trying to drink up the proceeds before he got home, lest his wife should take the money away from him. Heber, using the argument which he felt would be of most avail, tried to frighten the man into soberness by picturing his wife's wrath; whereupon the adroit scamp replied that he knew what *that* would be, and had taken the precaution to have his hair cut short, so that she could not get a grip on it. Martyn could no more have chuckled over this depravity than he could have chuckled over the fallen angels; but Saint Teresa could have laughed outright, her wonderful, merry, infectious laugh; and have then proceeded to plead, to scold, to threaten, to persuade, until a chastened and repentant pedlar, money in hand, and some dim promptings to goodness tugging at his heart, would have tramped bravely and soberly home.

It is so much the custom to obliterate from religious memoirs all vigorous human traits, all incidents which do not tend to edification, and all contemporary criticism which cannot be smoothed into praise, that what is left seems to the disheartened reader only a pale shadow of life. It is hard to make any biography illustrate a theme, or prove an argument; and the process by which such results are obtained is so artificial as to be open to the charge of untruth. Because General

Havelock was a good Baptist as well as a good soldier, because he expressed a belief in the efficacy of prayer (like Cromwell's "Trust in God, and keep your powder dry"), and because he wrote to his wife, when sent to the relief of Lucknow, "May God give me wisdom and strength for the work!" —which, after all, was a natural enough thing for any man to say—he was made the subject of a memoir determinedly and depressingly devout, in which his family letters were annotated as though they were the epistles of Saint Paul. Yet this was the man who, when Lucknow *was* relieved, behaved as if nothing out of the ordinary had happened to besiegers or besieged. "He shook hands with me," wrote Lady Inglis in her journal, "and observed that he feared we had suffered a great deal." That was all. He might have said as much had the little garrison been incommoded by a spell of unusual heat, or by an epidemic of measles.

As a matter of fact, piety is a by no means uncommon attribute of soldiers, and there was no need on the part of the Reverend Mr. Brock, who compiled these shadowy pages, to write as though General Havelock had been a rare species of the genius military. We know that what the English Puritans especially resented in Prince Rupert was his insistence on regimental prayers. They could pardon his raids, his breathless charges, his bewildering habit of appearing where he was least expected or desired; but that he should usurp their own especial prerogative of piety was more than they could bear. It is probable that Rupert's own private petitions resembled the memorable prayer offered by Sir Jacob Astley (a hardy old Cavalier who was both devout and humourous) before the battle of Edgehill: "Oh, Lord, Thou knowest how busy I must be this day. If I forget Thee, do not Thou forget me. March on, boys!"

If it were not for a few illuminating anecdotes, and the thrice blessed custom of letter writing, we should never know what manner of thing human goodness, exalted human goodness, is; and so acquiesce ignorantly in Sir Leslie Stephen's judgment. The sinners of the world stand out clear and distinct, full of vitality, and of an engaging candour. The saints of Heaven shine dimly through a nebulous haze of hagiology. They are embodiments of inaccessible virtues, as remote from us and from our neighbours as if they had lived on another planet. There is no more use in asking us to imitate these incomprehensible creatures than there would be in asking us to climb by easy stages to the moon. Without some common denominator, sinner and saint are as aloof from each other as sinner and archangel. Without some clue to the saint's spiritual identity, the record of his labours and hardships, fasts, visions, and miracles, offers nothing more helpful than bewilderment. We may be edified or we may be sceptical, according to our temperament and training; but a profound unconcern devitalizes both scepticism and edification. What have we mortals in common with these perfected prodigies of grace?

It was Cardinal Newman who first entered a protest against "minced" saints, against the pious and popular custom of chopping up human records into lessons for the devout. He took exception to the hagiological licence which assigns lofty motives to trivial actions. "The saint from humility made no reply." "The saint was silent out of compassion for the ignorance of the speaker." He invited us to approach the Fathers of the Church in their unguarded moments, in their ordinary avocations, in their moods of gayety and depression; and, when we accepted the invitation, these figures, lofty and remote, became imbued with life. It is one thing to know that Saint Chrysostom retired at twenty-three to a monastery near Antioch, and there spent six years in seclusion and study. It is another and more enlightening thing to be made aware, through the medium of his own letters, that he took this step with reasonable doubts and misgivings—doubts which extended to the freshness of the monastery bread, misgivings which concerned themselves with the sweetness of the monastery oil. And when we read these candid expressions of anxiety, Saint Chrysostom, by virtue of his healthy young appetite, and his distaste (which any poor sinner can share) for rancid oil, becomes a man and a brother. It is yet more consoling to know that when well advanced in sainthood, when old, austere, exiled, and suffering many privations for con- science' sake, Chrysostom was still disposed to be a trifle fastidious about his bread. He writes from Cæsarea to Theodora that he has at last found clean water to drink, and bread which can be chewed. "Moreover, I no longer wash myself in broken crockery, but have contrived some sort of bath; also I have a bed to which I can confine myself."

If Saint Chrysostom possessed, according to Newman, a cheerful temper, and "a sunniness of mind all his own," Saint Gregory of Nazianzus was a fair humourist, and Saint Basil was a wit. "Pensive playfulness" is Newman's phrase for Basil, but there was a speed about his retorts which did not always savour of pensiveness. When the furious governor of Pontus threatened to tear out his liver, Basil, a confirmed invalid, replied suavely, "It is a kind intention. My liver, as at present located, has given me nothing but uneasiness."

To Gregory, Basil was not only guide, philosopher, and friend; but also a cherished target for his jests. It has been wisely said that we cannot really love anybody at whom we never laugh. Gregory loved Basil, revered him, and laughed at him. Does Basil complain, not unnaturally that Tiberina is cold, damp, and muddy, Gregory writes to him unsympathet- ically that he is a "clean-footed, tip-toeing, capering man." Does Basil promise a visit, Gregory sends word to Amphil- ochus that he must have some fine pot-herbs, "lest Basil should be hungry and cross." Does Gregory visit Basil in his solitude at Pontus, he expresses in no measured terms his sense of the discomfort he endures. It would be hard to find, in all the annals of correspondence, a letter written with a more laud- able and well-defined intention of teasing its recipient, than the one dispatched to Basil by Gregory after he has made good his escape from the austerities of his friend's house-keeping.

"I have remembrance of the bread and of the broth,—so they were named,—and shall remember them; how my teeth stuck in your hunches, and lifted and heaved themselves as out of paste. You, indeed, will set it out in tragic style, taking a sublime tone from your own sufferings; but for me, unless that true Lady Bountiful, your mother, had rescued me quickly, showing herself in my need like a haven to the tempest-tossed, I had been dead long ago, getting myself little honour, though much pity, from Pontic hospitality."

This is not precisely the tone in which the lives of the saints (of any saints of any creeds) are written. Therefore is it better to read what the saints say for themselves than what has been said about them. This is not precisely the point of view which is presented unctuously for our consideration, yet it makes all other points of view intelligible. It is contrary to human nature to court privations. We know that the saints did court them, and valued them as avenues to grace. It is in accord with human nature to meet privations cheerfully, and with a whimsical sense of discomfiture. When we hear the echo of a saint's laughter ringing down the centuries, we have a clue to his identity; not to his whole and heroic self, but to that portion of him which we can best understand, and with which we claim some humble brotherhood. We ourselves are not hunting assiduously for hardships; but which one of us has not summoned up courage enough to laugh in the face of disaster?

There is no reading less conducive to good spirits than the recitals of missionaries, or than such pitiless records as those compiled by Dr. Thomas William Marshall in his two portly volumes on "Christian Missions." The heathen, as portrayed by Dr. Marshall, do not in the least resemble the heathen made familiar to us by the hymns and tracts of our infancy. So far from calling on us to deliver their land "from error's chain," they mete out prompt and cruel death to their deliverers. So far from thirsting for Gospel truths, they thirst for the blood of the intruders. This is frankly discouraging, and we could never read so many pages of disagreeable happening, were it not for the gayety of the letters which Dr. Marshall quotes, and which deal less in heroics than in pleasantries. Such men as Bishop Berneux, the Abbé Rétord, and Father Féron, missionaries in Cochin-China and Corea, all possessed that protective sense of humour which kept up their spirits and their enthusiasms. Father Féron, for example, hidden away in the "Valley of the Pines," six hundred miles from safety, writes to his sister in the autumn of 1858 :–

"I am lodged in one of the finest houses in the village, that of the catechist, an opulent man. It is considered to be worth a pound sterling. Do not laugh; there are some of the value of eightpence. My room has a sheet of paper for a door, the rain filters through my grass-covered roof as fast as it falls outside, and two large kettles barely suffice to receive it. . . . The Prophet Elisha, at the house of the Shunamite, had for furniture a bed, a table, a chair, and a candlestick,—four pieces in all. No superfluity there. Now if I search well, I can also find four articles in my room; a wooden candlestick, a trunk, a pair of shoes, and a pipe. Bed none, chairs none, table none. Am I, then, richer or poorer than the Prophet? It is not an easy question to answer, for, granting that his quarters were more comfortable than mine, yet none of the things belonged to him; while in my case, although the candlestick is borrowed from the chapel, and the trunk from Monseigneur Berneux, the shoes (worn only when I say Mass) and the pipe are my very own."

Surely if one chanced to be the sister of a missionary in Corea, and apprehensive, with good cause, of his personal safety, this is the kind of a letter one would be glad to receive. The comfort of finding one's brother disinclined to take what Saint Gregory calls "a sublime tone" would tend—illogically, I own,—to ease the burden of anxiety. Even the remote reader, sick of discouraging details, experiences a renewal of confidence, and all because Father Féron's good humour is of the common kind which we can best understand, and with which it befits every one of us to meet the vicissitudes of life.

I have said that the ardent reformer is seldom gay. Small wonder, when his eyes are turned upon the dark places of earth, and his whole strength is consumed in combat. Yet Saint Teresa, the most redoubtable reformer of her day, was gay. No other word expresses the quality of her gladness. She was not only spiritually serene, she was humanly gay, and this in the face of acute ill-health, and many profound discouragements. We have the evidence of all her contemporaries—friends, nuns, patrons, confessors; and we have the far more enduring testimony of her letters, in proof of this mirthfulness of spirit, which won its way into hearts, and lightened the austerities of her rule. "A very cheerful and gentle disposition, and excellent temper, and absolutely void of melancholy," wrote Ribera. "So merry that when she laughed, every one laughed with her, but very grave when she was serious."

There is a strain of humour, a delicate and somewhat biting wit in the correspondence of Saint Teresa, and in her admonitions to her nuns. There is also an inspired common sense which we hardly expect to find in the writings of a religious and a mystic. But Teresa was not withdrawn from the world. She travelled incessantly from one end of Spain to the other, establishing new foundations, visiting her convents, and dealing with all classes of men, from the soldier to the priest, from the prince to the peasant. The severity of her discipline was tempered by a tolerant and half-amused insight into the pardonable foibles of humanity. She held back her nuns with one hand from "the frenzy of self-mortification," which is the mainstay of spiritual vanity, and with the other hand from a too solicitous regard for their own comfort and convenience. They were not to consider that the fear of a headache,—a non-existent headache threatening the future—was sufficient excuse for absenting themselves from choir; and, if they were too ailing to practise any other austerities, the rule of silence, she reminded them, could do the feeblest no harm. "Do not contend wordily over matters of no consequence," was her counsel of perfection. "Fly a thousand leagues from such observations as 'You see I was right,' or 'They did me an injustice.' "

Small wonder that peace reigned among the discalced Carmelites so long as Teresa ruled. Practical and fearless (save when a lizard ran up her sleeve, on which occasion she confesses she nearly "died of fright,") her much-sought advice was always on the side of reason. Asceticism she prized; dirt she abhorred. "For the love of Heaven," she wrote to the Provincial, Gratian, then occupied with his first foundation of discalced friars, "let your fraternity be careful that they have clean beds and tablecloths, even though it be more expensive, for it is a terrible thing not to be cleanly." No persuasion could induce her to retain a novice whom she believed to be unfitted for her rule:—"We women are not so easy to know," was her scornful reply to the Jesuit, Olea, who held his judgment in such matters to be infallible; but nevertheless her practical soul yearned over a well-dowered nun. When an "excellent novice" with a fortune of six thousand ducats presented herself at the gates of the poverty-stricken convent in Seville, Teresa, then in Avila, was consumed with anxiety lest such an acquisition should, through some blunder, be lost. "For the love of God," wrote the wise old saint to the prioress in Seville, "if she enters, bear with a few defects, for well does she deserve it."

This is not the type of anecdote which looms large in the volumes of "minced saints" prepared for pious readers, and its absence had accustomed us to dissever humour from sanctity. But a candid soul is, as a rule, a humorous soul, awake to the tragi-comic aspect of life, and immaculately free from self-deception. And to such souls, cast like Teresa's in heroic mould, comes the perception of great moral truths, together with the sturdy strength which supports enthusiasm in the face of human disabilities. They are the lantern-bearers of every age, of every race, of every creed, *les âmes bien nées* whom it behooves us to approach fearlessly out of the darkness, for so only can we hope to understand.

The Great Mystery

BY

PATRICK A. SHEEHAN

THE MYSTERY OF suffering! The great eternal problem! And yet no problem at all, if we only consider it as a Law of Being. Apart altogether from the higher and transcendent and beautiful teachings of religion, which place an aureole around the crown of thorns on each wounded head, and throw the iridescence of hope athwart the gloomiest and darkest sky, is it not in the nature of things that suffering is inevitable? I look at it under three aspects: (1) As a necessary condition of imperfect beings; (2) as a necessary motive power in carry-ing on the work of existence; (3) as an unconscious but most noble revelation to higher beings than we are of facts and principles in the great economy of creation that perhaps other-wise would be hidden from them for ever. I know perfectly that all these philosophical reasonings cannot mitigate pain any more than reasoning can disarm Death of its terrors, or soothe an excruciating physical torment. I know no philo-sophical talisman for anguish or sorrow, except that final hope of suffering humanity: All things have an end. But, nevertheless, it may be in our painless moments a soothing thought that suffering is not the unreasoning and inconsiderate

From *Parerga*, by Patrick A. Sheehan. Reprinted by permission of the copyright owner, His Lordship, the Bishop of Cloyne, Ireland.

infliction on helpless beings of pain from the hands of a supreme and arbitrary power; but that behind it there may be grave motives and far-reaching designs which our imperfect knowledge may feebly grasp, if we cannot always hold fast to them as a consolatory remedy for our weakness and our woes.

It is strange that men will not see how suffering is the inevitable accompaniment of our state of existence. Whether man has fallen from a state of perfection according to Christian truth and belief, keeping still some vague tradition of that happy condition in his eternal dream of the perfectability of the race; or whether, in the evolutionist theory, he is supposed to be struggling upwards from primary elements towards more spacious conditions and final developments, it must be admitted that this his intermediate state is a state of imperfection, with all the blunted senses, stunted faculties, darkened intellect, and weakened will, that denote a fallen or struggling being. In such a state, suffering is inevitable. Death must be preluded by disease; and the aspiring soul must beat its wings in fruitless efforts to touch an ideal that is ever present, and ever unattainable. Hence, the sublime dissatisfaction that ever haunts the dreams of mortals,—the never-satisfied craving and hunger after an indefinable something that ever eludes us, and that is not to be attained, no matter how frequently we change the surroundings of life and seek to satisfy our unquenchable desires. Hence come mental pain and anxiety,— "the looking before and after and pining for what is not," of which the poet speaks,—the restlessness and irritability, the exaggeration of trifles, the sad presentiments of the future, the bitter remorse for neglected opportunities that beset the weary way,—the *via dolorosa* of human life.

> *Nothing begins and nothing ends,*
> *That is not paid with moan;*
> *For we are born in others' pain,*
> *And perish in our own.*

Again, there can be no progress without pain. In pain are we brought forth into the world; in pain do we grow and increase; in pain, perhaps painless pain, do we die. But never a forward step is taken by man or society without pain and suffering. The whole development of human character is wrought, and can only be wrought, by self-denial and suffering, by the patient bearing of weary burdens, by the crushing of one's own will, by the forehead wrinkled and the face agonised under the pressure of torture. All the finest faculties of our nature remain dormant until they wake under the sharp *accolade* of pain. We all know the beauty of a suffering creature, —the unspeakable beauty of death. It is only the sharp chisel of pain that can round the lineaments into such perfect and ethereal loveliness. . . .

The social body, too, is moved ahead along the wheels of suffering. It is a sad truth that the horrors of war appear to be the necessary preliminaries to advancing civilisation. Every great forward movement in human history has been preluded by conquest. Degeneracy is the adjunct of continued peace. Hence the school of thinkers who maintain that war is a necessity for eliminating the weaker elements of a nation and developing its strength!

> *Is it peace or war? better, war! loud war by land and sea,*
> *War with a thousand battles, and shaking a hundred thrones.*

It is famine, too, that scattered the civilising races over the earth. The surplus populations in the old countries, driven to distress and despair by over-crowding, fled their own land with its congested millions, and carried civilisation across seas and lands to black and tawny savages. These in turn yielded under the sword, and the "white man" triumphed. We cannot say much for the morality of such progress: but we are speaking of facts. Famine drove forth the conquerors; the conquered perished by the sword. Civilisation followed in the wake of the latter; that is, along the valleys of suffering and death. The path of progress is the path of pain. Bleached bones and broken hearts mark every inch of its way.

But there is a third consideration, which is for ever rising up before my mind. I can hardly conceive anything so absurd as the proud claim made by us, denizens of this little planet, that we represent the acme of perfection in God's universe; that we are the objective of all evolutionary processes,—the sum total and crowning-point of all the mysterious designs and occult operations of the universe. Man has always seemed to me to be the lowest representative of intellect in the Universe, if he is the highest animal. And I never had the least doubt that there are species and types beyond the limit, of spiritual and intellectual essences, either resident, as we are, in planetary worlds, or diffused universally through the ether in which the universe is enveloped. Our conceptions of the seraphim and the cherubim would represent the highest attainable grade in spiritual perfections. But between the seraphim and man, what a mighty gulf interposes! What a vast space to be peopled with great spirits! And what tremendous possibilities for the exercise of the never-tiring, ever-plastic attribute of God's omnipotence!

. . . Now each tiniest item of creation works outward and upward, subserving some higher species. Its energies are not limited to its own existence or welfare; nor even to the continuance and preservation of its own kind. It is the Altruism of Nature—the design of making all things coöperate in one single plan; each working for some higher existence than its own, and subserving some higher and hidden purpose far beyond its ken. For, just as each drop of rain serves the ulterior purpose of carrying salts to the sea; as the coral insect builds an island, and then a continent, while it perishes; as the tiny shellfish dies, after extracting from its viscera the material that goes to build yonder cathedral; so every human life has some ulterior purpose, as yet but dimly guessed, but yet most certainly to be revealed. And, as the rabbit or guinea-pig in the hands of the scientist knows nothing in its pain of the vast purposes it subserves, and only knows that it is passing through a mysterious trial under the hands of some superior and powerful being, so we, too, are ignorant of the purposes which we serve throughout the universe of God by the mysterious agency of labour and pain and suffering.

And may it not happen that, as the shrinking animal gives ideas that are helpful to the higher species of its own creation, so we also may be the means, through labour, agony, and even death, of communicating larger knowledge, nay, perhaps wider help, to beings of whose existence we can form but a vague comprehension, but who are as far beyond us as we are beyond the beasts that perish and are dumb? And may there not be some supreme science, some synthesis of all earthly sciences, such as we are always seeking after, but never attaining; and that all this human pain and suffering under which we blindly labour, and which sometimes seems to us such an infliction of unnecessary cruelty on the part of an all-powerful but capricious Being, are contributory to the perfecting of that science, just as the toxin in the veins of an afflicted beast reveals some secret to the eye of a scientist, who in turn builds therefrom some great theory fraught with illimitable and beneficial consequences to suffering mankind?

On the Delights of an Incognito

BY

LOUISE IMOGEN GUINEY

PERFECT HAPPINESS, WHICH we pretend is so difficult to get at, lies at either end of our sentient pole: in becoming intimately recognized, or else in evading recognition altogether. An actor finds it inspiring to step forth from the wings, steeled cap-à-pie in self-consciousness, before a great houseful of enthusiastic faces and hands; but if he ever knows a moment yet more ecstatic, it is when he is alone in the hill-country, swimming in a clear pool, and undemonstratable as human save by his habiliments hanging on a bush, and his dog, sitting on a margin under, doubtfully eyeing now these, now the unfamiliar large white fish which has shed them. Thackeray once said that the purest satisfaction he ever took, was in hearing one woman name him to another as the author of *Vanity Fair,* while he was going through a ragged and unbookish London lane. It is at least as likely that Aristides felt pleasure in accosting his own ostracizer, and helping him to ruin the man whom he was tired of hearing called The Just. And the young Charles the Second, between his defeat at Worcester, and his extraordinary escape over sea, was able to report, with exquisite relish, the conduct of that honest Hambletonian, who "dranke a goode glass of beare to me, and called me Brother Roundhead." To be indeed the King, and to masquerade as Will Jackson, *alias* Jones, "in a green cloth jump coat and breeches worn to shreds," in Pepys' sympathetic detail, with "little rools of paper between his toes," and "a long thorn stick crooked three or four several ways" in his artificially-browned hand, has its dangers; but it is the top, nevertheless, of mundane romance and felicity.

In fact, there is no enjoyment comparable to walking about "unwept, unhonored, and unsung," once you have become, through your misfortune rather than your fault, ever so little of a public personage. Lucky was the good Haroun al Raschid, inasmuch as, being duly himself by day, he could stroll abroad, and be immeasurably and magnificently himself by night. Nothing but duty dragged him back from his post of spectator and speculator at the street-corner, to the narrow concrete humdrum of a throne. There are, and always have been, in every age, men of genius who cling to the big

cloak and the dark lantern, and who travel pseudonymously
from the cradle to the grave; who keep apart, meddle not at
all, have only distant and general dealings with their kind,
and, in an innocent and endearing system of thieving, come
to understand and explain everything social, without being
once understood or explained themselves, or once breaking
an inviolable privacy.

> *Not even the tenderest heart and next our own,*
> *Knows half the reason why we smile or sigh.*

The arrangement is excellent: it induces and maintains dignity. Most of us who suffer keenly from the intolerable
burden of self, are grateful to have our fits of liberty by the
hour or the week, when we may eat lotos and fern-seed, and
die out of the ken of *The Evening Bugaboo*. To be clean of
mortal contact, to resolve into grass and brooks, to be a royal
nobody, or a dim imbecile spectrum not suspected to be you,
by your acquaintanceship, is the privilege which the damned
on a Saratoga piazza are not even blest enough to groan for.
"Oh," cried Hazlitt, heartily inhaling liberty at the door of a
country inn, after a march. "Oh, it is great to shake off the
trammels of the world and public opinion, to lose our impor-
tunate, tormenting, everlasting personal identity in the elements of Nature, and to become the creature of the moment
clear of all ties; to hold to the universe only by a dish of sweet-
breads, and to owe nothing but the score of the evening; and,
no longer seeking for applause or meeting with contempt, to
be known by no other title than "The Gentleman in the Parlour." Surely, surely, to be Anonymous is better than to be
Alexander, and to have no care is a more sumptuous wealth
than to have sacked ten cities. Cowley says engagingly, in his
little essay on *Obscurity*: *"Bene qui latuit, bene vixit*: he lives
well, that has lain well hidden; in which, if it be a truth, I'll
swear the world has been sufficiently deceived. For my part, I
think it is; and that the pleasantest condition of life is in
incognito. . . . It is, in my mind, a very delightful pastime

for two good and agreeable friends to travel up and down together, in places where they are by nobody known, nor know anybody. It was the case of Æneas and his Achates, when they walked invisibly about the fields and streets of Carthage. Venus herself

> *"A veil of thickened air around them cast,*
> *That none might know or see them as they passed."*

The atmosphere was so liberally allowed, in the Middle Ages, to be thick with spirits, that the subject is said to have arisen in the debates of the schools whether more than a thousand and fifty-seven of them could execute a saraband on the point of a needle. We are not informed by what prior necessity they desired to dance; but something, after all, must be left to the imagination. Dancing, in their case, must be, as with lambs and children, the spontaneous witness of light hearts; and what is half so likely to make a shade whimsically frolicsome, as the sense of his own complete intangibility in our world of wiseacres and mind-readers and myopic Masters of Arts? To watch, to listen, to know the heretofore and the hereafter, and to be at the same time dumb as a nail, and skilful at dodging a collision with flesh and blood, must be, when you come to think of it, a delightful vocation for ghosts. It is, then, in some sort, anticipatory of part of our business in the twenty-sixth century of the Christian era, to becloud now our name and nativity, and,

> *Beholding, unbeheld of all,*

to move musingly among strange scenes, with the charity and cheerfulness of those delivered from death. I once had an odd spiritual adventure, agreeable and memorable, which demonstrated how much pleasure there is to be had out of these moods of detachment and non-individuality. I had spent the day at a library desk, and had grown hazy with no food and much reading. As I walked homeward in the evening, I felt, for sheer buoyancy of mind, like that thin Greek who had to fill his pockets with lead, for fear of being blown away by the wind. It happened that I was obliged to pass, on the way to my solitary lodging of the night, the house where I was eternally the expected guest: the house of one with whom and with whose family I was on a most open and affectionate footing. Their window-shades were drawn, not so low but that one could see the shining dinner-table dressed in its pomp, and the cosy ring of merry faces closing it in. There was S., the bonniest of wives, smiling, in her pansy-colored gown, with a pearl comb in her hair: and opposite her was little S., in white, busy with the partridge; and there was A. H., the jolly artist cousin; and, facing the window at the head of his own conclave, *(quos inter Augustus recumbens purpureo bibit ore nectar)*, sat dear O., with his fine serious genial head bobbing over the poised carving-knife, as he demolished, perhaps, some quoted sophism of Schopenhauer. There were welcome and warmth inside there for me: how well I knew it! But the silent day just over had laid a spell upon my will; I looked upon them all, in their bright lamplight, like any vagrant stranger from the street, and hurried on, never quite so paradoxically happy in my life as when I quitted that familiar pane without rapping, and went on into the dark and the frost, unapprehended, impersonal, aberrant, a spirit among men.

On Lying

BY

HILAIRE BELLOC

HE THAT WILL set out to lie without having cast up his action and judged it this way and that, will fail, not in his lie, indeed, but in the object of it; which is, *imprimis,* to deceive, but *in ultimis* or fundamentally, to obtain profit by his deceit, as Aristotle and another clearly show. For they that lie, lie not vainly and wantonly as for sport (saving a very few that are habitual), but rather for some good to be got or evil to be evaded: as when men lie of their prowess with the fist, though they have fought none—no, not even little children—or in the field, though they have done no more than shoot a naked blackamoor at a furlong. These lie for honour. Not so our stockers and jobbers, who lie for money direct, or our parliament men, who lie bestraught lest worse befall them.

Lies are distinguished by the wise into the Pleasant and the Useful, and again into the Beautiful and the Necessary. Thus a lie giving comfort to him that utters it is of the Lie Pleasant, a grateful thing, a cozening. This kind of lie is very much used among women. This sort will also make out good to the teller, evil to the told, for the pleasure the cheat gives; as, when one says to another that his worst actions are now known and are to be seen printed privately in a Midland sheet, and bids him fly.

The lie useful has been set out *ut supra,* which consult; and may be best judged by one needing money. Let him ask for the same and see how he shall be met; all answers to him shall

From *This, That and the Other,* by Hilaire Belloc. Reprinted by permission of the publishers, Dodd, Mead and Company, Inc., New York, and Methuen & Co., Ltd., London.

be of this form of lie. It is also of this kind when a man
having no purse or no desire to pay puts sickness on in a
carriage, whether by rail or in the street, crying out: "Help!
help!" and wagging his head and sinking his chin upon his
breast, while his feet patter and his lips dribble. Also let
him roll his eyes. Then some will say: "It is the heat! The
poor fellow is overcome!" Others, "Make way! make way!"
Others, men of means, will ask for the police, whereat the
poorer men present will make off. But chiefly they that should
have taken the fare will feel kindly and will lift the liar up
gently and convey him and put him to good comfort in some
waiting place or other till he be himself—and all the while
clean forget his passage. For such is the nature of their rules.
Lord Hincksey, now dead, was very much given to this kind
of lie, and thought it profitable.

You shall lie at large and not be discovered; or a little,
and for once, and yet come to public shame, as it was with
Ananias and his good wife Sapphira in Holy Scripture, who
lied but once and that was too often. While many have lied
all their lives long and come to no harm, like John Ade, of
North-Chapel, for many years a witness in the Courts that
lied professionally, then a money-lender, and lastly a parlia-
ment-man for the county: yet he had no hurt of all this that
any man could see, but died easily in another man's bed, being
eighty-three years of age or thereabouts, and was very hon-
ourably buried in Petworth at a great charge. But some say
he is now in Hell, which God grant!

There is no lie like the winsome, pretty, flattering, dilating
eyelid-and-lip-brow-lifting lie such as is used by beauty im-
poverished, when land is at stake. By this sort of lie many
men's estates have been saved, none lost, and good done at
no expense save to holiness. Of the same suit also is the lie
that keeps a parasite in a rich man's house, or a mixer attendant upon a painter, a model upon a sculptor, and beggars
upon all men.

Fools will believe their lies, but wise men also will take

delight in them, as did the Honourable Mr. Gherkin, for some time His Majesty's Minister of State for the Lord Knows What, who, when policemen would beslaver him, and put their hands to their heads and pay court in a low way, told all that saw it what mummery it was; yet inwardly was pleased. The more at a loss was he when, being by an accident in the Minories too late and his hat lost, his coat torn and muddy, he made to accost an officer, and civilly saying, "Hi—" had got no further but he took such a crack on the crown with a truncheon as laid him out for dead, and he is not now the same as he was, nor ever will be.

Ministers of religion will both show forth to the people the evil of lying and will also lie themselves in a particular manner, very distinct and formidable: as was clear when one denounced from the pulpit the dreadful vice of hypocrisy and false seeming, whereat a drunkard not yet sober, hearing him say, "Show me the hypocrite!" rose where he was, full in church, and pointed to the pulpit, so that he was thrust out for truth-telling by gesture in that sacred place; as was that other who, when the preacher came to "Show me the drunkard," jerked his thumb over his shoulder at the parson's wife: a very mutinous act. But to Lying.

He that takes lying easily will take life hardly; as the saw has it, "Easy lying makes hard hearing," but your constructed and considered, your well-drafted lie—that is the lie for men grown, men discreet and fortunate. To which effect also the poet Shakespeare says in his *Sonnets*—but no matter! The passage is not for our ears or time, dealing with a dark woman that would have her Will: as women also must if the world is to wag, which leads me to that sort of lie common to all the sex of which we men say that it is the marvellous, the potent, the dextrous, the thorough, or better still, the mysterious, the uncircumvented and not explainable, the stopping-short and confounding-against-right-reason lie, the triumphant lie of Eve our mother: Iseult our sister: Judith, an aunt of ours, who saved a city, and Jael, of holy memory.

But if any man think to explain that sort of lie, he is an ass for his pains; and if any man seek to copy it he is an ass sublimate or compound, for he attempts the mastery of women.

Which no man yet has had of God, or will.

Amen.

2

FELLOW-TRAVELERS

An Introduction to Michael Burt

BY

LEONARD FEENEY

THROUGH THE KINDNESS of a very dear lady with snow-white hair I became acquainted with Michael Burt. I might have called her an *old* lady, but Michelangelo says one shouldn't on the score that innocence never grows old. This nice lady received from a priest friend of hers in Ireland one of Michael Burt's pamphlets. Pamphlet is too big a name for it. It is no more than a single sheet folded. It bears no publisher's inscription, no indication of having originated in a book or a magazine; it carries no copyright and makes no claims to rights reserved. It is simply called: *More Litterae Scriptae* by Michael Burt, presumably one of many little literary delectables distributed by the kind author for the amusement of his friends.

It is possible to know the quality of a splendid bird by one feather dropped from its plumage. It is this way with Michael Burt. One senses in his slightest performance the abundance of wit and idea at his command. For Michael Burt is a consumate artist. Working in the smallest possible medium he achieves imperishable results. What novelist could ever fix

From *America* (Dec. 25, 1937). Reprinted by permission of the Editor.

so sharply the complete character of Georgetta Smugge in two letters; or account for the whole of Chaplain O'Shaughnessy in a telegram? The juxtaposition of these two, Lady Smugge and Father O'Shaughnessy, is a masterpiece of dramatic device bringing to the fore the full force of his stolid, adamantine charity, and her dazzling, lovable asininity. Not only that, but we are given a perfect etching of the character of the overwhelming A. Karpett-Knight (Major). A Vicar General and an indefinite Stacey Smugge occur in the proper proportions. Even Sir Ephraim and the Pope play effective roles in the piece, the one in the form of "a fez" and the other in the form of "an ear."

But I shall not impede Michael Burt's Sketch with any more preamble. Other than to say that I hope my introduction of him to an American audience will be at least remotely the cause of his being brought into the full light of the fame which he deserves, possibly even of being undisguised of a pseudonymity. Here's Michael Burt—and you're going to enjoy him!

I.

Sir Ephraim and Lady Smugge
request the pleasure of the Company of
The Reverend Seamus O'Shaughnessy
at Dinner on Friday, the 24th December, at 7:30
Fancy Dress.

Government House   R. S. V. P. to
Chutnipur   The Private Secretary
12th December   to H.E. the Governor

II.

The Reverend Seamus O'Shaughnessy is greatly honoured by the kind invitation of His Excellency the Governor and Lady Smugge to dinner on Friday, the 24th December, and deeply regrets that he is unable to accept.

The Presbytery
Chutnipur   13th December

III.

Private   Government House
                                                          Chutnipur
                                                      14th December

Dear Father O'Shaughnessy,

I hope you will forgive the liberty I take in writing to you, but I feel it only right to point out that you have taken a somewhat unprecedented step in declining their Excellencies' invitation to dinner on the 24th, without giving any kind of reason. Perhaps you will allow one who is presumably better acquainted than yourself with Lady Smugge to suggest that, if through some totally unavoidable engagement you are really unable to attend, you might perhaps care to amplify your refusal accordingly, before I submit it to her Excellency. Believe me,

Sincerely yours,

A. Karpett-Knight (Major)
Private Secretary

IV.

The Reverend Seamus O'Shaughnessy is greatly honoured by the kind invitation of His Excellency the Governor and Lady Smugge to dinner on Friday, the 24th December, and very deeply regrets that he is unable to accept, owing to the occurrence of Christmas Eve on that date.

The Presbytery   15th December

V.

Private   Government House
                                                          Chutnipur
                                                      16th December

My dear Father O'Shaughnessy,

I am so sorry to have to trouble you again, but your amended refusal of their Excellencies' invitation is *(si j'ose m'exprimer ainsi)* even more opaque than the original. I should have thought it clear that their Excellencies had chosen the 24th for their dinner-party *because* it was Christmas Eve, whereas your letter would seem to imply that this is an impediment. With the utmost deference I would seriously urge you to vouchsafe just a little more information before I show your letter to Lady Smugge, whose feelings, I am sure, you have no desire to wound. I do hope that you will accept this friendly hint in the spirit in which it is offered.

With all good wishes,
Yours very sincerely,
A. Karpett-Knight (Major)
Private Secretary

VI.

The Presbytery
Chutnipur
17th December

Dear Major Karpett-Knight,

I am truly sorry to be causing you all this anxiety. I certainly have no wish to offend Lady Smugge, but I assure you that it is quite impossible for me to accept her kind invitation. In the first place Christmas Eve (or the Vigil of the Nativity, as we call it) is a day of fasting and abstinence, and I have no desire to be either literally or metaphorically, a skeleton at the feast. Then again, but for a brief interval for a hasty collation, I shall be in the confessional from 4 p.m. till nearly midnight; and lastly, I have to sing the Midnight Mass.

Now that I have placed you in possession of the facts I feel sure you will agree that I am quite unable to dine out that evening, and that you will be able to make satisfactory excuses on my behalf to Lady Smugge.

Thanking you for all the trouble you have taken,

I remain,
Yours very sincerely,
Seamus O'Shaughnessy
Catholic Chaplain

VII.

Government House
18th December

Dear Father O'Shaughnessy,

Major Karpett-Knight has shown me your letters, and I am writing *at once* to see if I cannot persuade you to change your mind. We are not Roman Catholics, of course, but we are not at all *bigoted,* and we are always ready to make allowances for other peoples' *scruples*. Nevertheless I am sure it cannot be right for you to *fast* at Xmastide—surely it is the traditional season for *feasting* and *merrymaking?*—but in any case my husband has *great influence* at the Vatican (his nephew, Stacey Smugge, of whom you have doubtless heard—his mother was one of the *Shropshire* Watt-Prices, you know, *not* the Berkshire branch, who are really *Price-Watts*—is *Third* Secretary to our Embassy in Rome and therefore has the *Ear* of the Pope, though he is not himself an R.C., of course—Stacey, I mean, not the Pope) and I am sure that in the event of any *unpleasantness* he could make it *quite* all right for you.

Now, do come, will you not? We shall be *so* glad to have you with us, for I always say R.C.'s are so *broadminded* and between ourselves our *dear* Canon Blenkins is a bit of a Wet Blanket and it would be so nice to have you to cheer him up.

Never mind about fancy dress if you haven't any—your biretta would do *Splendidly*. My husband *never* wears anything but a *fez* and he looks just like a Turk—truly *Oriental*—which is so nice as it matches my *Sultana* Costume—so you will come, won't you?

Very cordially Yours,
Georgetta Smugge

P.S. —*Surely* you can get someone else to take your evening service or else have it *after tea,* as dear Canon Blenkins is doing. In any case, surely midnight is a most inconvenient and *unconventional* hour to choose, but I am sure you will change this to please me. Thanks *so* much.

VIII.

The Presbytery
Chutnipur
19th December

Dear Lady Smugge,

It was really extremely good of you to write me such a charming letter, and I am sincerely sorry to be unable to accept your kind invitation. Unfortunately it would be impossible for me, without embarking upon a detailed dissertation on highly technical and controversial subjects, to explain exactly why I must appear to be so discourteous, but I beg you to accept my assurance that, in any case, such matters are not left to my personal discretion, but are strictly controlled by Canon Law.

Once again, please believe that I am deeply sensible of both the honour and the kindness you have done me, and am truly sorry that circumstances do not permit me to avail myself of them.

With kind regards to Sir Ephraim and yourself,

I am, dear Lady Smugge,

Yours sincerely,

Seamus O'Shaughnessy

IX.

(Telegram)

Father O'Shaughnessy, Chutnipur.

Urgent and confidential; who or what is georgetta smugge, wire received addressed Very Reverend Canon Law requesting you to be dispensed fasting abstinence confessions Midnight Mass to attend fancy-dress revels; bishop deeply moved, requests immediate explanation and guidance for reply.

X.

(Telegram)

Vicar-General, Bishop's House, Mangopur.

Corporal work of mercy, if you snub smugge hip and thigh; governor's wife, bane of life, well-meaning heretic claiming vicarious tenure pope's ear; please assure his lordship have neither desire nor intention attend her carousals; grateful if you emphatically refuse dispensation in name of canon law.

O'Shaughnessy

XI.

(Telegram)

Smugge, Chutnipur.

Utterly impossible; canon law adamantine.

Vicar-General

XII.

Government House
22nd December

Dear Father O'Shaugnessy,

It will, I am sure, be a matter of grief to you to know that I have been *deeply wounded* and set at *naught* by the contumely and opprobium meted out to me by your *odius* Canon Law, to whom I *naturally* wired for some relaxation of the narrow and *bigoted* regimen to which you appear to be subjected, and who has not even had the courtesy to reply himself but has deputed some *minion* to answer my telegram—*who* or *what* is a "general vicar," pray? However, this is to assure you, dear Father, that I shall leave *no stone unturned* to have this nauseating oppression brought to the *Pope's ear.* Stacey Smugge, Sir Ephraim's nephew, has always spoken most highly of the Pope's *broad-mindedness,* and I am confident that he will not allow this narrow and fanatical *Canon* to ride *roughshod* over my feelings like a *juggernaut.*

Meanwhile, dear Father O'Shaughnessy, you may rest assured that I have yet another *arrow* in my *quiver,* and that even if we are to be bereft of your company at our little party Friday night, I am taking steps to ensure that you shall at least have a *nourishing meal* before your evening service, instead of the *dried lentils* on which absurd Law person doubtless expects you to subsist.

Wishing you a Right *Hearty* Yule-tide, and a *Bright* New Year.

Most sympathetically yours,
Georgetta Smugge

Josephine:
Girlhood and Girls

BY

CHARLES FAIRBANKS

A BRIGHT-EYED, fair, young maiden, whose satchel I should insist upon carrying to school for her every morning if I were half a century younger, came to me a day or two after the publication of my last essay, and, placing her white, taper fingers in my rough, Esau-like hand, said, "I liked your piece about

From *My Unknown Chum,* by Aguecheek (Charles Fairbanks). Reprinted by permission of the publisher, The Devin-Adair Company, New York.

the boys very much; and now I hope that you'll write something about girls." "My dear Nellie," replied I, "if I should do that I should lose all my female acquaintances. I have a weakness for telling the truth, and there are some subjects concerning which it is very dangerous to speak out 'the whole truth and nothing but the truth.' " The gentle damsel smiled, and looked

> Modest as justice, and did seem a palace
> For the crown'd truth to dwell in,

as she still urged me on, and refused to see any danger in my giving out the plainest truth about girlhood. *She* had no fear, though all the truth were told; and I suppose that if we had some of Nellie's purity and gentleness remaining in our sere and selfish hearts, we should be much better and happier men and women, and should dread the truth as little as she does. But I must not begin my truth-telling by seeming to praise too highly, though it must be confessed, even at my time of life, if I were to describe the charming young person I have referred to, with the merciless fidelity of a daguerreotype and an absence of hyperbole worthy of the late Dr. Bowditch's work on Navigation, I should seem to the unfortunate "general reader" who does not know Nell, to be indulging in the grossest flattery, and panting poesy would toil after me in vain. So I will put aside all temptations of that kind, and come down to the plain prose of my subject.

There is, in fact, very little that can be said about girlhood. Those calm years that come between the commencement of the bondage of the pantalettes and emancipation from the tasks of school, present few salient points upon which the essayist (observe he never so closely) may turn a neat paragraph. They offer little that is startling or attractive either to writer or reader—

> As times of quiet and unbroken peace,
> Though for a nation times of blessedness,
> Give back faint echoes from the historian's page.

The rough sports of boyhood, the out-door life which boys always take to so naturally, and all their habits of activity, give a strength of light and shade to their early years which is not to be found in girlhood. It is not enough to say that there is no difference in kind, but simply one in degree—that the years of boyhood are calm and happy, and that those of girlhood are so likewise—that the former resemble the garish sunshine, and the latter the mitigated splendour of the moon; for the characters of boys seem to be struck in a sharper die than those of girls, which gives them an absoluteness quite distinct from the feminine grace we naturally look for in the latter. The free-hearted boy, plunging into all sorts of fun without a thought of his next day's arithmetic lesson, and with a charming disregard of the expense of jackets and trousers, and the gentle girl, who clings to her mother's side, like an attendant angel, and contents herself with teaching long lessons to docile paper pupils in a quiet corner by the fireside, are representatives of two distinct classes in the order of nature, and (untheologically, of course, I might add) of grace. There is not a greater difference between a hockey and a crochet needle than there is between them.

I have, as a general thing, a greater liking for boys than for girls; for the vanity so common to all mankind is not developed in them at so early an age as in the latter. Still I must acknowledge that I have seen some splendid exceptions, the mere recollection of which almost tempts me to draw my pen through that last sentence. Can I ever forget—I can never forget—one into whose years of girlhood the beauty and grace of a long, pure life seemed to have been compressed? It was many years ago, and I was younger than I am now—so pardon me if I should seem to catch a little enthusiasm of spirit from the remembrance of those days. Like the ancient Queen of Carthage, *Agnosco veteris vestigia flammae.* I was living in London at that time, or rather at Hampstead, which had not then become a mere suburb of the great metropolis, but was a quiet town, whose bright door-plates, and well-scoured doorsteps, and clean window curtains contrasted finely with the dingy brick walls of its houses, and impressed the visitor with the general prosperity and quiet respectability of its inhabitants. In my daily walks to and from the city, I frequently met a gentleman whose gray hairs and simple dignity of manners always attracted me towards him, and exacted from me an involuntary tribute of respectful recognition. One day he overtook me in a shower, and gave me the benefit of his umbrella and his friendship—for an intimacy which ended only with his death commenced between us from that hour. He was a gentleman of good family and education, who had seen thirty years of responsible service in the employ of the Honourable East India Company, had attained a competency, and had forsworn Leadenhall Street for a pension and a quiet retreat on the heights of Hampstead. His wife was a lady of cultivated tastes, whose sober wishes never learned to stray from the path of simple domestic duty, and the presence of the books in which she found her daily pleasures.

Type of the wise, who soar, but never roam;
True to the kindred points of Heaven and Home.

Their only child, "one fair daughter, and no more," was a gentle and merry-hearted creature, who, in the short and murky days of November, filled that cottage with a more than June-like sunshine. Her parents always had a deep sympathy with that unfortunate Empress of France whose dismission from the throne was the commencement of the downward career of the first Napoleon, and bore witness to it by giving her name to their only child. They lived only three or four doors from my lodgings, and there were few days passed after the episode of the umbrella in which I did not find a welcome in their quiet home. Their daughter was their only idol, and I soon found myself a convert to their innocent system of paganism. We all three agreed that Josey was the incarnation of all known perfections, and the lapse of forty years has not sufficed to weaken that conviction in my mind. She had risen just above the horizon of girlhood, and the natural beauty of her character made the beholder content to forget even the promise of her riper years. I do not think she was what the world calls handsome. I sometimes distrust my judgment in the matter of female beauty; indeed, some of my candid friends have told me that I had no judgment in such things. Well, as I was saying, Josey was not remarkable for personal beauty—in fact, I think I remember some persons of her own sex who thought her "very plain"—"positively homely"—and wondered what there was attractive about her. There are circumstances under which I should not have hesitated to attribute such remarks to motives of envy and jealousy; but as they came from girls whose attractions of every kind were far below those of the gentle creature whom they delighted to criticise, how can I account for them? Josey's complexion was dark— her forehead, like those of the best models of female comeliness among the ancients, low. Her teeth were pearly and uniform, and her clear, dark eyes seemed to reflect the happiness and hope which were the companions of her youth. Her beauty was not of that kind which consists in mere regularity of features; it was far superior to that. You could discern under those traits, none of which were conspicuous, a combination of mental and social qualities which were far above the fleeting charms that delight so many, and which age, instead of destroying, would increase and perfect. She was quiet and gentle, without being dull or moody; light-hearted and cheery, without being frivolous; and witty, without being pert or conceited. Her unaffected goodness of heart found many an opportunity of exercise. I often heard of her among the poor, and among those who needed words of consolation even more than the necessaries of life. It was her delight to intercede with the magistrate who had inflicted a punishment on some disorderly brother of one of her poor clients, and to obtain his pardon by promising to watch over him and insure his future good behaviour; and there were very few, among the most reckless, who were not restrained by the thought that their offences would give pain to the kind-hearted girl who had so willingly become their protector.

During the months that I lived at Hampstead my intercourse with that excellent family was as familiar as if I had been one of their own kindred. A little attack of rheumatism, which confined me to my lodging for a fortnight or three weeks, proved the constancy of their friendship. The old gentleman came daily to see me—told me all the news from the city, and read to me; the mother sent me some of her favourite books; and Josey came to get assistance in her Latin and French, and brought me sundry little pots of grape jelly and other preserves, which tasted all the sweeter for being the work of her fair hands. It was a sad parting when I was called away to America—sad for me; for I told them that I hoped that my absence from England would be but temporary, when I felt inwardly that it might extend to several years.

Two or three months after my arrival at home, I received a letter from the old gentleman, written in his deliberate, round, clerk-like style, informing me of his wife's death. A note was enclosed from Josey, in which she described with her pencil the spot where her mother was buried in the old churchyard, and told me of her progress in her studies. More than a year passed by without my hearing from them at all, two or three of my letters to them having miscarried. Nearly seven years elapsed before I visited England again. Two years before that, I had read the decease of the old gentleman, in a stray London newspaper. I had written to Josey, sympathizing with her in her desolation, but had received no answer. So, the day after my arrival in London, I determined to make a search for the beloved Josey. I went to Hampstead, and my heart beat quicker as I approached the cottage where I had spent so many happy hours. My throat felt a little choky, as I recognized the neat bit of hedge before the door, the graceful vine which overhung it, and the familiar arrangement of the flower pots in the frames outside the windows; but my hopes received a momentary check when I found a strange name on the plate above the knocker. I knocked, and inquired concerning the former occupants of the house. After a severe effort to overcome the Bœotian stupidity of the housemaid, she ushered me into the little breakfast room, and said she would "call her missus." Almost before I had time to look about me, Josey entered the room. The little girl whose Latin exercises I had corrected, and who had always lived in my memory as she appeared in those days, suddenly came before me

> *A perfect woman, nobly planned,*
> *To warn, to comfort, and command;*
> *And yet a spirit still and bright*
> *With something of an angel light.*

Yet she was hardly changed at all. She had lost none of those charming qualities which had made the thought of her precious to me during long years of absence. She had gained the maturity and dignity of womanhood without losing any of the simplicity and light-heartedness of girlhood. She was married. Her husband was a literary man of considerable reputation. Though only in middle age, he was a great sufferer with the gout. He was, generally speaking, a patient man; but I found, after I became intimate with him, that his pains sometimes made him express himself with a force of diction somewhat in advance of the religious prejudices of his gentle Josey, who tended him and ministered to his wants like an angel, as she was. But excuse me for wandering so far from my theme. To make a long story short, Josey went to Italy with her husband, who had been ordered thither by his physicians, and I never saw her afterwards. She deposited her husband's remains in the cemetery where those of Shelley and Keats repose, and found for two or three years a consolation for her bereaved spirit in residence in that city which more than all others proclaims to our unwilling hearts the vanity and transitoriness of this world's hopes, and the glory of the unseen eternal. Years after, I met one of her husband's friends in Paris, who told me that some four years after his death, she had entered a convent of a religious order devoted to the reclaiming of the degraded of her sex, in Brussels. There she had found a fitting occupation for the natural benevolence of her heart, and the peace which the world could not give. She had concealed the glory of her good works under her vow of obedience—her personality was hidden under the common habit of her Order—the very name which was so dear to me had been exchanged for another on the day that saw her covered with the white veil of the novice. I was about returning to England from the continent when I heard this, and I resolved to take Belgium's fair capital in my route. I found the convent readily enough, and waited in its uncarpeted but scrupulously clean parlour some time for the Lady Superior. She was a lady of dignified mien, with the clear complexion, the serene brow, and the dovelike eyes so common among nuns, and her face lighted up, as she spoke, with a gentle smile, which seemed almost like a presage of immortality. I explained my errand, and she told me that the good English sister had been dead more than a year. The intelligence pained me, and it gave me a feeling of self-reproach to notice that the nun, who had been with her in her last hour, spoke of her as if she had merely passed into another part of the convent we were in. The Superior, perceiving my emotion, conducted me through the garden of the convent to a shady corner of the grounds, where there were several graves. She stopped before a mound, over which a rose bush bent affectionately, as if its white blossoms craved something of the purity which was enshrined beneath it. At its head was a simple wooden cross, on which was inscribed the name of "Sister Helen Agnes," the date of her death, and the common supplication that she might rest in peace; and that was the only memorial of Josey that remained to me.

I have not forgotten, dear reader, that I am writing about girls; but having brought forward one who always seemed to me to be about as near perfection as it is vouchsafed to poor humanity to approach, I could not help following her to the end, and showing how she went from a beautiful girlhood to a still more beautiful womanhood, and a death which all of us might envy; and how lovely and harmonious was her whole career. For I feel that the consideration of the contrast which most of the young female readers of these pages will discover between themselves and Josey, will do them some good.

I do not know of a more quietly funny sight than a group of school-girls, all talking as fast as their tongues can wag, (forty-woman power), and clinging inextricably together like a parcel of macaroni, *à la Napolitaine.* Their independence is quite refreshing. Lady Blessington in her diamonds never descended the grand staircase at Covent Garden Opera House with half the consciousness of making a sensation, that you may notice in these school-girls whenever you take your walks abroad. It is delightful to see them step off so proudly, and look you in the face so coolly, thinking all the time of just nothing at all. Their boldness is the boldness of innocence; for perfect modesty does not even know how to blush. How vain they grow as they advance in their teens! How careful they are that the crinoline "sticks out" properly before they venture on the road to school! If Mother Goose (of blessed memory) could take a look into this world now, she would wish to revise her ancient rhyme to her patrons—

Come with a whoop—come with a call,

for she would find that it is now their custom to come with a *hoop* when they come for a call.

When unhappy Romeo stands in old Capulet's garden, under the pale beams of the "envious moon," and watches the unconscious Juliet upon the balcony, he utters, in the course of his incoherent soliloquial apostrophe, these remark-able words concerning that interesting young person:—

She speaks, yet she says nothing.

I have seen many young ladies of Juliet's time of life in my day of whom the same thing might be said. They indeed speak, yet say nothing. Yet take them on such a subject as the trimming of the new bonnet for Easter Sunday, or any of those entertaining topics more or less connected with the adornment of their persons, and how voluble they are! To the stronger sex, which of course cares nothing about dress, being entirely free from vanity, the terms used in their never-ending colloquies on such themes are mere unmeaning words; but I must do the gentler side of humanity the justice to say that they are not all vanity, as their fathers and husbands find to their dismay, when the quarterly bills come in, that gimp, and flounces, and trimming generally, have a real, tangible existence.

How sentimental they are! In my young days albums were all the rage among young ladies; but now they seem to be somewhat out of date, and young ministers have taken their place. What pains will they not take to get a bow from the Rev. Mr. Simkins! They swarm around him after service, like flies around the bung of a molasses cask. Raphael never had such a face as his; Massillon never preached as he does. What a wilderness of worsted work are they not willing to travel over for his sake! How do they exhaust their inventive faculties in the search after new patterns for lamp mats, watch cases, pen wipers, and slippers to encase the feet at which they delight to sit! But when Simkins marries old Thompson's youngest daughter and a snug property, he finds a sad abatement in his popularity. The Rev. Mr. Jenkins, a young preacher with a face every whit as milk-and-watery as his own, succeeds to the throne he occupied, and reigns in his stead among the volatile devotees; and Simkins then sees that his popularity was no more an evidence of the favour his preaching of the gospel found among those thoughtless young people than was the popularity of the good-looking light comedian, after whom the girls ran as madly as they did after his own white neckerchief and nicely-brushed black frock coat.

Exaggeration is one of the great faults of girlhood. Whatever meets their eyes is either "splendid" or "horrid." They delight to exaggerate their likes and dislikes. Self-restraint seems to be a term not contained in their lexicon. They take a momentary fancy to a young man, and flatter him with their smiles until some new face takes his place in their fleeting memory. In this way many young hearts are frittered away in successive flirtations before their possessors have reached womanhood. But it would be wrong to confine action from mere blind impulse and exaggeration to young girls alone. I think it is St. Paul who gives us some good counsel about "speaking the truth in love." I fear that very few victims of the tender passion, from Pyramus and Thisbe down to Petrarch and Laura, and from the latter couple down to Mr. Smith with Miss Brown hanging on his arm—who have not sadly needed the advice of the Apostle of the Gentiles. I have seen very few people in my day who really speak the truth in love. Therefore I will not blame girls for a fault which is common to all mankind.

Impulse is commonly supposed to be inconsistent with cunning; but in most girls I think the two things are singularly combined. I am told that there is an academy in this city, frequented by many young women, known as the School of Design. The fact is a gratifying one to me; for my observation of girlish nature had led me to suppose that there were very few indeed of the young ladies of these days who required any tuition in the arts of design. I hail the fact as a good omen for the sex. Action from impulse carries its young victims to the extremes of good and evil. Queen Dido is a fair type of the majority of her sex. Defeated in their hopes, they are willing to make a funeral pile of all that remains to them. But there is a spirit of generosity in them which does not find a place in the hearts of men. It was the part of Eve to bring death into this world, and all our woe, by her inquisitiveness and credulity; but it was reserved for Adam to inaugurate the meanness of mankind by laying all the blame to his silly little wife. The accusation ought to have blistered Adam's cowardly tongue.

But I am making a long preachment, and yet I have said very little. I must leave my young friends, however, to draw their own lessons from the portrait I have given of one whose perfections would far outweigh the silliness and vanity of a generation of girls. Let them take the gentle Josey as the model of their youth, and they will not wish to sculpture their later career after any less perfect shape. There will then be fewer heartless flirts, fewer vain exhibitors of the works of the milliner and dressmaker parading the streets, and more true women presiding over the homes of America. The imitation of her virtues will be found a better preservative of beauty than any *eau lustrale;* for it will create a beauty which "time's effacing fingers" are powerless to destroy, and give to those who practise it a serene and lovely old age, whose recollection of the past, instead of awakening any self-reproach shall be a source of perpetual benediction.

Children in Midwinter

BY

ALICE MEYNELL

CHILDREN ARE SO flowerlike that it is always a little fresh surprise to see them blooming in winter. Their tenderness,

From *The Children,* by Alice Meynell. Reprinted by permission of the copyright owner, Mr. Wilfrid Meynell.

their down, their colour, their fulness—which is like that of a thick rose or of a tight grape—look out of season. Children in the withering wind are like the soft golden-pink roses that fill the barrows in Oxford Street, breathing a southern calm on the north wind. The child has something better than warmth in the cold, something more subtly out of place and more delicately contrary; and that is coolness. To be cool in the cold is the sign of a vitality quite exquisitely alien from the common conditions of the world. It is to have a naturally, and not an artificially, different and separate climate.

We can all be more or less warm—with fur, with skating, with tea, with fire, and with sleep—in the winter. But the child is fresh in the wind, and awakes cool from his dreams, dewy when there is hoar-frost everywhere else; he is "more lovely and more temperate" than the summer day and than the winter day alike. He overcomes both heat and cold by another climate, which is the climate of life; but that victory of life is more delicate and more surprising in the tyranny of January. By the sight and the touch of children, we are, as it were, indulged with something finer than a fruit or a flower in untimely bloom. The childish bloom is always rare. The fruit and flower will be common later on; the strawberries will be a matter of course anon, and the asparagus dull in their day. But a child is a perpetual *primeur*.

Or rather he is not in truth always untimely. Some few days in the year are his own season—unnoticed days of March or April, soft, fresh and equal, when the child sleeps and rises with the sun. Then he looks as though he had his brief season, and ceases for a while to seem so strange.

It is no wonder that we should try to attribute the times of the year to children; their likeness is so rife among annuals. For man and woman we are naturally accustomed to a longer rhythm; their metre is so obviously their own, and of but a single stanza, without repetition, without renewal, without refrain. But it is by an intelligible illusion that we look for a quick waxing and waning in the lives of young children—for a waxing that shall come again another time, for a waning that shall not be final, shall not be fatal. But every winter shows us how human they are, and how they are little pilgrims and visitants among the things that look like their kin. For every winter shows them free from the east wind; more perfectly than their elders, they enclose the climate of life. And, moreover, with them the climate of life is the climate of the spring of life; the climate of a March that is sure to make a constant progress, and of a human April that never hesitates. The child "breathes April and May"—another April and his own May.

The winter child looks so much the more beautiful for the season as his most brilliant uncles and aunts look less well. He is tender and gay in the east wind. Now more than ever must the lover beware of making a comparison between the beauty of the admired woman and the beauty of a child. He is indeed too wary ever to make it. So is the poet. As comparisons are necessary to him, he will pay a frankly impossible homage, and compare a woman's face to something too fine, to something it never could emulate. The Elizabethan lyrist is safe among the lilies and cherries, roses, pearls, and snow. He understands the beautiful office of flattery, and flatters with courage. There is no hidden reproach in the praise. Pearls and snow suffer, in a sham fight, a mimic defeat that does them no harm, and no harm comes to the lady's beauty from a competition so impossible. She never wore a lily or a coral in the colours of her face, and their beauty is not hers. But here is the secret: she is compared with a flower because she could not endure to be compared with a child. That would touch her too nearly. There would be the human texture and the life like hers, but immeasurably more lovely. No colour, no surface, no eyes of woman have ever been comparable with the colour, the surface, and the eyes of childhood. And no poet has ever run the risk of such a defeat. Why, it is defeat enough for a woman to have her face, however well-favoured, close to a child's even if there is no one by who should be rash enough to approach them still nearer by a comparison.

This, needless to say, is true of no other kind of beauty than that beauty of light, colour, and surface to which the Elizabethans referred, and which suggested their flatteries in disfavour of the lily. There are, indeed, other adult beauties, but those are such as make no allusions to the garden. I do but aver that the beautiful woman, widely and wisely likened to the flowers, which are inaccessibly more beautiful, must not, for her own sake, be likened to the always accessible child.

Besides light and colour, children have a beauty of finish which is much beyond that of more finished years. This gratuitous addition, this completeness, is one of their unlooked for advantages. Their beauty of finish is the peculiarity of their first childhood, and loses, as years are added, that little extra character and that surprise of perfection. A bloom disappears, for instance. In some little children the whole face, and especially all the space between the growth of the eyebrows and the growth of the hair, is covered with hardly perceptible down as soft as bloom. Look then at the eyebrows themselves. Their line is as definite as in later life, but there is in the child the finish given by the exceeding fineness of the delicate hairs. Moreover, what becomes, afterwards, of the length and the curl of the eyelash? What is there in growing up that is destructive of a finish so charming as this?

Queen Elizabeth forbade any light to visit her face "from the right or from the left" when her portrait was a-painting. She was an observant woman, and liked to be lighted from the front. It is a light from the right or from the left that marks an elderly face with minute shadows. And you must place a child in such a light, in order to see the finishing and parting caress that infancy has given to his face. The down will then be found even on the thinnest and clearest skin of the middle red of his cheek. His hair, too, is imponderably fine, and his nails not much harder than petals.

But another word of the child in January. It is his month

for the laying up of dreams. No one can tell whether it is so with all children, or even with a majority, but with some children of passionate fancy there occurs now and then a children's dance, or a party of any kind, which has a charm and glory mingled with uncertain dreams. Never forgotten, and yet never certainly remembered as a fact of this life, is such an evening. When many and many a later pleasure, about the reality of which there was any kind of doubt, has been long forgotten, that evening—as to which all is doubt—is impossible to forget. In a few years it has become so remote that the history of Greece derives antiquity from it. In later years it is still doubtful, still a legend.

The child never asked how much was fact. It was always so immeasurably long ago that the sweet party happened—if indeed it happened. It had so long taken its place in that past wherein lurks all the antiquity of the world. No one would know, no one could tell him, precisely what occurred. And who can know whether—if it be indeed a dream—he has dreamt it often, or has dreamt once that he had dreamt it often? That dubious night is entangled in repeated visions during the lonely life a child lives in sleep; it is intricate with allusions. It becomes the most mysterious and the least worldly of all memories, a spiritual past. The word pleasure is too trivial for such a remembrance. A midwinter long gone by contained the suggestion of such dreams. And the midwinter of every year must doubtless prepare for the heart of many an ardent young child a like legend and a like antiquity. For us it is a mere present.

Lady Macbeth's Trouble

BY

MAURICE BARING

Letter from Lady Macbeth to Lady Macduff

Most Private.

The Palace, Forres,
October 10.

My dearest Flora,

I am sending this letter by Ross, who is starting for Fife tomorrow morning. I wonder if you could possibly come here for a few days. You would bring Jeamie of course. Macbeth is devoted to children. I think we could make you quite comfortable, although of course palaces are never very comfortable, and it's all so different from dear Inverness. And there is the tiresome Court etiquette and the people, especially the Heads of the Clans, who are so touchy, and insist on one's observing every tradition. For instance, the bagpipes begin in the early morning; the pipers walk round the castle a little after sunrise, and this I find very trying, as you know what a bad sleeper I am. Only two nights ago I nearly fell out of the window walking in my sleep. The doctor, who I must say is a charming man (he was the late King's doctor and King Duncan always used to say he was the only man who really understood his constitution), is giving me mandragora mixed with poppy and syrup; but so far it has not done me any good; but then I always was a wretched sleeper and now I am worse, because—well, I am coming at last to what I really want to say.

From *Dead Letters,* by Maurice Baring. Reprinted by permission of the late Maurice Baring.

I am in very great trouble and I beg you to come here if you can, because you would be the greatest help. You shall have a bedroom facing south, and Jeamie shall be next to you, and my maid can look after you both, and as Macduff is going to England I think it would really be wiser and *safer* for you to come here than to stay all alone in that lonely castle of yours in these troublesome times, when there are so many robbers about and one never knows what may not happen.

I confess I have been very much put about lately. (You quite understand if you come we shall have plenty of opportunities of seeing each other alone in spite of all the tiresome etiquette and ceremonies, and of course you must treat me just the same as before; only in *public* you must just throw in a "Majesty" now and then and curtchey and call me "Ma'am" so as not to shock the people.) I am sorry to say Macbeth is not at all in good case. He is really not at all well, and the fact is he has never got over the terrible tragedy that happened at Inverness. At first I thought it was quite natural he should be upset. Of course very few people know how fond he was of his cousin. King Duncan was his favourite cousin. They had travelled together in England, and they were much more like brothers than cousins, although the King was so much older than he is. I shall never forget the evening when the King arrived after the battle against those horrid Norwegians. I was very nervous as it was, after having gone through all the anxiety of knowing that Macbeth was in danger. Then on the top of that, just after I heard that he was alive and well, the messenger arrived telling me that the King was on his way to Inverness. Of course I had got nothing ready, and Elspeth our housekeeper put on a face as much as to say that we could not possibly manage in the time. However, I said she *must* manage. I knew our cousin wouldn't expect too much, and I spent the whole day making those flat scones he used to be so fond of.

I was already worried then because Macbeth, who is superstitious, said he had met three witches on the way (he said something about it in his letter) and they had apparently been uncivil to him. I thought they were gipsies and that he had not crossed their palm with silver, but when he arrived he was still brooding over this, and was quite *odd* in his way of speaking about it. I didn't think much of this at the time, as I put it down to the strain of what he had gone through, and the reaction which must always be great after such a time; but now it all comes back to me, and now that I think over it in view of what has happened since, I cannot help owning to myself that he was not himself, and if I had not known what a sober man he was, I should almost have thought the 1030 (Hildebrand) whisky had gone to his head—because when he talked of the old women he was quite incoherent: just like a man who has had an hallucination. But I did not think of all this till afterwards, as I put it down to the strain, as I have just told you.

But now! Well, I must go back a little way so as to make everything clear to you. Duncan arrived, and nothing could be more civil than he was. He went out of his way to be nice to everybody and praised the castle, the situation, the view, and even the birds' nests on the walls! (All this, of course, went straight to my heart.) Donalbain and Malcolm were with him. They, I thought at the time, were not at all well brought up. They had not got their father's manners, and they talked in a loud voice and gave themselves airs.

Duncan had supper by himself, and before he went to bed he sent me a most beautiful diamond ring, which I shall always wear. Then we all went to bed. Macbeth was not himself that evening, and he frightened me out of my wits by talking of ghosts and witches and daggers. I did not, however, think anything serious was the matter and I still put it down to the strain and the excitement. However, I took the precaution of pouring a drop or two of my sleeping draught into the glass of water which he always drinks before going to bed, so that at least he might have a good night's rest. I suppose I did not give him a strong enough dose. (But one cannot be too careful with drugs, especially mandragora, which is bad for the heart.) At any rate, whether it was that or the awful weather we had that night (nearly all the trees in the park were blown down, and it will never be quite the same again) or whether it was that the hall porter got tipsy (why they choose the one day in the year to drink when one has guests, and it really matters, I never could understand!) and made the most dreadful noise and used really disgraceful language at the front door about five o'clock in the morning, I don't know. At any rate, we were all disturbed long before I had meant that we should be called (breakfast wasn't nearly ready and Elspeth was only just raking out the fires). But, as I say, we were all woken up, and Macduff went to call the King, and came back with the terrible news.

Macbeth turned quite white and at first my only thought was for him. I thought he was going to have a stroke or a fit. You know he has a very nervous, high-strung constitution, and nothing could be worse for him than a shock like this. I confess that I myself felt as though I wished the earth would open and swallow me up. To think of such a thing happening in our house!

Banquo, too, was as white as a sheet; but the only people who behaved badly (of course this is strictly between ourselves, and I do implore you not to repeat it, as it would really do harm if it got about that I had said this, but you are safe, aren't you, Flora?) were Donalbain and Malcolm. Donalbain said nothing at all, and all Malcolm said when he was told that his father had been murdered was: "Oh! by whom?" I could not understand how he could behave in such a heartless way before so many people; but I must say in fairness that all the Duncans have a very odd way of showing grief.

Of course the first thing I thought was "Who can have done it?" and I suppose in a way it will always remain a mystery. There is no doubt that the chamber grooms actually did the deed; but whether they had any accomplices, whether it was just the act of drunkards (it turned out that the whole household had been drinking that night and not only the hall porter) or whether they were *instigated* by any one else (of course don't quote me as having suggested such a thing) we shall never know. Much as I dislike Malcolm and Donalbain, and shocking as I think their behaviour has been, and not only shocking but *suspicious,* I should not like any one to think that I suspected them of so awful a crime. It is one thing to be bad-mannered, it is another to be a parricide. However, there is no getting over the fact that by their conduct, by their extraordinary behaviour and flight to England, they made people suspect them.

I have only just now come to the real subject of my letter. At first Macbeth bore up pretty well in spite of the blow, the shock, and the extra worry of the coronation following immediately on all this; but no sooner had we settled down at Forres than I soon saw he was far from being himself.

His appetite was bad; he slept badly, and was cross to the servants, making scenes about nothing. When I tried to ask him about his health he lost his temper. At last one day it all came out and I realized that another tragedy was in store for us. Macbeth is suffering from hallucinations; this whole terrible business has unhinged his mind. The doctor always said he was highly strung, and the fact is he has had another attack, or whatever it is, the same as he had after the battle, when he thought he had seen three witches. (I afterwards found out from Banquo, who was with him at the time, that the matter was even worse than I suspected.) He is suffering from a terrible delusion. He thinks (of course you will never breathe this to a soul) that he killed Duncan! You can imagine what I am going through. Fortunately, nobody has noticed it.

Only last night another calamity happened. Banquo had a fall out riding and was killed. That night we had a banquet we could not possibly put off. On purpose I gave strict orders that Macbeth was not to be told of the accident until the banquet was over, but Lennox (who has no more discretion

than a parrot) told him, and in the middle of dinner he had
another attack, and I had only just time to get every one to
go away before he began to rave. As it was, it must have
been noticed that he wasn't himself.

I am in a terrible position. I never know when these fits
are coming on, and I am afraid of people talking, because if
it once gets about, people are so spiteful that somebody is sure
to start the rumour that it's true. Imagine our position, then!
So I beg you, dear Flora, to keep all this to yourself, and if
possible to come here as soon as possible.

I am, your affectionate,

Harriet R.

P.S.—Don't forget to bring Jeamie. It will do Macbeth
good to see a child in the house.

The Pensioner of the Pied Brothers

BY

HELEN PARRY EDEN

IF EVER I become a trifle eccentric I shall take it very ill of
my friends and relatives if they shut me up with anyone more
demented than themselves. It has always seemed to me both
extravagant and unkind to put a more or less amateur and
occasional lunatic among hard-bitten professionals. Mild madmen are better with their families and their families better
with them. As for madmen with no or reluctant families,
why not attach them to religious communities as jesters were
attached to royal households in the Middle Ages? This, I

From *Whistles of Silver and Other Stories,* by Helen Parry Eden. Reprinted by permission of the publisher, The Bruce Publishing Company, Mil-
waukee.

feel, would be an excellent plan. The community could concentrate on one official imbecile the forbearance they now exercise on each other; and the imbecile, unlike the average Religious, could lap himself around with forbearance as with a garment, and hug the warmth. This, at any rate, was how it worked with the only lunatic I ever met in such circumstances—John-Theodore de la Vigne of Cope in the county of Wessex, the Pensioner of the Pied Brothers.

John-Theodore, you must understand, was consigned at the age of sixteen by his highly respectable (some say inconspicuously noble) Walloon relatives to the guardianship of the Pied Brothers: and in particular to the Prior, for the time being, of the Priory of Cope. In thus establishing their half-witted nephew and cousin in virtuous and dignified surroundings, at a sufficient distance from the hereditary estate near Nivelles, the De la Vignes certainly thought they were doing their best for themselves, religion, and the object of their solicitude. And though success does not always attend performances on this gamut of interests, in the particular case I mention the upshot was extremely harmonious.

John-Theodore came to Cope in the wake of an old French Prior, and in charge of a young English lay-brother, at the age of sixteen. He was sixty when I first knew him and sixty-six when he died, and I never heard that he had a day's unhappiness. Certainly I never saw it. To begin with, he was highly popular at the Priory. His status with the Fathers in general I have already defined in my allocution on forbearance, but a few unchastened spirits loved John-Theodore for his own sake. To the lay-brothers he was acceptable because the care of his little room and some slight assistance with the inaccessible buttons of his toilet were a change from scrubbing the refectory flags and polishing the church candle-sticks. While to the boys of the Priory School—for Cope was the House of Studies for the province—he provided a not only good-tempered but positively appreciative butt for jests too elementary or outworn to play off on each other.

It would be hard to say which John-Theodore loved best, to be noticed or to be left alone. He was so radiantly happy in either case. In the nature of things he was more often alone, for a monastery school is, or should be, a place of fixed hours and settled functions, of never-ending class-bells and refectory bells and church-bells. The last two John-Theodore punctually regarded, always turning up at Mass and meat before any other enthusiast for either. But the boys' long study hours he spent all alone out of doors the whole year round: dozing under the acacia on the lawn in summer; drifting down the avenue with the dead leaves in the autumn; stopping out, as late as he dared, in the mild winter dusk to listen to the distilled rime dripping through the elms; and standing amazed every spring before the winter-greens in the kitchen-garden, when the April rains suddenly shot them up into tropical yellow flowers. Sometimes he strayed off to his prayers in the little church alongside the avenue; especially if a strain of music from the choir put him in mind of the claims of heaven. And many a Pied Brother has paused at the organ with the stops out and his hands hovering hawk-like over a chord, to hear John-Theodore ushering himself with indistinguishable murmurs of devotion into his humble place at the end of the nave.

Yet I think it was with his fellow-Christians that John-Theodore drank in life at its fullest; and could he have thought it out, he would have been quite of St. Thomas's opinion that the presence of friends is a fit concomitant to the bliss of heaven. Devout strangers he particularly affected on account of the extra measure of compassion they bestowed on him. For the compassion of the devout was to John-Theodore what the confidence of the vulgar is to a politician, and he was not much more scrupulous as to how he obtained it.

Towards the end of his days he was more than a trifle blind; yet not so blind but that he could find his way down the sanctuary steps with the rest of the school when it filed into church from the sacristy door for Mass or Meditation. But if there was a high feast kept, and strangers were present, John-Theodore would hang behind the rest and fumble dismally for the first step with his foot, his half-sightless eyes raised appealingly to heaven; until ten to one, some humane outsider, with or without an indignant glance at the callous scholars (who never failed to enjoy the little drama as far as its sacred setting permitted), would hasten up the shallow flight of marble inside the altar rails and lead John-Theodore, radiant as a prima-donna, safely down the steps and into his place.

There was only one person in the world with whom John-Theodore was not on good terms, and that was Father Caffyn. I never knew the precise ins and outs of the feud myself, because the good Father had been happily transferred from Cope before my acquaintance with the place began. But there was a rumour that he had a very cutting way with him, and that women, cats, and idiots—the three chief objectives of his scorn—used to flee at the sound of his voice like rooks at the crack of a rifle. John-Theodore never exactly fled; but they say he used to tack, with something more purposeful than his usual erratic change of course, whenever Father Caffyn appeared in the avenue. Moreover, being an expert at ritual himself, he lay in wait for little slips whenever the good Father said Mass or gave Benediction. And who so happy as John-Theodore when he caught the unfortunate priest reading the wrong Epistle, or leaving some recent Papal interpolation out of the Litany? He would hasten to the Prior of the day, with a zest so undisguised as to be shorn of half its malice, and accuse his enemy of substituting *Beatus vir* for *Memores estote* on the Feast of St. Silverius—or some such piece of inconspicuous heedlessness. And if he could delate the culprit to the Provincial in person, his jubilation knew no bounds.

When John-Theodore came to die—which he did, as I said, at the age of sixty-six—the memory of Father Caffyn whom he had not set eyes on for at least eight years, was the staple

amusement of his painless and leisurely decline. The Prior
could not bring him a glass of milk or a bunch of grapes without the invalid pluming himself between every sip and berry
on the anguish it would have caused his old traducer to see
him so pampered.

"Father Caffyn would never have fetched me grapes, eh
Father?" "Father Caffyn would never have brought me
milk!" he babbled over and over again; and the stray smiles
that crossed his quiet face as he lay speechless for hours on
his bed were probably referable to the same unholy satisfaction.

On the day he died he asked pardon of all he had ever offended with extraordinary meekness and dignity. But when
he had done this, and received the Last Sacraments, he was
allowed to slip back and enjoy his half-wittedness to the end.
The retrospective marvel of his Communion (which he had
never been encouraged to make before, save on high feasts
and holidays) became yet another triumph of compassion ex-
torted from the soft-hearted Prior by the piteousness of John-
Theodore; and yet another signal frustration of the malice
of his ancient foe.

"Father Caffyn would never have brought Him to me, eh
Father?" he said with serene exultation, as the bell which had
escorted the Blessed Sacrament to his bedside died away down
the corridor.

They will tell you, if you ever go to Cope—the Prior with
a smile and the Community with a sigh—that this monstrous
and entirely unfounded accusation was the last coherent
speech of The Pensioner of the Pied Brothers.

A Date for Saturday Night

BY

FRANCIS X. TALBOT

WHEN ADRIAN SUGGESTED that we might dine at the Half Moon Hotel, Coney Island, North America, I was a bit hesitant in my answer. Priests sometimes go to Coney Island, I admitted to myself; they even live there and have a church there. They are therefore not unknown. Walking along the Boardwalk or Surf Avenue, with a Roman collar confining me, would probably cause no more stir or scandal than a dwarf from one of the side-shows, or the fat woman who usually sits before the gaping mob. But Coney Island, even at an early dinner hour, encloses everybody visiting it in the aroma of a bright-light district and characterizes every visitor as a frequenter of broadways and manners. There might be a church in Coney Island, but Coney Island is not reputed for its churchiness.

"The 'Half Moon' is decent enough for a Monsignor," Adrian advised me. Since the young man has less respect for Monsignori than he has for Cardinals, his reference increased my suspicions. Contra, whatever is not too scandalous for a Monsignor is edifying enough for me, and, contra, there did seem an impelling reason other than idle curiosity. I turned to Adrian and admonished him: "To Coney Island."

"To Coney Island, James," he repeated, in turn, to the roadster. As if the Ford understood him, it smoothly slid away from the curb and into the lane of the street. "Whoopee," Adrian exulted, with a rising inflection on the first and a purr on the second. The roadster, being sensitive to its driver's emotion, quickened its pace.

From *America*, XLII (1929). Reprinted by permission of the Editor.

Perhaps Adrian needs some explanation. He is somewhat younger than I am, but more maturely radical. He is youthful enough to write poetry, but old enough to recognize how wretched are his verses, even when published. He was a Vers Librist, before he became a Symbolist. He professed to see something in the Dadists and, at the moment, was debating the ultimate influences on English Literature of the Transition group. Several Transitionists who had acquired the habit of suppressing all capital letters in their names, and who believed the language would be purified if commas and periods were annihilated, had issued a proclamation which attracted him.

"What can they mean by that fifth declaration: 'The expression of these concepts can be achieved only through the rhythmic "hallucination of the word" '? And the sixth: 'The literary creator has the right to disintegrate the primal matter of words imposed on him by text books and dictionaries'? And the seventh: 'He—' "

"He, he! to interflipt," I cut him short. He was driving, and the roadster was such a sensitive Ford that when he said fifth, the indicator rose to fifty, when he said sixth it swung to sixty, and now on the seventh it was struggling to keep up with him. I had to take the conversation away from him.

"Interflipt is a perfect transitional word. It means to interrupt flippantly. Joyce uses 'eithou' to indicate 'I,' 'you,' 'either,' all at once. Do you remember that beautiful storiette by Theo Rutra which begins: 'Abyssblue hosannaed into spring. Platonics stood horizontal song. He lingered in a sassaslab. It was so alcohol'?"

The last word had suggested gasoline to Adrian, and gasoline speed, and speed had recalled the tenth declaration: "Time is a tyranny to be abolished." My interlude had brought Adrian's eyes back on the road and his mind on the roadster. So we reached the Half Moon safely.

"You are not the first priest that ever walked into this hotel," Adrian reminded me, as he boldly packed me into a compartment of the revolving doors. "It's all very sedate and conservative. It's a good hotel and there's no scandal about a Roman collar being seen here—especially in my company." He ended in the lordly manner that is sometimes so irritating in Adrian.

With a flourish that would impress any check-girl, he skimmed his hat on to the table where the silver coins in a little dish were displayed. We marched up the softly carpeted steps to the dining room. A gentleman, as aged as he was distinguished looking, glanced at us from his deeply cushioned chair. A solidly, respectable couple observed us coldly and with utter detachment. It was more like the Mayflower than the Half Moon, and not like Coney Island in any respect.

Adrian chose a table in a quiet corner of the long-sweeping, high-ceilinged dining room. We looked out over the ocean and heard the music of the waves playing upon the sands. Sunset was upon the crests of the waters and night was black in the hollows. A white ship floated nearer, and afar was a shadowy ship vaguely silhouetted. The ocean was at its loveliest.

"Beautiful," I murmured, as I turned towards Adrian. The man was thinking of meters and rhymes. The beauty of it all was just the subject of a poem he was creating. "It will be another wretched poem," I thought to myself. "While he is thinking of his own poems he is neglecting to read this obvious poem of God."

"Yes sir! Yes sir!" said the smiling waiter. "Yes, sir! Yes, sir!" he repeated as he poised his pencil over his order pad. The preliminaries passed quickly, for Adrian was more interested in his rhymes than he was in fish and cauliflower. Instead of talking to me, he was quite clearly composing verses within his own mind, verses, I could not help reflecting, that I shall most assuredly, within the next week, reject as "not being found available for publication."

Left to myself, my eyes wandered down the long rows of immaculately clothed tables. A girl was coming towards us,

a blond head in contrast with a black dress. She did not seem
to walk, but to dance rhythmically with the abandonment of
restraint. As she passed the diners, she cast her smiles upon
them as a child would toss the petals of a daisy upon her dolls.
She sparkled like the waves with sunshine upon them. Now
and then she stopped at the tables, and uncovered the tray on
which she was carrying the hot buns. "A cabaret effect," I
thought to myself. "She could easily get a job as a night-club
queen." Adrian's back was toward her and his face was towards the sea, still fascinated.

The cabaret girl turned abruptly to the right a few tables
above us. She did not offer us of her buns. I could see the
diners responding to her smiles as she encircled the dining
room. She lilted towards our table a second time, just as the
soup was arriving and Adrian was returning from the ocean
view. Without a glance she spurned us again.

"Call that girl that is serving the buns," I told Adrian.
He turned as she was the third time rhythmically turning
away from us and loudly motioned her. The smile left her
face for a moment, but she came. He appraised her, and he
scowled. He thought I might not be favorably impressed by
her rouge and carmined lips and the black thread of her eyebrows.

"You have been neglecting us," I said, not without a touch
of asperity.

"Have I?" she answered, not without a touch of brazen-
ness.

"You were going to pass us the third time, without offering
us a bun," I told her. Adrian said nothing, but chose two
muffins.

She was serious when I looked up at her. She folded the
napkin over her tray, and as she turned to go she leaned towards me and whispered: "I was afraid of you." With a light
laugh, she tripped away.

"What did she say?" Adrian inquired. I did not tell him.
Her words had startled me, for why should she be afraid

of *me*? Was I the sort of being that would inspire fear in a painted young lady? Did her instinct set her against me? Why was the smile frozen on her pretty face when we forced her to come to us? Why *should* she be afraid of me? Adrian, who concluded that I had been insulted and was burning to demand an apology from the manager of the hotel, kept asking me what she said.

With smiles for all, she floated towards us again. As she passed, I asked: "Why?"

She stared at me for a moment from her sea-blue eyes, and in a low tone said: "You reminded me of something."

Adrian did not hear her words. His napkin was now clutched in his hand and both his fists were on the table.

"What did she say to you?" he demanded. He suspected something outrageous. I suppressed him partially by telling him to keep on searching for his wretched rhymes. What did I remind her of, I reflected. I examined my conscience quickly, and buttered my bun abstractedly, and struggled with the chicken on my plate. Adrian called the nymph to our table.

"Give me a muffin," he growled viciously. "And what are you saying to him?" he demanded. She looked at him along the length of her dainty nose. She excluded him completely from the world by injecting her shoulder between us.

"Do you know what you remind me of?" she whispered. She was frightfully serious.

I shook my head, fearful of the revelation. Doom was impending.

"I'll tell you. I haven't 'been' for three weeks. And when I saw you coming into the dining room, I thought of it. That is why I was afraid to come near. I am *never* going again."

I began to smile. She smiled. I had to laugh outright. She tittered guiltily. She blithely danced away, play-acting to the diners.

Adrian's face was really funny to look on as he turned from me to her and back and forth.

"What's the joke?" he asked testily. Since he was completely left out of it, he felt fearful and outraged. He had the greatest confidence in me, but he was scandalized that I should be talking and laughing with the painted thing that was dispensing buns. He was troubled, and he made no secret of it. The girl had returned. "How about going?" I asked. She rested her tray on the table and leaned towards me. Adrian heard my question, and was easing forward to hear the answer; but I waved him off. He leaned back against his chair and looked sulkily out towards the ocean. Adrian is gentleman enough to know when he is intruding. She, too, cast a look on him that would have put anybody, even though he was not a gentleman, in his proper place.

"The priests in our Church are cranky. They scolded me the last time," she confided. "I missed Mass two Sundays. I have to work here all Sunday morning, and I would lose my job if I went to Mass. Mother is sick now, and can't work. But when I tell the priest about missing Mass, oh, la-la."

The headwaiter was ostentatiously making his presence felt. She made a funny little noise towards Adrian who had been keeping his eyes on the darkling waves. "Ta, ta," she said to him sweetly, for the benefit of the headwaiter who looked as if he, too, would like to scold her. She was off with her smiles and her buns.

"Finished?" snapped Adrian to me. The dinner was a failure.

"This coffee is delicious," I assured him. "I like to sip my coffee slowly after dinner." I was waiting for the girl with the buns. She had eluded the headwaiter and in the course of her wanderings among the diners she was casually approaching our table.

"Will you go on Saturday night?" I asked her.

"I'm never going *again,*" she answered flatly.

"Why be afraid? Everything will be all right. Say yes. Come on. Say that you'll go next Saturday."

"I don't finish work until half-past nine," she weakened.

"That's not too late," I told her.

The head waiter hovered near again. She did not deign to notice him but sauntered off to a group of men that were growing hungry for her muffins.

Adrian motioned to me to precede him out of the dining room. He had heard enough of what I had said to make him suspicious and angry. We passed her on the way out.

"Next Saturday?" I pleaded with her.

"No," she snapped. "Yes. I'll go. Sure." She almost sang the word. Sure. She gave her word.

When we were settled in the roadster, Adrian looked at me before he stepped on the gas. He was ineffably polite.

"It's probably okay," he exploded. "But I feel bound to tell you, Father, that I didn't like to see you flirting with that girl, and what is more, making a date with her. I couldn't help hearing about Saturday night. I don't know what it's all about, but I don't like it. And I want to tell you something more. I'm responsible for bringing you down here to Coney Island, but I'm not responsible for anything else that happened." He was really angry when he finished his speech.

"Adrian, my friend," I said kindly, "please don't worry. I think your poem about the sunset on the sea at Coney Island is going to be very good. But the best poems are sometimes not written. My dear Adrian! You haven't the slightest idea as to the reason why we came down to Coney Island. You were not responsible for our coming. You were only the poor sap that drove the machine."

He stared at me. The sun rose in his eyes.

"I'll recite the poem as we drive along," he said, and a happy ring was in his voice. "It came on me like a flash. I hope you are going to like it."

3

LENGTH AND BREADTH

The Vision of the Alps

BY ·

HILAIRE BELLOC

THE WOOD WENT up darkly and the path branched here and there so that I was soon uncertain of my way, but I followed generally what seemed to me the most southerly course, and so came at last up steeply through a dip or ravine that ended high on the crest of the ridge.

Just as I came to the end of the rise, after perhaps an hour, perhaps two, of that great curtain of forest which had held the mountain side, the trees fell away to brushwood, there was a gate, and then the path was lost upon a fine open sward which was the very top of the Jura and the coping of that multiple wall which defends the Swiss Plain. I had crossed it straight from edge to edge, never turning out of my way.

It was too marshy to lie down on it, so I stood a moment to breathe and look about me.

It was evident that nothing higher remained, for though a new line of wood—firs and beeches—stood before me, yet nothing appeared above them, and I knew that they must be the fringe of the descent. I approached this edge of wood, and saw that it had a rough fence of post and rails bounding

From *The Path to Rome,* by Hilaire Belloc. Reprinted by permission of the publisher, George Allen and Unwin, Ltd., London.

it, and as I was looking for the entry of a path (for my original path was lost, as such tracks are, in the damp grass of the little down) there came to me one of those great revelations which betray to us suddenly the higher things and stand afterwards firm in our minds.

There, on this upper meadow, where so far I had felt nothing but the ordinary gladness of The Summit, I had a vision.

What was it I saw? If you think I saw this or that, and if you think I am inventing the words, you know nothing of men.

I saw between the branches of the trees in front of me a sight in the sky that made me stop breathing, just as great danger at sea, or great surprise in love, or a great deliverance will make a man stop breathing. I saw something I had known in the West as a boy, something I had never seen so grandly discovered as was this. In between the branches of the trees was a great promise of unexpected lights beyond.

I pushed left and right along that edge of the forest and along the fence that bound it, until I found a place where the pine-trees stopped, leaving a gap, and where on the right, beyond the gap, was a tree whose leaves had failed; there the ground broke away steeply below me, and the beeches fell, one below the other, like a vast cascade, towards the limestone cliffs that dipped down still further, beyond my sight. I looked through this framing hollow and praised God. For there below me, thousands of feet below me, was what seemed an illimitable plain; at the end of that world was an horizon, and the dim bluish sky that overhangs an horizon.

There was brume in it and thickness. One saw the sky beyond the edge of the world getting purer as the vault rose. But right up—a belt in that empyrean—ran peak and field and needle of intense ice, remote, remote from the world. Sky beneath them and sky above them, a steadfast legion, they glittered as though with the armour of the immovable armies of Heaven. Two days' march, three days' march away, they stood up like the walls of Eden. I say it again, they stopped my breath. I had seen them.

So little are we, we men: so much are we immersed in our muddy and immediate interests that we think, by numbers and recitals, to comprehend distance or time, or any of our limiting infinities. Here were these magnificent creatures of God, I mean the Alps, which now for the first time I saw from the height of the Jura; and because they were fifty or sixty miles away, and because they were a mile or two high, they were become something different from us others, and could strike one motionless with the awe of supernatural things. Up there in the sky, to which only clouds belong and birds and the last trembling colours of pure light, they stood fast and hard; not moving as do the things of the sky. They were as distant as the little upper clouds of summer, as fine and tenuous; but in their reflection and in their quality as it were of weapons (like spears and shields of an unknown array) they occupied the sky with a sublime invasion: and the things proper to the sky were forgotten by me in their presence as I gazed.

To what emotion shall I compare this astonishment? So, in first love one finds that *this* can belong to *me*.

Their sharp steadfastness and their clean uplifted lines compelled my adoration. Up there, the sky above and below them, part of the sky, but part of us, the great peaks made communion between that homing creeping part of me which loves vineyards and dances and a slow movement among pastures, and that other part which is only properly at home in Heaven. I say that this kind of description is useless, and that it is better to address prayers to such things than to attempt to interpret them for others.

These, the great Alps, seen thus, link one in some way to one's immortality. Nor is it possible to convey, or even to suggest, those few fifty miles, and those few thousand feet; there is something more. Let me put it thus: that from the height of Weissenstein I saw, as it were, my religion. I mean, humility, the fear of death, the terror of height and of distance, the glory of God, the infinite potentiality of reception whence springs that divine thirst of the soul; my aspiration also towards completion, and my confidence in the dual destiny. For I know that we laughers have a gross cousinship with the most high, and it is this contrast and perpetual quarrel which feeds a spring of merriment in the soul of a sane man.

Since I could now see such a wonder and it could work such things in my mind, therefore, some day I should be part of it. That is what I felt.

A Day in the Bog

BY

SEUMAS MacMANUS

Do you mind the turf-cutting? The turf-cutting in Donegal! the turf-cutting in the lone bogs, away from the far hills, in the merry May time, when the sun was bright and the air was balmy, and the first flowers were showing on the slopes, and the marsh-mallows by the wayside; and the milky-white *cean-a-bhans* were broidering the bogs; and the bee was humming, and the water-wagtail twittering; and the lark spilling his melody from above—when the bog, at most times lonely, was at length lively with the quick-working little groups that dotted it—the men and bigger boys fast plying the spade, and slinging the clean-cut turf high up into the eager hands that waited to catch it soft and sodden, and bear it back to the clear, dry ground behind, where the sun, and the wind, and the air would win the peat that should serve to feed a fine

From *Yourself and the Neighbors,* by Seumas MacManus. Reprinted by arrangement with the publisher, The Devin-Adair Company, New York.

fire. Oh, the turf-cutting! the glorious turf-cutting! the happy turf-cutting! the turf-cutting in the bogs of Ireland!

But, to be sure, 'twasn't *all* merriment, and 'twasn't *all* poetry, the same turf-cutting in your lovely, lonely bogs. It ever meant a long day's work, and a strong day's work and hard—bracingly begun before the sun rolled above the rim of the bog, and ended, with aching back and raging appetite, after he had gone to rest again, and was pulling black curtains between him and the world.

At four o'clock in the morning your father, who never seemed to sleep when there was anything to do, was already afoot in the little mountain cabin, and noisily awaking every mother's son and daughter of you, and hastening you from your beds before you got the gates of dreamland shut. By five o'clock the clan-jaffrey of you had stowed away a breakfast of oaten stirabout that would provision a privateer, and with bottles of new milk, and fadges of well-hardened, thickly buttered oatcake, and pocketsful of hard-boiled eggs, leave behind you the little house with the candle in its little window, and, in the breaking dawn, are treading an uncertain way down the uneven *cassey* that leads from your door to the road, cheerily chattering and heartily laughing at one another's mishaps as you go. On the road, your father is impatiently holding a donkey by the head, waiting for the girls to take their place in the high-caged cart. The cage swings open; the girls bounce in; the donkey is released, and off along the hard, white road it trots, click-clack, click-clack, the girls laughing gleefully, while your father and yourselves, by long and hasty strides, kill yourselves trying to keep up to the mighty wise little animal, which knows well, since such early start is made, that a big day's work lies ahead, and extraordinary haste is called for.

On the way you fall in with many another hurrying party. So, in the bog, the round red sun rises upon a lively scene—a pleasant contrast with the usually dreary aspect of the white-patched, great and wide stretches of waste. Here and there over the vast surface of it you see high-caged carts, little and big, up-ended; and the animals that drew them, the donkeys and horses, picking stray blades of grass and soft tops of heather, as they wander wide. Reeks of blue smoke are mounting on the morning air from a hundred small fires nigh the carts, and a hundred family parties, bareheaded and bare-footed, each upon a turf-bank near their own fire, are hard at work plying the spade, or catching, or throwing, or carry-ing, or wheeling the fresh turf, or setting drier ones on end, four or five together—"footing" them. The father's spade, or elder brother's, works mortal fast indeed; carving its way through the soft bank, sharp and quick, the bright blade, for a second deep-buried, is flashing aloft the next instant, and a clean turf is flying from it into the waiting hands that quickly pass it far from its bed. Four, or five, or six sweating people, father, and sisters, and brothers, take little time—you'd think —to hearken to the lark's song or the bees' hum, to enjoy the blue sky, or the bright hills beyond the bog, or the white sun-shine that is frisking upon them, or the sweet-smelling smoke that is curling above. Keeping hands and eyes close upon their labour, they work hard and still harder as the sun mounts high and still higher. But, for all that, don't conceit yourself that the beauty is lost on them. It is in their hearts as they work, their blood leaps the quicker for it; the lively tune, and glad song, and merry joke, come lightly from their lips. The black bog is bright, and the lone bog full of life, and the silent bog filled with music, with whistle and song, with laughter, chat and cheery hail.

Till the white sun has reached its height, and passed it, there is neither cease nor pause. Many a suddenly-sprung turf-cutting contest has been hotly fought out, and many a victor loudly acclaimed. "Patrick's Andy walked his floor * at the rate of a weddin', but Manis Gildea swept his like a blaze o' whins." But, then, "The match of Manis wasn't within the five baronies, and his bate couldn't be got though

---

* A "floor" is a strip or bog-bank cleaned for cutting.

you screenged Ireland with a herrin' net; and as for Andy, his aiqual was far to find." For the champion turf-cutter is a hero not without honour in his own country, and in his own way he may gather to himself nigh as much glory as the school-master. His name is spoken proudly at wedding, wake and fair, and he holds a high place in the councils of his neigh-bours. He toils hard for the fame that finally comes to him, and has the consolation of knowing that for a generation after the "daisy quilt" is pulled over him his name will be passed with pride, and his deeds paraded by the wondering ones he leaves behind.

After midday, when appetites are keen as a March blast, your father, to the joy of all, says:

"That'll do, childer. Let us in God's name have food to eat, and rest for our limbs." And turf and turf-barrows are instantly dropped, and, with a rousing cheer, you all rush for the cart where the coveted things are stored. Close to the fire the Cloth of Plenty is untied, and stacks of buttered oatcake, mounds of eggs, and mountains of milk-bottles disclosed to hungering eyes. Into the fire the eggs are put for roasting. Down on the bog-floor, by the piles of eatables and drink-ables, you all squat. Your father, taking off his hat, blesses himself, and you all follow the good example. With hearty good-will you then "fall-to," and the carnage begins.

Notwithstanding the ravenous hunger that each of you brings to the feast, there is always time for a joke between bites, and the gay laughter goes forward without cessation. At the tail of the feasting your father draws out his pipe, and fills and lights it, stretches his legs from him, gets his back against a pile of turf and smokes, in high content with him-self and the world. You and your brothers step across to the neighbouring parties, and have your whispers with the blush-ing *cailini* there; while, just to strike a balance, the boys from there cross over to tell your girls what sort the weather is going to be tomorrow. But there's only little time for inter-course just now. The call of a dozen fathers: "To your work, brave boys!" soon rings out. And, with brightness in your eyes and merry music on your lips, tripping you come to your task once more, and in a few minutes' time the bog is again busy with a toiling multitude.

When, after a long day and a glad day, the sun has at last left the pearly sky, and the shadows, waving their dark wands, come after you all, now tired and songless, but still merry, you drop spade and barrow, gather your alls, pursue, bring back and harness the donkey, get the girls into the cart, and, wearing a pleasant cloak of fatigue, set your steps on the homeward way. A supper fit for a king is before you as you burst into the warm kitchen of your cabin, nigh to bedtime— a mountain of flowery potatoes, still steaming, and laughing through their jackets, hillocks of yellow butter flanking it, and lochs of thick-milk—for, surely, little less than lochs are the great bowls of it that are set down, one for each man, and boy, and girl. The envy of a king would be the appetites that each of you brings home with you from the bog; and the envy of a king might well be the relish with which you attack the mountain of laughing potatoes; and certainly the envy of a king would be the happy hearts and the sleep-filled heads, and glad, tired limbs, which, when Rosary is said, you stretch upon welcome beds.

Before yet the turf is fully won, and dragged home, and stacked in the garden, there's many another long and toil-some, joyous, bright day in the bog still ahead of you. And after the turf is won, and safely stacked at home, on many a winter's night will the high-leaping, bright-blazing turf fire warm you and cheer you, as you propound riddles, and sing songs, and hearken to the old, old, beautiful tales and *laoidhs* that happily while away the surly, burly, rainy, stormy, blowy, snowy winter nights, and repay you, happy-hearted children of all ages, for many a sore, toilsome, glorious day in the bog!

The Great Nickel Adventure

BY

JOYCE KILMER

WHENEVER I READ Mr. Chester Firkins' excellent poem "On a Subway Express" I am filled with amazement. It is not strange that Mr. Firkins turned the subway into poetry, it is strange that the subway does not turn every one of its passengers into a poet.

There are, it is true, more comfortable means of locomotion than the subway; there are conveyances less crowded, better ventilated, cooler in Summer, warmer in Winter. A little discomfort, however, is an appropriate accompaniment of adventure. And subway-riding is a splendid adventure, a radiant bit of romance set in the gray fabric of the work-a-day world.

The aëroplane has been celebrated so enthusiastically in the course of its brief life that it must by now be a most offensively conceited machine. Yet an aëroplane ride, however picturesque and dangerous, has about it far less of essential romance than a ride in the subway. He who sails through the sky directs, so nearly as is possible, his course; he handles levers, steers, goes up or down, to the left or right. Or if he is a passenger, he has, at any rate, full knowledge of what is going on around him, he sees his course before him, he can call out to the man at the helm: "Look out for that comet's hair! Turn to the left or the point of that star will puncture our sail!"

Now, unseen dangers are more thrilling than those seen; the aëroplane journey has about it inevitably something pro-

saic. This is the great charm of the subway, that the passengers, the guards, too, for that matter, give themselves up
to adventure with a blind and beautiful recklessness. They
leave the accustomed sunlight and plunge into subterranean
caverns, into a region far more mysterious than the candid
air, into a region which since mankind was young has been
associated with death. Before an awed and admiring crowd,
the circus acrobat is shut into a hollow ball and catapulted
across the rings; with not even a sense of his own bravado,
the subway passenger is shut into a box and shot twenty miles
through the earth.

Once there lived on West One Hundred and Eighty-second
Street a man of uncompromising practicality, a stern rationalist. He was as advanced as anything! He believed in the
materialistic interpretation of history, economic determinism,
and radium; this, he said, with some pride, was his Creed.
Often he expressed his loathing for "flesh-food," more frequently for "Middle Class morality," most frequently for
faith. "Faith is stupidity," he would say. "Look before you
leap! It makes me sick to see the way people have been hum-
bugged in all ages. The capitalist class has told them something was true, something nobody could understand, and
they've blindly accepted it, the idiots! I believe in what I see
—I don't take chances. I don't trust anybody but myself."

Yet every day this man would give himself up to the subway with a sweet and child-like faith. As he sat in the speed-
ing car, he could not see his way, he had no chance of directing
it. He trusted that the train would keep to its route, that it
would stop at Fourteenth Street and let him off. He could
not keep it from taking him under the river and hurling him
out into some strange Brooklyn desert. When he started for
home in the evening, he read the words "Dyckman Street" on
the car window with a medieval simplicity, and on the guarantee of these printed words, placed there by minions of
the capitalist class, he gave up the privilege of directing his
course. The train, he believed, would not at Ninety-sixth

Street be switched off to a Bronx track; the sign told him that he was safe, and he believed it.

So the subway caused him to exercise the virtue of faith, made him, for a time, really a human being. Perhaps it is the sharing of this faith that makes a subway crowd so democratic. Surely there is some subtly powerful influence at work, changing men and women as soon as they take their seats, or straps.

For one thing, they become alike in appearance. The glare of the electric light unifies them, modifying swarthy faces and faces delicately rouged until they are nearly of one hue. Then, the differences of attitude are lost, and attitudes are great instruments of subordination. The ragged bootblack does not kneel at the broker's feet; he sits close beside him, or perhaps, comfortably at rest, watches the broker clutch a strap and struggle to keep his footing.

"Tired clerks, pale girls, street-cleaners, business men, boys, priests and sailors, drunkards, students, thieves"—all gain a new sincerity. Neither the millionaire's imperiousness nor the beggar's professional humility can make the train go faster, so both are laid aside. Distinctions of race and caste grow insignificant, as in a company confronting one peril or one God. This is not theory, it is fact. The subway passenger purchases a nickel's worth of speed and he must take with it a nickel's worth of democracy.

Perhaps it is the youthful romanticism of America which makes our subways so much more exciting than those of Europe. The Englishman is too cautious and too conservative to trust himself away from the earth's surface more than two minutes at a time. So the trains that run through the London tube are tame, cowardly things. They timidly run underground for half a mile or so and pop their heads out into the air and sunlight or fog at every station.

But the New York subway train is ready to take a chance. It dives into the earth and "stays under," like a brave diver, for an hour at a time. And when it does emerge, what splendor attends its coming! There is a glimmer of sunshine at the One Hundred and Sixteenth Street Station; the blue and white of the walls and pillars reflect a light not wholly artificial. Then there is a brief stretch of fantastically broken darkness. Passengers in the first car can see ahead of them, at Manhattan Street, a great door of sunshine. At last there is a strange change in the rumble of the wheels, for the echoing roof and walls are gone, and the train leaves its tunnel not to run humbly over the ground, but to rise higher and higher until it comes to a sudden halt above chimneys and tree tops. To say that the grub becomes a butterfly does not fit the case, for the grub is a slow-moving beast and a butterfly's course is capricious. Rather, it is as if, by some tremendous magic, a great snake became a soaring eagle.

And how keenly all the passengers enjoy their few seconds in the open air! When they hurried down the steps to the train, they were scornful of the atmosphere they were leaving, they had no thought of tasting wind and watching sunlight. Now they are become, for the moment, connoisseurs of these delectable things; they wish the train would linger at Manhattan Street, not inevitably plunge at once into its roaring cavern. But the train is wise, it knows brevity is essential to all exquisite things, so it gives its passengers only an evanescent glimpse of the glories they have just now learned to appreciate.

This is a part of the great conspiracy of the subway. It is regarded only as a swift and convenient and uncomfortable carrier, and it has no wish to be otherwise interpreted. But those who have studied it know the hidden purposes it constantly and effectively serves. It is showing our generation the value of mankind's commonest and most precious gifts, by taking them away.

Now, it is good for man or beast to stand on solid ground in the sunlight, breathing clean air. Also fellowship is good, and the talk of friends. We forgot the value of these, we shut ourselves up in dark rooms and we spared no time to social exercise. Then—to punish and cure our folly—came the subway, making our journeys things close and dark in which conversation is a matter of desperate effort. And now how kind and talkative are people who go home together from the subway station after their daily disciplinary ride! They are grateful, too—although it may be subconsciously —for the familiar sights and sounds of the earth, for houses and streets and light that does not come from a wire in a bottle. They take gladly the great common things; they are simple, natural, democratic.

So they spend much of their leisure out of doors, these men and women who are underground two hours every weekday. In the evenings and on Sunday afternoons, they walk the pleasant streets with eager delight. They are curious about the loveliness far beneath which they daily speed. They have learned something of the art of life.

Of course, the subway has its incidental charms—its gay fresco of advertisements, for instance, and its faint mysterious thunder when it runs near the surface of the street on which we stand. But its chief service to man—perhaps its reason for existence—is that it gives him adventure. In this adventure he meets the spirit of faith and the spirit of democracy, which is an aspect of charity. And by their influence he becomes, surely though but for a time, as a little child.

Romantic Sligo

BY

SÉAN O'FAOLÁIN

MYTHS SUFFUSE THE air like spray. They fall on the simplest things and cover them like hoar-frost; or the shimmering webs that mist the fields in summer. The eye obscures itself. Objectivity is impossible where so many reliques excite the mind; dolmens, cairns, stone circles, forts, cromlechs, trilithons, all suggestive of events not merely great but superhuman. One look at that flat-topped plateau of Knocknarea, one hint of its associations, one glimpse of the enormous cairn surmounting it—as large at close quarters as one of those man-dwarfing slag-heaps of the Black Country—is enough to subdue all disbelief; and since it is one of the first natural objects to catch the eye, one approaches this region subject to it even before one has well entered it. People say this vast cairn is the tomb of Queen Maeve, the legendary Queen of Connaught, an amazon who emerges from the epic tales about her with a stature greater than any Boadicea or Brunhild. Yet the name, in local tradition, means the Hill of Kings rather than "of the queens" (more romantic antiquaries wished to call it the Mountain of the Moon), and that tremendous mythical battle fought back on the Plain of Moytura, beside Lough Mask, is also traced here in an epic flight through the entire length of Connaught, to end with a battle where the remnants of the Firbolg were cut to pieces on the sands below by the following Tuatha de Danaan. In ordinary conversation any intelligent Sligo man will point you out the track of that flight, and resurrect from the place-names

From *An Irish Journey,* by Séan O'Faoláin. Reprinted by arrangement with the publisher, Longmans, Green & Co., New York.

the evidence for whatever version of the tradition has come down to him. Yet another tradition relates Knocknarea and Carrowmore (both sets of monuments are connected) to a revolt supported by Ulstermen, against a Connaught king of the sixth century, Eoghan Bel. He was killed in that fight, but before he died ordered his men to bury him standing, his red spear in his hand, facing the route of the fleeing Ulstermen; and some hold that he was buried under the great cairn of Knocknarea. Only stone implements have been found about both Knocknarea and Carrowmore, marking them as reliques of semi-civilization.

To the north, across Rosses Point, rises the broken snout of Ben Bulben. With that blunt promontory goes the far later epic of the Fenian cycle—the story of Fionn, and Oisin, Diarmuid and Grainne, Oscar and Caoilte and Diorruing. It is the place where the second great Irish love-story came to its tragic end, the counterpart, and probable derivative of the magnificent, earlier story of Deirdre. As the high-king Conchubar desired Deirdre, and she loved Naoisi, so the leader of the Fianna, Fionn, desired Grainne, and she loved Diarmuid. She eloped with him. They fled all over Ireland, and everywhere you are pointed out those caverns and cromlechs which the people call "Leabuidh Dhiarmada agus Grainne," the Bed of Diarmuid and Grainne. In the end Diarmuid made peace with Fionn, but Fionn harboured a relentless jealousy, and planned a boar-hunt to which Diarmuid was enticed. The hunt ended on Ben Bulben, where the boar ripped the bowels of Diarmuid. Even then Fionn might have saved him by bringing to him magic water in his hands from a well not nine paces away. Three times Fionn, under threats from Oscar, came with the water, but each time his jealous heart made him spill it between his fingers, and Diarmuid died.

It is a story less noble in its conclusion, as it is less ancient, than the Deirdre story; where Deirdre fell with her lover into his grave, Grainne let the old man wean her from her loyalty, and married him. "Fionn," records the old story, "left not playing her with sweet words until he had brought her to his own will, and he had his desire of her. After that Fionn and Grainne went their way, and no tidings are told of them until they reached the Fianna." The Fianna had, in their hatred of Fionn's treachery revolted against him. "When they saw Fionn and Grainne coming towards them in that guise they raised a shout of derision and mockery at her, and she bowed her head in shame. . . ."

Yeats, looking up at Knocknarea, mingled the two periods:

> The host is riding from Knocknarea
> And over the grave of Clooth-na-bare,
> Caoilte tossing his flaming hair,
> And Niamh calling, "Away, come away."

He offended against no canon. The folk mingle them as wildly. An old nurse of a friend of mine, in Sligo, used tell him the story of Deirdre and of her exile in Scotland in terms of the modern Burns and Laird direct route from Sligo to Glasgow, saying, "They then wint on a honeymoon to Glashgow." Yeats himself heard an old man tell stories of Fionn in one of which Fionn threw a bailiff over a haycock while on the way to a police-court, and I have, myself, worked over several of these Ossianic tales which the people have confused and mixed up to their hearts' content for greater relevance to their own humble lives, bringing stories as old as Knocknarea into the period of Michael Davitt and landlordism.

There is a strong Protestant colony in Sligo, and a solid and well-to-do colony. Yeats alone of all their generations seized on the magic of the Gaelic world. It is moving, today, so soon after his death, when somebody points out a place, say Glencar, and adds a half-line of a poem, "the woods above Glencar." They take on a new quality at once. It is the same when you go up the lovely, dreaming water of Lough Gill and see Innisfree, and Dooney Rock, and if you can go ashore you may find a rock where he lay one night as he recalls half-seriously, half self-teasingly, in *Reveries:*

"My father read me some passage out of *Walden* and I planned some day to live in a cottage on a little island called Inishfree, and Inishfree was opposite to Slish Wood where I meant to sleep. I thought that having conquered bodily desire and the inclination of my mind towards women and love, I should live, as Thoreau lived, seeking wisdom. I set out from Sligo about six in the evening, walking slowly, for it was an evening of great beauty, but though I was well into Slish Wood by bedtime I could not sleep, not for the discomfort of the dry rock I had chosen for my bed but from my fear of the wood-ranger. . . ." Then he tells of his weary return and how the servant chuckled a ribald chuckle at the notion that he had been sleeping in a wood: she thought that she knew far better what he had been up to, and would go into fits of laughter for months after if any reference was made to the expedition, saying, "You had good right to be fatigued."

I was touched to find a photograph of this rock in Tadgh Kilgannon's guide to Sligo, marked, *Inishfree. Yeats' Bed in the Foreground,* with a note, which some of our more pious folk might find irreverent, that "in centuries to come it will, no doubt, be known as Yeats' Bed, and as frequented and reverenced by the ubiquitous, inquiring tourist as St. Kevin's Bed (in Glendalough) is today."

The town has its later, stirring, associations—Red Hugh O'Donnell, Sarsfield, and not least Sir Tadgh O'Regan, the last native defender of Connaught, of whom one may conveniently read in Colonel Wood-Martin's local history. Sir Tadgh comes after the fall of the Gaelic world at Limerick, and the victory of the Williamites, as a link with the modern Ireland: one of the few leaders left behind by the Wild Geese when Sarsfield led them to France. He had held out in Tyrone only until his men were eating raw horse-skin. He was ragged, holes in his boots, a rag for a cravat, hunchbacked,

on an old spavined nag that kept kicking and whinnying as
he parleyed with Schomberg. When Connaught was cut off
he held out to the last, surrendered on honourable terms, and
thereafter the game was in the hands of the *raparees,* the on-
the-run men of the bad century, the progenitors of the I.R.A.
of our day.

It is a lovely site for a town, the Garravogue broadening
into a bay, big steamers lining the quays, the old seamen's
pubs, small, very cosy at night, with squared windows facing
the river where the lights from the opposite side fall dagger-
ing into the water. Every side street seems to lead to a bridge,
since the town is divided by the river, and though the main
streets are narrow and undistinguished, they have a busy, rattling, sociable air, and in no country southern town have I
seen so many cafés and tea-shops. Up the hill on the north
side of the town there are some fine old houses and some very
quaint and homely ones. Here and there the streets widen
into something that is almost a square, and in so small a town
to meet unexpectedly the Abbey, the cathedral, the lovely
Norman church of St. John's, several lesser churches and
chapels, gave added force to the first impression I got of a
varied and articulate society with a tradition behind it.

So ensconced in time, it is a town that could, I felt, wind
many tendrils about the heart. It is a welcoming town. In
others, through the west, I have felt "This is remote, but I
feel no sense of loss." Here I did not once even think that
I was remote. There was, more than in any other place that
I have been, of its size, extraordinary feeling of self-
sufficiency. They have done very well here in music and
drama; they hold two Feiseanna, or art-festivals, every summer, and the standards are extraordinarily high. And when
I began to consider this, and wonder why it is so, I could only
think that this is because the life-modes are more varied here
than in those other places, because there is a variety of classes,
and traditions—the best Protestant stock in all Ireland is in
Sligo—and because of that surrounding dignity of history and

fable which tempts one to liken this little port to some port-city on the Piraeus where the gods smiled on every hearth, or thundered in every storm, and no man thought that there existed beyond the hills any world but his own.

The Chapel of the Palms

BY

CHARLES WARREN STODDARD

OH, THE LONG suffering of him who threads a narrow trail over the brown crust of a hill where the short grass lies flat in tropical sunshine! On one side sleeps the blue, monotonous sea; on the other, crags clothe themselves in cool mist and look dreamy and solemn.

The boy Kahéle, who has no ambition beyond the bit of his foot-sore mustang, lags behind, taking all the dust with commendable resignation.

As for me, I am wet through with the last shower; I steam in the fierce noonday heat. I spur Hoké the mule into the shadow of a great cloud that drifts lazily overhead, and am grateful for this unsatisfying shade as long as it lasts. I watch the sea, swinging my whip by its threadbare lash like a pendulum—the sea, where very black rock is being drowned over and over by the tremendous swell that covers it for a moment; but somehow the rock comes to the surface again, and seems to gasp horribly in a deluge of breakers. That rock has been drowning for centuries, yet its struggle for life is as real as ever.

I watch the mountains, cleft with green, fern-cushioned

From *South Sea Idylls*, by Charles Warren Stoddard. Reprinted by permission of the publisher, Charles Scribner's Sons, New York.

chasms, where an occasional stream silently distills. Far up on a sun-swept ledge a white, scattering drift, looking like a rose-garden after a high wind, I know to be a flock of goats feeding. But the wind-dried and sunburnt grass under foot, the intangible dust that pervades the air, the rain-cloud in the distance, trailing its banners of crape in the sea as it bears down upon us—these are what fret me a little, and make life a burden for the time being; so I spur my faithless Hoké up a new ascent as forbidding as any that we have yet come upon, and slowly and with many pauses creep to the summit.

Kahéle, "the goer," belies his name, for he loiters everywhere and always; yet I am not sorry. I have the first glimpse of Wailua all to myself. I am not obliged to betray my emotion, which is a bore of the worst sort.

Wailua lies at my feet—a valley full of bees, butterflies and blossoms, the sea fawning at the mouth of it, the clouds melting over it; waterfalls gushing from numerous green corners; silver-white phaëtons floating in mid-air, at a loss to choose between earth and heaven, though evidently a little inclined earthward, for they no sooner drift out of the bewildering bowers of Wailua than they return again with noticeable haste.

Down I plunge into the depths of the valley, with the first drops of a heavy shower pelting me in the back; and under a great tree, that seems yearning to shelter somebody, I pause till the rain is over.

Anon the slow-footed Kahéle arrives, leaking all over, and bringing a peace-offering of *ohias,* the native apple, as juicy and sweet as the forbidden fruits of Paradise. As for these apples, they have a solitary seed, like a nutmeg, a pulp as white as wax, a juice flavored with roses, and their skins as red as a peony and as glossy as varnish. These we munch and munch while the forest reels under the impetuous avalanches of big rain-drops, and our animals tear great tufts of sweet grass from the upper roadside.

Is it far to the chapel, I wonder. Kahéle thinks not—

perhaps a *pari* or two distant. But a *pari*, a cliff, has many antecedents; and I feel that some dozen or so of climbs, each more or less fatiguing, still separate me from the rest I am seeking, and hope not to find until I reach the abode of Père Fidelis, at the foot of the cross, as one might say.

The rain ceases. Hoké once more nerves himself for fresh assaults upon the everlasting hills. Kahéle drops behind as usual, and the afternoon wanes.

How fresh seems the memory of this journey! yet its place is with the archives of the past. I seem to breathe the incense of orange-flowers and to hear the whisper of distant water-falls as I write.

It must have been toward sunset—we were threading the eastern coast, and a great mountain filled the west—but I felt that it was the hour when day ends and night begins. The heavy clouds looked as though they were still brimful of sun-light, yet no ray escaped to gladden our side of the world.

Finally, on the brow of what seemed to be the last hill in this life, I saw a cross—a cross among the palms. Hoké saw it, and quickened his pace: he was not so great an ass but he knew that there was provender in the green pastures of Père Fidelis, and his heart freshened within him.

A few paces from the grove of palms I heard a bell swing jubilantly. Out over the solemn sea, up and down that foam-crested shore, rang the sweet Angelus. One may pray with some fervor when one's journey is at an end. When the prayer was over I walked to the gate of the chapel-yard, lead-ing the willing Hoké, and at that moment a slender figure, clad all in black, his long robes flowing gracefully about him, his boyish face heightening the effect of his grave and serene demeanor, his thin, sensitive hands held forth in hearty wel-come—a welcome that was almost like benediction, so spiritual was the love which it expressed—came out, and I found my-self in the arms of Père Fidelis, feeling like one who has at least been permitted to kneel upon the threshold of his Mecca.

Why do our hearts sing *jubilate* when we meet a friend for

the first time? What is it within us that with its life-long yearning comes suddenly upon the all-sufficient one, and in a moment is crowned and satisfied? I could not tell whether I was at last waking from a sleep or just sinking into a dream. I could have sat there at his feet contented; I could have put off my worldly cares, resigned ambition, forgotten the past, and, in the blessed tranquillity of that hour, have dwelt joyfully under the palms with him, seeking only to follow in his patient footsteps until the end should come.

Perhaps it was the realization of an ideal that plunged me into a luxurious revery, out of which I was summoned by *mon père,* who hinted that I must be hungry. Prophetic father! hungry I was indeed.

Mon père led me to his little house with three rooms, and installed me host, himself being my ever-watchful attendant. Then he spoke: "The lads were at the sea, fishing: would I excuse him for a moment?"

Alone in the little house, with a glass of claret and a hard biscuit for refreshment, I looked about me. The central room, in which I sat, was bare to nakedness: a few devotional books, a small clock high up on the wall, with a short wagging pendulum, two or three paintings, betraying more sentiment than merit, a table, a wooden form against the window, and a crucifix, complete its inventory. A high window was at my back; a door in front opening upon a veranda shaded with a passion-vine; beyond it a green, undulating country running down into the sea; on either hand a little cell containing nothing but a narrow bed, a saint's picture, and a rosary. Kahéle, having distributed the animals in good pasturage, lay on the veranda at full length, supremely happy as he jingled his spurs over the edge of the steps and hummed a native air in subdued falsetto, like a mosquito.

Again I sank into a revery. Enter *mon père* with apologies and a plate of smoking cakes made of eggs and batter, his own handiwork; enter the lads from the sea with excellent fish, knotted in long wisps of grass; enter Kahéle, lazily sniffing the savory odors of our repast with evident relish; and then supper in good earnest.

How happy we were, having such talks in several sorts of tongues, such polyglot efforts toward sociability—French, English, and native in equal parts, but each broken and spliced to suit our dire necessity! The candle flamed and flickered in the land-breeze that swept through the house—unctuous waxen stalactites decorated it almost past recognition; the crickets sang lustily at the doorway; the little natives grew sleepy and curled up on their mats in the corner; Kahéle slept in his spurs like a born muleteer. And now a sudden conviction seized us that it was bedtime in very truth; so *mon père* led me to one of the cells, saying "Will you sleep in the room of Père Amabilis?" Yea, verily, with all humility; and there I slept after the benediction, during which the young priest's face looked almost like an angel's in its youthful holiness, and I was afraid I might wake in the morning and find him gone, transported to some other and more lovely world.

But I didn't. Père Fidelis was up before daybreak. It was his hand that clashed the joyful Angelus at sunrise that woke me from my happy dream; it was his hand that prepared the frugal but appetizing meal; he made the coffee, such rich, black, aromatic coffee as Frenchmen alone have the faculty of producing. He had an eye to the welfare of the animals also, and seemed to be commander-in-chief of affairs secular as well as ecclesiastical; yet he was so young!

There was a day of brief incursions mountainward, with the happiest results. There were welcomes showered upon me for his sake; he was ever ministering to my temporal wants, and puzzling me with dissertations in assorted languages.

By happy fortune a Sunday followed, when the Chapel of the Palms was thronged with dusky worshippers; not a white face present but the father's and mine own, yet a common trust in the blessedness of the life to come struck the key-note of universal harmony, and we sang the *Magnificat* with one voice. There was something that fretted me in all this admirable experience: Père Fidelis could touch neither bread nor water until after the last mass. Hour by hour he grew paler and fainter spite of the heroic fortitude that sustained his famishing body.

"*Mon père,*" said I, "you must eat, or go to heaven betimes." He would not. "You must end with an earlier mass," I persisted. It was impossible: many parishioners came from miles away; some of these started at daybreak, as it was, and they would be unable to arrive in season for an earlier mass. Excellent martyr! thought I, to offer thy body a living sacrifice for the edification of these savage Christians! At last he ate, but not until appetite itself had perished. Then troops of children gathered about him clamoring to kiss the hand of the priestly youth; old men and women passed him with heads uncovered, amazed at the devotion of one they could not hope to emulate.

Whenever I referred to his life, he at once led me to admire his fellow-apostle, who was continually in his thoughts. Père Amabilis was miles away, repairing a chapel that had suffered somewhat in a late gale; Père Amabilis would be so glad to see me; I must not fail to visit him; and for fear of some mischance, Père Fidelis would himself conduct me to him.

The way was hard—deep chasms to penetrate, swift streams to be forded, narrow and slippery trails to be threaded through forest, swamp, and wilderness. These obstacles separated the devoted friends, but not for long seasons. Père Fidelis would go to him whom he had not laid eyes on for a fortnight at least.

The boy Kahéle was glad of companionship; one of the small fishers, an acolyte of the chapel, would accompany us, and together they could lag behind, eating *ohias* and dabbling in every stream.

A long day's journey followed. We wended our way through jungles of *lauhala,* with slim roots in the air and long branches trailing about them like vines; they were like great cages of roots and branches in a woven snarl. We saw a rocky

point jutting far into the sea. "Père Amabilis dwells just beyond that cape," said my companion, fondly; and it seemed
not very far distant; but our pace was slow and wearisome,
and the hours were sure to distance us. We fathomed dark
ravines whose farther walls were but a stone's throw from
us, but in whose profound depths a swift torrent rushed madly
to the sea, threatening to carry us to our destruction—green,
precipitous troughs, where the tide of mountain-rain was
lashed into fury, and with its death-song drowned our voices
and filled our animals with terror.

Now and then we paused to breathe, man and beast panting
with fatigue; sometimes the rain drove us into the thick wood
for shelter; sometimes a brief deluge, the offspring of a rent
cloud at the head of the ravine, stayed our progress for half
an hour, until its volume was somewhat spent and the stream
was again fordable. Here we talked of the daily miracles in
nature. Again and again the young fathers are called forth
into the wilderness to attend on the sick and dying. Little
chapels are hidden away among the mountains and through
the valleys; all these must be visited in turn. Their life is an
actual pilgrimage from chapel to chapel, which nothing but
physical inability may interrupt.

At one spot I saw a tree under which Père Fidelis once
passed a tempestuous night. On either side yawned a ravine
swept by an impassable flood. There were no houses within
reach. On the soaked earth, with a pitiless gale sweeping
over the land, from sunset to sunrise he lay without the consolation of one companion. Food was frequently scarce: a
few limpets, about as palatable as parboiled shoe-leather, a
paste of roast yams and water, a lime perhaps, and nothing
besides but lumpy salt from the sea-shore.

While we were riding, a herald met us bearing a letter for
mon père. It was a greeting from Père Amabilis, who announced the chapel as rapidly nearing its complete restoration.
Père Fidelis fairly wept for joy at this intelligence, and burst
into a panegyric upon the unrivalled ingenuity of his spiritual

associate. We were sure to surprise him at work, and this trifling episode seemed to be an event of some importance in the isolated life they led.

At sunset we passed into the open vale of Wailuanui, and saw the chapel looking fresh and tidy on the slope of the hill toward the sea. Two waterfalls that fell against the sunset flashed like falling flame, and a soft haze tinged the slumberous solitudes of wood and pasture with the dream-like loveliness of a picture. There seemed to be but one sound audible —the quick, sharp blows of a hammer. Père Fidelis listened with eyes sparkling, and then rode rapidly onward.

Behold! from the chapel wall, high up on a scaffolding of boughs, his robes gathered about him, his head uncovered, and hammer in hand, Père Amabilis leaned forth to welcome us. The hammer fell to the earth. Père Amabilis loosened his skirts and clasped his hands in unaffected rapture. We were three satisfied souls, asking for nothing beyond the hem of that lonely valley in the Pacific.

Of course there was the smallest possible house that could be lived in, for our sole accommodation, because but one priest needed to visit the district at a time, and a very young priest at that. A tiny bed in one corner of the room was thought sufficient, together with two plates, two cups, and a single spoon. Luxuries were unknown and unregretted.

"Well, father, what have you at this hotel?" said Père Fidelis as we came to the door of the cubby-house.

"Water," replied our host, with a grave tone that had an undercurrent of truth in it.

But we were better provided for. Within an hour's time a reception took place: native parishioners came forth to welcome Père Fidelis and the stranger, each bringing some voluntary tribute—a fish, a fowl lean enough to quiet the conscience of Père Fidelis, an egg or two, or a bunch of taro.

Long talks followed; the news of the last month was discussed with much enthusiasm, and some few who had no opportunity of joining in the debate gave expression to their sentiments through such speaking eyes as savages usually are possessed of.

The welcome supper-hour approached. Willing hands dressed a fowl; swift feet plied between the spring and the kettle swung over the open camp-fire; children danced for very joy before the door of the chapel, under the statue of the Virgin, whose head was adorned with a garland of living flowers. The shadows deepened; stars seemed to cluster over the valley and glow with unusual fervor; the crickets sang mightily—they are always singing mightily over yonder; supper came to the bare table with its meagre array of dishes; and, since I was forced to have a whole plate and a bowl, as well as the solitary spoon, for my sole use, the two young priests ate together from the same dish and drank from the same cup, and were grateful and happy as the birds of the air under similar circumstances.

A merry meal, that! For us no weak tea, that satirical consoler, nor tea whose strength is bitterness, an abomination to the faithful, but *mon père's* own coffee, the very aroma of which was invigorating; and then our friendly pipes out under the starlight, where we sat chatting amicably, with our three heads turbaned in an aromatic Virginian cloud.

I learned something of the life of these two friends during that social evening. Born in the same city in the north of France, reared in the same schools, graduated from the same university, each fond of life and acquainted with its follies, each in turn stricken with an illness that threatened death, together they came out of the dark valley with their future consecrated to the work that now absorbs them, the friendship of their childhood increasing with their years and sustaining them in a remote land, where their vow of poverty seems almost like a sarcasm, since circumstance deprives them of all luxuries.

"Do you never long for home? do you never regret your vow?" I asked.

"Never!" they answered; and I believe them. "These old

people are as parents to us; these younger ones are as brothers and sisters; these children we love as dearly as though they were our own. What more can we ask?"

What more, indeed? With the rain beating down upon your unsheltered heads, and the torrents threatening to ingulf you; faint with journeyings; an hungered often; weak with fastings; pallid with prayer—what more *can* you ask in the same line? say I.

Père Fidelis coughed a little, and was somewhat feverish. I could see that his life was not elastic: his strength was even then failing him.

"Père Amabilis is an artisan: he built this house, and it is small enough; but some day he will build a house for me but six feet long and *so* broad," said Père Fidelis, shrugging his shoulders; whereat Père Amabilis, who looked like a German student with his long hair and spectacles, turned aside to wipe the moisture from the lenses, and said nothing, but laid his hand significantly upon the shoulder of his friend, as if imploring silence. Alas for him when those lips are silent forever!

I wondered if they had no recreation.

"Oh, yes. The poor pictures at the Chapel of the Palms are ours, but we have not studied art. And then we are sometimes summoned to the farther side of the island, where we meet new faces. It is a great change."

For a year before the arrival of Père Amabilis, who was not sooner able to follow his friend, Père Fidelis was accustomed to go once a month to a confessional many miles away. That his absence might be as brief as possible, he was obliged to travel night and day. Sometimes he would reach the house of his confessor at midnight, when all were sleeping: thereupon would follow this singular colloquy in true native fashion. A rap at the door at midnight, the confessor waking from his sleep.

Confessor. "Who's there?"
Père Fidelis. "It is I!"

Conf. "Who is I!"

Père F. "Fidelis!"

Conf. "Fidelis who?"

Père F. "Fidelis kahuna pule!" (Fidelis the priest.)

Conf. "Aweh!" (An expression of the greatest surprise.) "*Entre,* Fidelis kahuna pule."

Then he would rise, and the communion that followed must have been most cheering to both, for *mon père* even now is merry when he recalls it.

These pilgrimages are at an end, for the two priests confess to one another: conceive of the fellowship that hides away no secret, however mortifying!

The whole population must have been long asleep before we thought of retiring that night, and then arose an argument concerning the fittest occupant of the solitary bed. It fell to me, for both were against me, and each was my superior. When I protested, they held up their fingers and said, "Remember, we are your fathers and must be obeyed." Thus I was driven to the bed, while mine hosts lay on the bare floor with saddles for pillows.

It was this self-sacrificing hospitality that hastened my departure. I felt earth could offer me no nobler fellowship— that all acts to come, however gracious, would bear a tinge of selfishness in comparison with the reception I had met where least expected.

I am thankful that I had not the heart to sleep well, for I think I could never have forgiven myself had I done so. When I woke in the early part of the night, I saw the young priests bowed over their breviaries, for I had delayed the accustomed offices of devotion, and they were fulfilling them in peace at last, having me so well bestowed that it was utterly impossible to do aught else for my entertainment.

Once more the morning came. I woke to find Père Amabilis at work, hammer in hand, sending his nails home with accurate strokes that spoke well for his trained muscle. Père Fidelis was concocting coffee and directing the volunteer cooks, who were seeking to surpass themselves upon this last meal we were to take together. In an hour *mon père* was to start for the Chapel of the Palms, while I wended my way onward through a new country, bearing with me the consoling memory of my precious friends. I can forgive a slight and forget the person who slights me, but little kindnesses probe me to the quick. I wonder why the twin fathers were so very careful of me that morning! They could not do enough to satisfy themselves, and that made me miserable; they stabbed me with tender words, and tried to be cheerful with such evident effort that I couldn't eat half my breakfast, though, as it was, I ate more than they did—God forgive me!—and altogether it was a solemn and a memorable meal.

A group of natives gathered about us seated upon the floor; it was impossible for Père Fidelis to move without being stroked by the affectionate creatures who deplored his departure. Père Amabilis insisted upon adjusting our saddles, during which ceremony he slyly hid a morsel of cold fowl in our saddle-bags.

That parting was as cruel as death. We shall probably never see one another again; if we do, we shall be older and more practical and more worldly, and the exquisite confidence we have in one another will have grown blunt with time. I felt it then as I know it now—our brief idyl can never be lived over in this life.

Well, we departed; the corners of our blessed triangle were spread frightfully. Père Fidelis was paler than ever; he caught his breath as though there wasn't much of it, and the little there was wouldn't last long; Père Amabilis wiped his spectacles and looked utterly forsaken; the natives stood about in awkward, silent groups, coming forward, one by one, to shake hands, and then falling back like so many automatons. Somehow, genuine grief is never graceful; it forgets to pose itself; its muscles are perfectly slack and unreliable.

The sea looked gray and forbidding as it shook its shaggy breakers under the cliff; life was dismal enough. The animals were unusually wayward, and once or twice I paused in despair under the prickly sunshine, half inclined to go back and begin over again, hoping to renew the past; but just then Hoké felt like staggering onward, and I began to realize that there are some brief, perfect experiences in life that pass from us like a dream, and this was one of them.

In the poem to this idyl I seem to see two shadowy figures passing up and down over a lonesome land. Fever and famine do not stay them; the elements alone have power to check their pilgrimage. Their advent is hailed with joyful bells; tears fall when they depart. Their paths are peace. Fearlessly they battle with contagion, and are at hand to close the pestilential lips of unclean death. They have lifted my soul above things earthly, and held it secure for a moment. From beyond the waters my heart returns to them. Again at twilight, over the still sea, floats the sweet Angelus; again I approach the chapel falling to slow decay; there are fresh mounds in the churchyard, and the voice of wailing is heard for a passing soul. By and by, if there is work to do, it shall be done, and the hands shall be folded, for the young apostles will have followed in the silent footsteps of their flock. Here endeth the lesson of the Chapel of the Palms.

AMENITIES

The Fourth Order of Humanity

BY

FRANCIS THOMPSON

In the beginning of things came man, sequent to him woman; on woman followed the child, and on the child the doll. It is a climax of development; and the crown of these is the doll.

To the doll's supremacy in beauty woman's self bears testimony, implicit, if unconscious. For ages has she tricked her face in pigment, and her brows in alien hair; her *contours* she has filled to counterfeit roundness, her eyes and lashes tinged: and all in a frustrate essay to compass by Art what in the doll is right of Nature. Even the child exhibits distinct inferiorities. It is full of thwartness and eating and drinking, and selffulness (selfishness were a term too dully immitigate), and a plentiful lack of that repose wherein the doll is nearest to the quiet gods. For my own part, I profess that much acquaintance only increases my consideration for this fourth order of humanity: always excepting the very light-blue-eyed doll, in whose regard there is a certain chill *hauteur* against which my diffidence is not proof.

Consider the life of dolls. At the whim of some *debonair*

maternal tyranness, they veer on every wind of mutability; are the sport of imputed moods, suffer qualities over which they have no election—are sorry or glad, indocile or amiable, at their mistress' whim and mandate; they are visited with stripes, or the soft aspersion of kisses; with love delectably persecuted, or consigned to the clement quiet of neglect; exalted to the dimple of their mistress' cheek, or dejected to the servile floor; rent and mutilated, or rocked and murmured over; blamed or petted, be-rated or loved. Nor why it is thus or thus with them, are they any wise witting; wherefore these things should be, they know not at all.

> Consider the life of us—
> Oh, my cousins the dolls!

Some consciousness, I take it, there was; some secret sense of this occult co-rivalry in fate, which withheld me even in childhood from the youthful male's content for these short-lived parasites of the nursery. I questioned, with wounded feelings, the straitened feminine intolerance which said to the boy: 'Thou shalt not hold a baby; thou shalt not possess a doll.' In the matter of babies, I was hopeless to shake the illiberal prejudice; in the matter of dolls, I essayed to confound it. By eloquence and fine diplomacy I wrung from my sisters a concession of dolls; whence I date my knowledge of the kind.

But ineluctable sex declared itself. I dramatized them, I fell in love with them; I did not father them; intolerance was justified of its children. One in particular I selected, one with surpassing fairness crowned, and bowed before the fourteen inches of her skirt. She was beautiful. She was one of Shakespeare's heroines. She was an amity of inter-removed miracles; all wrangling excellencies at pact in one sole doll; the frontiers of jealous virtues marched in her, yet trespassed not against her peace. I desired for her some worthy name; and asked of my mother: Who was the fairest among living women? Laughingly was I answered that I was a hard questioner, but that perhaps the Empress of the French bore the

bell for beauty. Hence, accordingly, my Princess of puppet-
dom received her style; and at this hour, though she has long
since vanished to some realm where all sawdust is wiped for
ever from dolls' wounds, I cannot hear that name but the
Past touches me with a rigid agglomeration of small china
fingers.

But why with childhood and with her should I close the
blushing recital of my puppet-loves? Men are but children
of a larger growth; and your statue, I warrant me, is but your
crescent doll. Wherefore, then, should I leave unmemorized
the statue which thralled my youth in a passion such as feminine mortality was skill-less to instigate? Nor at this let any
boggle; for *she* was a goddess. Statue I have called her; but
indeed she was a bust, a head, a face—and who that saw that
face could have thought to regard further? She stood nameless in the gallery of sculptural casts which she strangely
deigned to inhabit; but I have since learned that men called
her the Vatican Melpomene. Rightly stood she nameless, for
Melpomene she never was: never went words of hers from
bronzèd lyre in tragic order; never through *her* enspelled lips
moaned any syllables of woe. Rather, with her leaf-twined
locks, she seemed some strayed Bacchante, indissolubly filmed
in a secular reverie. The expression which gave her divinity
resistless I have always suspected for an accident of the cast;
since in frequent engravings of her prototype I never met any
such aspect. The secret of this indecipherable significance, I
slowly discerned, lurked in the singularly diverse set of the
two corners of the mouth; so that her profile wholly shifted
its meaning according as it was viewed from the right or left.
In one corner of her mouth the little languorous firstling of a
smile had gone to sleep; as if she had fallen a-dream, and
forgotten that it was there. The other had drooped, as of its
own listless weight, into a something which guessed at sadness; guessed, but so as indolent lids are easily grieved by
the pricks of the slate-blue dawn. And on the full countenance
those two expressions blended to a single expression inexpress-

ible; as if pensiveness had played the Mænad, and now her arms grew heavy under the cymbals. Thither each evening, as twilight fell, I stole to meditate and worship the baffling mysteries of her meaning: as twilight fell, and the blank noon surceased arrest upon her life, and in the vaguening countenance the eyes broke out from their day-long ambuscade. Eyes of violet blue, drowsed-amorous, which surveyed me not, but looked ever beyond, where a spell enfixed them,

Waiting for something, not for me.

And I was content. Content; for by such tenure of unnoticedness I knew that I held my privilege to worship: had she beheld me, she would have denied, have contemned by gaze. Between us, now, are years and tears: but the years waste her not, and the tears wet her not; neither misses she me or any man. There, I think, she is standing yet; there, I think, she will stand for ever: the divinity of an accident, awaiting a divine thing impossible, which can never come to her, and she knows this not.

For I reject the vain fable that the ambrosial creature is really an unspiritual compound of lime, which the gross ignorant call plaster of Paris. If Paris indeed had to do with her, it was he of Ida. And for him, perchance, she waits.

On Lying in Bed

BY

G. K. CHESTERTON

LYING IN BED would be an altogether perfect and supreme experience if only one had a coloured pencil long enough to draw on the ceiling. This, however, is not generally a part of the domestic apparatus on the premises. I think myself that the thing might be managed with several pails of Aspinall and a broom. Only if one worked in a really sweeping and masterly way, and laid on the colour in great washes, it might drip down again on one's face in floods of rich and mingled colour like some strange fairy rain; and that would have its disadvantages. I am afraid it would be necessary to stick to black and white in this form of artistic composition. To that purpose, indeed, the white ceiling would be of the greatest possible use; in fact it is the only use I think of a white ceiling being put to.

But for the beautiful experiment of lying in bed I might never have discovered it. For years I have been looking for blank spaces in a modern house to draw on. Paper is much too small for any really allegorical design; as Cyrano de Bergerac says: "Il me faut des géants." But when I tried to find these fine clear spaces in the modern rooms such as we all live in I was continually disappointed. I found an endless pattern and complication of small objects hung like a curtain of fine links between me and my desire. I examined the walls; I found them to my surprise to be already covered with wall-paper, and I found the wall-paper to be already covered with very uninter-

From *Tremendous Trifles,* by G. K. Chesterton. Reprinted by permission of the publisher, Dodd, Mead & Company, Inc., New York; and the executrix of the estate of the late Gilbert Keith Chesterton.

esting images, all bearing a ridiculous resemblance to each other. I could not understand why one arbitrary symbol (a symbol apparently entirely devoid of any religious or philosophical significance) should thus be sprinkled all over my nice walls like a sort of small-pox.

The Bible must be referring to wall-papers, I think, when it says "Use not vain repetitions, as the Gentiles do." I found the Turkey carpet a mass of unmeaning colours, rather like the Turkish Empire, or like the sweetmeat called Turkish delight. I do not know exactly what Turkish delight really is; but I suppose it is Macedonian Massacres. Everywhere that I went forlornly, with my pencil or my paint brush, I found that others had unaccountably been before me, spoiling the walls, the curtains, and the furniture with their childish and barbaric designs.

.   .   .   .

Nowhere did I find a really clear place for sketching until this occasion when I prolonged beyond the proper limit the process of lying on my back in bed. Then the light of that white heaven broke upon my vision, that breadth of mere white which is indeed almost the definition of Paradise, since it means purity and also means freedom. But alas! like all heavens, now that it is seen it is found to be unattainable; it looks more austere and more distant than the blue sky outside the window. For my proposal to paint on it with the bristly end of a broom has been discouraged—never mind by whom; by a person debarred from all political rights—and even my minor proposal to put the other end of the broom into the kitchen fire and turn it into charcoal has not been conceded. Yet I am certain that it was from persons in my position that all the original inspiration came for covering the ceilings of palace and cathedrals with a riot of fallen angels or victorious gods. I am sure that it was only because Michelangelo was engaged in the ancient and honourable occupation of lying in bed that he ever realised how the roof of the Sistine

Chapel might be made into an awful imitation of a divine drama that could only be acted in the heavens.

The tone now commonly taken towards the practice of lying in bed is hypocritical and unhealthy. Of all the marks of modernity that seem to mean a kind of decadence, there is none more menacing and dangerous than the exultation of very small and secondary matters of conduct at the expense of very great and primary ones, at the expense of eternal public and tragic human morality. If there is one thing worse than the modern weakening of major morals it is the modern strengthening of minor morals. Thus it is considered more withering to accuse a man of bad taste than of bad ethics. Cleanliness is not next to godliness nowadays, for cleanliness is made an essential and godliness is regarded as an offence. A playwright can attack the institution of marriage so long as he does not misrepresent the manners of society, and I have met Ibsenite pessimists who thought it wrong to take beer but right to take prussic acid. Especially this is so in matters of hygiene; notably such matters as lying in bed. Instead of being regarded, as it ought to be, as a matter of personal convenience and adjustment, it has come to be regarded by many as if it were a part of essential morals to get up early in the morning. It is upon the whole part of practical wisdom; but there is nothing good about it or bad about its opposite.

.   .   .   .

Misers get up early in the morning; and burglars, I am informed, get up the night before. It is the great peril of our society that all its mechanism may grow more fixed while its spirit grows more fickle. A man's minor actions and arrangements ought to be free, flexible, creative; the things that should be unchangeable are his principles, his ideals. But with us the reverse is true; our views change constantly; but our lunch does not change. Now, I should like men to have strong and rooted conceptions, but as for their lunch, let them have it sometimes in the garden, sometimes in bed, sometimes on the roof, sometimes in the top of a tree.

Let them argue from the same first principles, but let them do it in a bed, or a boat, or a balloon. This alarming growth of good habits really means a too great emphasis on those virtues which mere custom can misuse, it means too little emphasis on those virtues which custom can never quite ensure, sudden and splendid virtues of inspired pity or of inspired candour. If ever that abrupt appeal is made to us we may fail. A man can get used to getting up at five o'clock in the morning. A man cannot very well get used to being burnt for his opinions; the first experiment is commonly fatal. Let us pay a little more attention to these possibilities of the heroic and the unexpected. I daresay that when I get out of this bed I shall do some deed of an almost terrible virtue.

For those who study the great art of lying in bed there is one emphatic caution to be added. Even for those who can do their work in bed (like journalists), still more for those whose work cannot be done in bed (as, for example, the professional harpooner of whales), it is obvious that the indulgence must be very occasional. But that is not the caution I mean. The caution is this: if you do lie in bed, be sure you do it without any reason or justification at all. I do not speak, of course, of the seriously sick. But if a healthy man lies in bed, let him do it without a rag of excuse; then he will get up a healthy man. If he does it for some secondary hygienic reason, if he has some scientific explanation, he may get up a hypochondriac.

The Puppy: A Portrait

BY

LOUISE IMOGEN GUINEY

HE IS THE twenty-sixth in direct descent, and his coat is like amber damask, and his blue eyes are the most winning that you ever saw. They seem to proclaim him as much too good for the vulgar world, and worthy of such zeal and devotion as you, only you, could give to his helpless infancy. And, with a blessing upon the Abbot of Clairvaux, who is popularly supposed to have invented his species, you carry him home from the Bench Show, and in the morning, when you are told that he has eaten a yard and a quarter of the new stair-carpet, you look into those dreamy eyes again: no reproach shall reach him, you swear, because you stand for evermore between. And he grows great in girth, and in character the very chronicle and log-book of his noble ancestry; he may be erratic, but he puts charm and distinction into everything he does. Your devotedness to his welfare keeps him healthful and honest, and absurdly partial to the squeak of your boots, or the imperceptible aroma which, as it would seem, you dispense, a mile away. The thing which pleases you most is his ingenuous childishness. It is a fresh little soul in the rogue's body:

> Him Nature giveth for defence
> His formidable innocence.

You see him touch pitch every day, associating with the sewer-building Italians, with their strange oaths; with affected and cynical "sales-ladies" in shops (she of the grape-stall being clearly his too-seldom-relenting goddess); and with the bony cat down the street, who is an acknowledged anarchist, infrequent suppers have made him sour-complexioned towards society, and "thereby disallowed him," as dear Walton would say, "to be a competent judge." But Pup loses nothing of his sweet congenital absent-mindedness; your bringing-up sits firmly upon him and keeps him young. He expands into a giant, and such as meet him on a lonely road have religion until he has passed. Seven, nine, ten months go over his white-hooded head; and behold, he is nigh a year old, and still Uranian. He begins to accumulate facts, for his observation of late has not been unscientific; but he cannot generalize, and on every first occasion he puts his foot in it. A music-box transfixes him; the English language, proceeding from a parrot in a cage, shakes his reason for days. A rocking-horse on a piazza draws from him the only bad word he knows. He sees no obligation to respect persons with mumps, or with very red beards, or with tools and dinner-pails; in the last instance, he acts advisedly against honest labor, as he perceives that most overalls have kicks in them. Following Plato, he would reserve his haughty demeanor for slaves and servants. Moreover, before the undemonstrated he comes hourly to a pause. If a wheelbarrow, unknown hitherto among vehicles, approach him from his suburban hill, he is aware of the supernatural; but he will not flinch, as he was wont to do once; rather will he stand four-square, with eyebrows and crinkled ears vocal with wonder and horror. Then the man behind the moving bulk speaks over his truck to you, in the clear April evening: "Begorra, 't is his furrust barry" and you love the man for his accurate affectionate sense of the situation. When Pup is too open-mouthed and curious, when he dilates, in fact, with the wrong emotion, it reflects upon you, and reveals the flaws in your educational system. He blurts out dire things before fine ladies. If he hear one of them declaiming, with Delsarte gestures, in a drawing-room, he appears in the doorway, undergoing symptoms of acutest distress, and singing her down, professedly for her own sake; and afterward he pities her so, and is so chivalrously drawn toward her in her aberrations, that he lies for hours on the flounce of her gown, eyeing you, meanwhile, and calumniating you somewhat by his vicarious groans and sighs. But ever after, Pup admits the recitation of tragic selections as one human folly more.

He is so big and so unsophisticated, that you daily feel the incongruity, and wish, in a vague sort of way, that there were a street boarding-school in your town, where he could rough it, away from an adoring family, and learn to be responsible and self-opinionated, like other dogs. He has a maternal uncle, on the estate across the field: a double-chinned tawny ogre, good-natured as a baby, but too rash and improvident; his society you cannot covet for your tender charge. One fine day, Pup is low with the distemper, and evidence is forthcoming that he has visited, under his uncle's guidance, the much-deceased lobster thrown into hotel tubs. After weeks of anxious nursing, rubbings in oil, and steamings with vinegar, during which time he coughs and wheezes in a heartbreaking imitation of advanced consumption, he is left alone a moment on his warm rug, with the thermometer in his special apartment steady at sixty-eight degrees, and plunges out into the winter blast. Hours later, he returns; and the vision of his vagabond uncle, slinking around the house, announces to you in what companionship he has been. Plastered to the skull in mud and icicles, wet to the bone, jaded, guilty, and doomed now, of course, to die, Pup retires behind the kitchen table. The next morning he is well. The moral, to him at least, is that our uncle is an astute and unappreciated person, and a genuine man of the world.

Yet our uncle, with all his laxity, has an honorable heart, and practises the *maxima reverentia puero*. It is not from him that Pup shall learn his modest share of iniquity. Meanwhile, illumination is nearing him in the shape of a little old white bull-terrier of uncertain parentage, with one ear, and a scar on his neck, and depravity in the very lift of his stumped tail. This active imp, recently come to live in the neighborhood, fills you with forebodings. You know that Pup must grow up sometime, must take his chances, must fight and be fooled, must err and repent, must exhaust the dangerous knowledge of the great university for which his age at last befits him. The ordeal will harm neither him nor you; and yet you cannot help an anxious look at him, full four feet tall from crown to toe, and with a leg like an obelisk, preserving unseasonably his ambiguous early air of exaggerated goodness. One day he follows you from the station, and meets the small Mephisto on the homeward path. They dig a bone together, and converse behind trees; and when you call Pup, he snorts his initial defiance, and dances away in the tempter's wake. Finally, your whistle compels him, and he comes soberly forward. By this time the ringleader terrier is departing, with a diabolical wink. You remember that, a moment before, he stood on a mound, whispering in your innocent's beautiful dangling ear, and you glance sharply at Pup. Yes, it has happened! He will never seem quite the same again, with

—*the contagion of the world's slow stain*

beginning in his candid eyes. He is a dog now. He knows.

A Meditation on Cakes

BY

PADRAIC COLUM

WHAT IS THIS, I say to myself, as, seated on an uncharged-for bench in the Luxembourg Gardens, I perceive faint smoke

From *A Half-Day's Ride or Estates in Corsica,* by Padraic Colum. Reprinted by permission of The Macmillan Company, publisher, and the author.

go up beside near-by trees. A tall, grey woman is beside where the smoke ascends; before her is a square, soot-black structure, and I can see that she has a ladle in her hand. Some priestess of a rite that has to be performed on a black altar in the open air, I permit myself to imagine. I look more intently on the scene. A string of people are before the altar-like structure, each with the peculiar intentness of those who are in expectation of some benefit: I watch the sibyl handing each a honey-coloured cake. Thereupon I approach the soot-black structure myself. The sibyl takes pieces of charcoal and puts them on a fire that is within the black square. Beside her is a great can of creamy paste. She takes up a ladleful: pulling out a pan she pours it in; she presses a cover down upon the paste, twists the pan upside down, and deftly pushes it within what is, after all, an oven set amongst trees. She draws it back in a minute; there, with diamond-like punches upon it, is an oblong cake. Shaking sugar on it she hands the cake to the first in line. It is a commercial transaction, I discover: there is an announcement "Gaufres, 80 centimes." And now I stand in line to receive one, with a soldier who wears a fez, a child who holds a toy-balloon, an old harridan, a very chic lady, and a man wearing velveteen trousers, a muffler and a cap, with an empty sack hanging across his shoulder, who nevertheless looks like an artist, and who (as I was to learn) supports a large family by collecting and marketing ants' eggs. I receive my gaufre. It is one of those cakes that are puffed into layers of paste; it is very tasty. I discover that it is rather like the American waffle, and am led to guess that "waffle" and "gaufre" are cognate words.

Back on my bench I can think of nothing else than cakes; my stream of consciousness flows around cakes. It is Shrove Tuesday, the eve of Lent. It has always been recognised that the most satisfactory way of preparing for a fast is to have a feast. The best part of a feast, it has always seemed to me, is the part in which cakes have a place; a feast in which no time is wasted getting to the cakes—in which the cakes constitute the feast—is the best of feasts. Pancake Night, Shrove Tuesday, as I discern now, is rightly placed before Ash Wednesday: the happiest feast before the longest fast.

It is true that the cakes eaten on this feast are cakes in their simplest form—to wit, pancakes. But pancakes made by a practised pancake-maker (and there are, the Lord be praised, many such!) make a dish fit for a better man than a king—a dish fit for a sage. When I think of sages eating pancakes, I think of them as eating pancakes made thin and with much butter on their surfaces. As a youth I used to tramp from house to house in a certain district in Ireland on Shrove Tuesday evening. I had forty aunts (well, not quite forty) all adepts in pancake-making, and all living conveniently near to one another. I managed to visit nearly every one of them on Pancake Night.

The best story I ever read has the making of pancakes for its central incident. You will find it in the Thousand and One Nights; not in any of the abbreviated versions; it is somewhere in Burton's seventeen volumes, or if not in Burton, in Payne, or if not in Burton or Payne, in Monsieur Mardrus's French version. It is entitled "The Caliph and the Daughter of Kisra." The central incident, the luminous point which, as Robert Louis Stevenson tells us, should be recognisable in every well-constructed story, is where the Daughter of Kisra is sent pancakes by the Caliph. They are in a silver dish and the Daughter of Kisra, with the generosity that characterises her royal house, has dish and pancakes sent to the young man who gave her a cruse of water when she was in need of refreshment in the streets of Bagdad. The silver dish is offered for sale in the market; the Caliph recognises it, and this leads to very remarkable developments. It may not be the best story ever written, but it is the best instance I know of pattern in story-telling. And the central incident, as I have stated, is the making of the pancakes; they are made by the Caliph himself; Haroun al-Raschid tucks up his sleeves, makes the batter, pours it on the pan, holds it on the brazier, and repeats this over and over until the great silver dish is packed with pancakes. A most memorable incident, I maintain.

I had a grandmother. I don't remember her pancakes, but I have a distinct memory of a special cake she used to make for me. This cake was named in Irish "Keestha Bosca," which means "the cake of the palm"; it had this name because it was shaped in the palm of the maker out of dough left over from baking the bread for next day. In my grandmother's house (this is a long time ago and things have changed since) most of the bread we ate was baked in the pot-oven at night. Probably the mixing and the kneading and the putting of the dough into the oven took place at no great length of time after candle-light. But to a child lying in bed and keeping awake to watch such proceedings they seemed to be at a very remote time in the night. My grandmother's bread was mixed in buttermilk and with soda. When it was put in the oven, the coals and ashes of a turf-fire were put around the oven and over it. And on the lid of the pot was placed "the cake of the palm," after sugar and sweet milk had been placed on the top of it.

I have never lost my taste for cakes. After the cakes of folk-culture such as pancakes and "the cake of the palm," came cakes that were still popular but approaching the cakes of higher cultivation: squares of ginger-bread sold off carts at little fairs or in little shops; ginger-cakes which were very vitalizing as one faced a mile of road on a chill evening (in those remote days one could get a bagful for twopence). Later on there was a heavy, clammy cake that one bought in pennyworths—Chester-cake it was called. It was related that the ingredients of this cake were always mixed in beer—in porter—and this rumour added to the worth of the cake, to our minds, by giving it a dark and secret origin. And, still on the border between the cakes of folk-culture and the cakes of higher cultivation, there were spiced cakes and cream tarts.

Then came cakes of the higher cultivation—cakes with icings, cakes with rare fruits crowning them and embedded in them, cakes that are the creations of meditative and daring intelligences. All such cakes are a temptation to me—all, I should say, except cakes that have chocolate outside or inside of them. I think such cakes are mistakes. I see people whose tastes I know to be indisputable eating them, and it is as if I saw them reading the longer poems of Dante Gabriel Rossetti. Chocolate cakes are not for me.

I do not know what ingredients should go into a cake, nor how the ingredients should be combined, nor how the combination should be baked. But I know the temper in which cakes should be made. The temper should be that of affection and light-heartedness. Soups can be made by slaves. Meats may be cooked by mockers and salads mixed by suspicious, cross-eyed servitors. Fish and fowl can be prepared by fleshly men sunk in infamies. But cakes can only be made by the candid. Everyone knows that Cinderella could make cakes and that her jealous half-sisters couldn't, and it is clear to Shakespearean scholars that Cordelia was a cake-maker. "I offer you cakes and friendship," said a remarkable lady to me once. She, being the most experienced lady in Dublin, knew that these two went together. I cherish her friendship still and have happy memories of her cakes. And I know a lady in Chicago whose cakes (or should I call them cates?) are the sort that the Queen of Sheba gave Solomon when full of friendship for him.

I remember that there used to be a cake-maker in this quarter who made cakes in his own little stall. He was a Constantinopolitan; perhaps he made cakes as the Caliph did, tucking up his sleeves and holding the pan above the brazier. But I could not recall his method and was teased into going in search of his stall. Three little shops were together: I remember them; the first sold firewood and had, as is the pleasant fashion in Paris, logs painted all over its front, the round ends showing notches and the grain: intended to be representational, this shining pattern of logs was so stylized as to be symbolic, evoking the lives of wood-cutters dwelling in huts in château-surrounding forests. Almost touching upon this shop was another outside of which were hanging three deep, richly glowing copper basins. The Constantinopolitan's was between the two. The stall was small and bare: there was in it room for the stove, the kneading-board, the cauldron of oil, and the cake-maker himself. At the back was an unremarkable curtain, behind which, no doubt, birds sang, and fountains played, and odalisques awaited their master. I ordered a couple of his cakes. He punched out a circle in the dough on his kneading-board, and punched a hole in that circle of dough; then he plunged the piece into the cauldron of boiling oil. He took it out, crisp and swollen, oily, ring-shaped, and golden-brown. He made another and put the couple in paper for me. They were the sort that is known in America as doughnuts, and were admirable of their kind.

Agrippina

BY

AGNES REPPLIER

SHE IS SITTING now on my desk, and I glance at her with deference, mutely begging permission to begin. But her back is turned to me, and expresses in every curve such fine and delicate disdain that I falter and lose courage at the very threshold of my task. I have long known that cats are the most contemptuous of creatures, and that Agrippina is the most contemptuous of cats. The spirit of Bouhaki, the proud Theban beast that sat erect, with gold earrings in his ears, at the feet of his master, King Hana; the spirit of Muezza,

From *Essays in Idleness*. Reprinted by permission of the publisher, Houghton, Mifflin Company, Boston.

whose slumbers Mahomet himself was not bold enough to
disturb; the spirit of Micetto, Chateaubriand's ecclesiastical
pet, dignified as a cardinal, and conscious ever that he was the
gift of a sovereign pontiff—the spirits of all arrogant cats that
have played scornful parts in the world's great comedy look
out from Agrippina's yellow eyes, and hold me in subjection.
I should like to explain to her, if I dared, that my desk is
small, littered with many papers, and sadly overcrowded with
the useful inutilities which affectionate friends delight in giving me at Christmas time. Sainte-Beuve's cat, I am aware, sat
on his desk, and roamed at will among those precious manuscripts which no intrusive hand was ever permitted to touch;
but Sainte-Beuve probably had sufficient space reserved for his
own comfort and convenience. I have not; and Agrippina's
beautifully ringed tail flapping across my copy distracts my
attention, and imperils the neatness of my penmanship. Even
when she is disposed to be affable, turns the light of her countenance upon me, watches with attentive curiosity every stroke
I make, and softly, with curved paw, pats my pen as it travels
over the paper—even in these halcyon moments, though my
self-love is flattered by her condescension, I am aware that I
should work better and more rapidly if I denied myself this
charming companionship.

But in truth it is impossible for a lover of cats to banish
these alert, gentle, and discriminating little friends, who give
us just enough of their regard and complaisance to make us
hunger for more. M. Fée, the naturalist, who has written
so admirably about animals, and who understands, as only a
Frenchman can understand, the delicate and subtle organization of a cat, frankly admits that the keynote of its character
is independence. It dwells under our roof, sleeps by our fire,
endures our blandishments, and apparently enjoys our society,
without for one moment forfeiting its sense of absolute freedom, without acknowledging any servile relation to the human
creature who shelters it. "The cat," says M. Fée, "will never
part with its liberty; it will neither be our servant, like the

horse, nor our friend, like the dog. It consents to live as our guest; it accepts the home we offer and the food we give; it even goes so far as to solicit our caresses, but capriciously, and when it suits its humor to receive them."

Rude and masterful souls resent this fine self-sufficiency in a domestic animal, and require that it should have no will but theirs, no pleasure that does not emanate from them. They are forever prating of the love and fidelity of the dog, of the beast that obeys their slightest word, crouches contentedly for hours at their feet, is exuberantly grateful for the smallest attention, and so affectionate that its demonstrations require to be curbed rather than encouraged. All this homage is pleasing to their vanity; yet there are people, less magisterial perhaps, or less exacting, who believe that true friendship, even with an animal, may be built upon mutual esteem and independence; that to demand gratitude is to be unworthy of it; and that obedience is not essential to agreeable and healthy intercourse. A man who owns a dog is, in every sense of the word, its master; the term expresses accurately their mutual relations. But it is ridiculous when applied to the limited possession of a cat. I am certainly not Agrippina's mistress, and the assumption of authority on my part would be a mere empty dignity, like those swelling titles which afford such innocent delight to the Freemasons of our severe republic. If I call Agrippina, she does not come; if I tell her to go away, she remains where she is; if I try to persuade her to show off her one or two little accomplishments, she refuses, with courteous but unswerving decision. She has frolicsome moods, in which a thimble, a shoe-buttoner, a scrap of paper, or a piece of string will drive her wild with delight; she has moods of inflexible gravity, in which she stares solemnly at her favorite ball rolling over the carpet, without stirring one lazy limb to reach it. "Have I seen this foolish toy before?" she seems to be asking herself with musing austerity; "and can it be possible that there are cats who run after such frivolous trifles? Vanity of vanities, and all is vanity, save only to lie upon the hearth-rug, and be warm, and 'think grave thoughts to feed a serious soul.'" In such moments of rejection and humiliation, I comfort myself by recalling the words of one too wise for arrogance. "When I play with my cat," says Montaigne, "how do I know whether she does not make a jest of me? We entertain each other with mutual antics; and if I have my own time for beginning or refusing, she too has hers."

This is the spirit in which we should approach a creature so reserved and so utterly self-sufficing; this is the only key we have to that natural distinction of character which repels careless and unobservant natures. When I am told that Agrippina is disobedient, ungrateful, cold-hearted, perverse, stupid, treacherous, and cruel, I no longer strive to check the torrent of abuse. I know that Buffon said all this, and much more, about cats, and that people have gone on repeating it ever since, principally because these spirited little beasts have remained just what it pleased Providence to make them, have preserved their primitive freedom through centuries of effete and demoralizing civilization. Why, I wonder, should a great many good men and women cherish an unreasonable grudge against one animal because it does not chance to possess the precise qualities of another? "My dog fetches my slippers for me every night," said a friend triumphantly, not long ago. "He puts them first to warm by the fire, and then brings them over to my chair, wagging his tail, and as proud as Punch. Would your cat do as much for you, I'd like to know?" Assuredly not! If I waited for Agrippina to fetch me shoes or slippers, I should have no other resource save to join as speedily as possible one of the barefooted religious orders of Italy. But, after all, fetching slippers is not the whole duty of domestic pets. As La Fontaine gently reminds us:—

Tout animal n'a pas toutes propriétés.

We pick no quarrel with a canary because it does not talk like a parrot, nor with a parrot because it does not sing like a canary. We find no fault with a King Charles spaniel for not flying at the throat of a burglar, nor with a St. Bernard because we cannot put it in our pocket. Agrippina will never make herself serviceable, yet nevertheless is she of inestimable service. How many times have I rested tired eyes on her graceful little body, curled up in a ball and wrapped round with her tail like a parcel; or stretched out luxuriously on my bed, one paw coyly covering her face, the other curved gently inwards, as though clasping an invisible treasure! Asleep or awake, in rest or in motion, grave or gay, Agrippina is always beautiful; and it is better to be beautiful than to fetch and carry from the rising to the setting of the sun. She is droll, too, with an unconscious humor, even in her most serious and sentimental moods. She has quite the longest ears that ever were seen on so small a cat, eyes more solemn than Athene's owl blinking in the sunlight, and an air of supercilious disdain that would have made Diogenes seem young and ardent by her side. Sitting on the library table, under the evening lamp, with her head held high in air, her tall ears as erect as chimneys, and her inscrutable gaze fixed on the darkest corner of the room, Agrippina inspires in the family sentiments of mingled mirthfulness and awe. To laugh at her in such moments, however, is to incur her supreme displeasure. I have known her to jump down from the table, and walk haughtily out of the room, because of a single half-suppressed but wholly indecorous giggle.

Schopenhauer has said that the reason domestic pets are so lovable and so helpful to us is because they enjoy, quietly and placidly, the present moment. Life holds no future for them, and consequently no care; if they are content, their contentment is absolute; and our jaded and wearied spirits find a natural relief in the sight of creatures whose little cups of happiness can so easily be filled to the brim. Walt Whitman expresses the same thought more coarsely when he acknowledges that he loves the society of animals because they do not sweat and whine over their condition, nor lie awake in the dark and weep for their sins, nor sicken him with discussions of their duty. In truth, that admirable counsel of Sydney Smith's, "Take short views of life," can be obeyed only by the brutes; for the thought that travels even to the morrow is long enough to destroy our peace of mind, inasmuch as we know not what the morrow may bring forth. But when Agrippina has breakfasted, and washed, and sits in the sunlight blinking at me with affectionate contempt, I feel soothed by her absolute and unqualified enjoyment. I know how full my day will be of things that I don't want particularly to do, and that are not particularly worth doing; but for her, time and the world hold only this brief moment of contentment. Slowly the eyes close, gently the little body is relaxed. Oh, you who strive to relieve your overwrought nerves, and cultivate power through repose, watch the exquisite languor of a drowsy cat, and despair of imitating such perfect and restful grace! There is a gradual yielding of every muscle to the soft persuasiveness of slumber; the flexible frame is curved into tender lines, the head nestles lower, the paws are tucked out of sight; no convulsive throb or start betrays a rebellious alertness; only a faint quiver of unconscious satisfaction, a faint heaving of the tawny sides, a faint gleam of the half-shut yellow eyes, and Agrippina is asleep. I look at her for one wistful moment, and then turn resolutely to my work. It were ignoble to wish myself in her place, and yet how charming to be able to settle down to a nap, *sans peur et sans reproche*, at ten o'clock in the morning!

These, then, are a few of the pleasures to be derived from the society of an amiable cat; and by an amiable cat I mean one that, while maintaining its own dignity and delicate reserve, is nevertheless affable and condescending in the company of human beings. There is nothing I dislike more than newspaper and magazine stories about priggish pussies—like the children in Sunday-school books—that share their food with hungry beasts from the back alleys, and show touching fidelity to old blind masters, and hunt partridges, in a spirit of noble self-sacrifice, for consumptive mistresses, and scorn to help themselves to delicacies from the kitchen tables, and arouse their households so often in cases of fire that I should suspect them of starting the conflagrations in order to win applause by giving the alarm. Whatever a real cat may or may not be, it is never a prig, and all true lovers of the race have been quick to recognize and appreciate this fact.

"I value in the cat," says Chateaubriand, "that independent and almost ungrateful temper which prevents it from attaching itself to any one; the indifference with which it passes from the salon to the housetop. When you caress it, it stretches itself out and arches its back responsively; but that is caused by physical pleasure, and not, as in the case of the dog, by a silly satisfaction in loving and being faithful to a master who returns thanks in kicks. The cat lives alone, has no need of society, does not obey except when it likes, pretends to sleep that it may see the more clearly, and scratches everything that it can scratch."

Here is a sketch spirited enough, and of good outline, but hardly correct in detail. A cat seldom manifests affection, yet is often distinctly social, and likes to see itself the petted minion of a family group. Agrippina, in fact, so far from living alone, will not, if she can help it, remain for a moment in a room by herself. She is content to have me as a companion, perhaps in default of better; but if I go upstairs or downstairs in search of a book, or my eyeglasses, or any one of the countless things that are never where they ought to be, Agrippina follows closely at my heels. Sometimes, when she is fast asleep, I steal softly out of the door, thinking to escape her vigilance; but before I have taken a dozen steps she is under my feet, mewing a gentle reproach, and putting on all the injured airs of a deserted Ariadne. I should like to think such behavior prompted by affection rather than by curiosity; but in my candid moments I find this "pathetic fallacy" a difficult sentiment to cherish. There are people, I am aware, who trustfully assert that their pets love them; and one such sanguine creature has recently assured the world that "no man who boasts the real intimacy and confidence of a cat would dream of calling his four-footed friend 'puss.' " But is not such a boast rather ill-timed at best? How dare any man venture to assert that he possesses the intimacy and confidence of an animal so exclusive and so reserved? I doubt if Cardinal Wolsey, in the zenith of his pride and power, claimed the intimacy and confidence of the superb cat who sat in a cushioned armchair by his side, and reflected with mimic dignity the full-blown honors of the Lord High Chancellor of England. Agrippina, I am humbly aware, grants me neither her intimacy nor her confidence, but only her companionship, which I endeavor to receive modestly, and without flaunting my favors to the world. She is displeased and even downcast when I go out, and she greets my return with delight, thrusting her little gray head between the banisters the instant I open the house door, and waving a welcome in mid-air with one ridiculously small paw. Being but mortal, I am naturally pleased with these tokens of esteem, but I do not, on that account, go about with arrogant brow, and boast of my intimacy with Agrippina. I should be laughed at, if I did, by everybody who is privileged to possess and appreciate a cat.

As for curiosity, that vice which the Abbé Galiani held to be unknown to animals, but which the more astute Voltaire detected in every little dog that he saw peering out of the window of its master's coach, it is the ruling passion of the feline breast. A closet door left ajar, a box with half-closed lid, an open bureau drawer—these are the objects that fill a cat with the liveliest interest and delight. Agrippina watches breathlessly the unfastening of a parcel, and tries to hasten matters by clutching actively at the string. When its contents are shown her, she examines them gravely, and then, with a sigh of relief, settles down to repose. The slightest noise disturbs and irritates her until she discovers its cause. If she hears a footstep in the hall, she runs out to see whose it is, and, like certain troublesome little people I have known, she dearly loves to go to the front door every time the bell is rung. From my window she surveys the street with tranquil scrutiny, and, if boys are playing below, she follows their games with a steady, scornful stare, very different from the wistful eagerness of a friendly dog, quivering to join in the sport. Sometimes the boys catch sight of her, and shout up rudely at her window; and I can never sufficiently admire Agrippina's conduct upon these trying occasions, the well-bred composure with which she affects neither to see nor to hear them, nor to be aware that there are such objectionable creatures as children in the world. Sometimes, too, the terrier that lives next door comes out to sun himself in the street, and, beholding my cat sitting well out of reach, he dances madly up and down the pavement, barking with all his might, and rearing himself on his short hind legs, in a futile attempt to dislodge her. Then the spirit of evil enters Agrippina's little heart. The window is open, and she creeps to the extreme edge of the stone sill, stretches herself at full length, peers down smilingly at the frenzied dog, dangles one paw enticingly in the air, and exerts herself with quiet malice to drive him to desperation. Her sense of humor is awakened by his frantic efforts, and by her own absolute security; and not until he is spent with exertion, and lies panting and exhausted on the bricks, does she arch her graceful back, stretch her limbs lazily in the sun, and with one light bound spring from the window to my desk. Wisely has Moncrif observed that a cat is not merely diverted by everything that moves, but is convinced that all nature is occupied exclusively with catering to her diversion.

There is a charming story told by M. Champfleury, who has written so much and so admirably about cats, of a poor hermit whose piety and asceticism were so great that in a vision he was permitted to behold his place in heaven, next to that of St. Gregory, the sovereign pontiff of Christendom. The hermit, who possessed nothing upon earth but a female

cat, was abashed by the thought that in the next world he was
destined to rank with so powerful a prince of the Church;
and perhaps—for who knows the secret springs of spiritual
pride?—he fancied that his self-inflicted poverty would win
for him an even higher reward. Whereupon a second revelation made known to him that his detachment from the world
was by no means so complete as he imagined, for that he loved
and valued his cat, the sole companion of his solitude, more
than St. Gregory loved and valued all his earthly possessions.
The Pope on his throne was the truer ascetic of the two.

This little tale conveys to us, in addition to its excellent
moral—never more needed than at present—a pleasing truth
concerning the lovability of cats. While they have never attained, and never deserve to attain, the widespread and somewhat commonplace popularity of dogs, their fascination is a
more potent and irresistible charm. He who yields himself
to the sweet seductiveness of a cat is beguiled forever from
the simple, honorable friendship of the more generous and
open-hearted beast. The small domestic sphinx whose inscrutable eyes never soften with affection; the fetich animal that
comes down to us from the far past, adored, hated, and feared
—a god in wise and silent Egypt, a plaything in old Rome, a
hunted and unholy creature, suffering one long martyrdom
throughout the half-seen, dimly-fathomed Middle Ages—
even now this lovely, uncanny pet is capable of inspiring
mingled sentiments of horror and devotion. Those who are
under its spell rejoice in their thralldom, and, like M. Champfleury's hermit, grow strangely wedded to this mute, unsym-
pathetic comradeship. Those who have inherited the old,
half-fearful aversion render a still finer tribute to the cat's
native witchery and power. I have seen middle-aged women,
of dignified and tranquil aspect, draw back with unfeigned
dismay at the sight of Agrippina, a little ball of gray and
yellow fir, curled up in peaceful slumber on the hearth rug.
And this instinctive shrinking has nothing in common with
the perfectly reasonable fear we entertain for a terrier snap-

ping and snarling at our heels, or for a mastiff the size of a calf, which our friend assures us is as gentle as a baby, but which looks able and ready to tear us limb from limb. It may be ignominious to be afraid of dogs, but the emotion is one which will bear analysis and explanation; we know exactly what it is we fear; while the uneasiness with which many people behold a harmless and perfectly indifferent cat is a faint reflection of that superstitious terror which the nineteenth century still borrows occasionaly from the ninth. We call it by a different name, and account for it on purely natural principles, in deference to progress; but the Mediæval peasant who beheld his cat steal out, like a gray shadow, on St. John's Eve, to join in unholy rites, felt the same shuddering abhorrence which we witness and wonder at today. He simplified matters somewhat, and eased his troubled mind by killing the beast; for cats that ventured forth on the feast of St. John, or on Halloween, or on the second Wednesday in Lent, did so at their peril. Fires blazed for them in every village, and even quiet stay-at-homes were too often hunted from their chimney-corners to a cruel death. There is a receipt signed in 1575 by one Lucas Pommoreux—abhorred forever be his name!—to whom has been paid the sum of a hundred *sols parisis* "for having supplied for three years all the cats required for the fire on St. John's Day"; and be it remembered that the gracious child, afterwards Louis XIII, interceded with Henry IV for the lives of these poor animals, sacrificed to wicked sport and an unreasoning terror.

Girt around with fear, and mystery, and subtle associations of evil, the cat comes down to us through the centuries; and from every land fresh traditions of sorcery claim it for their own. In Brittany is still whispered the dreadful tale of the cats that danced with sacrilegious glee around the crucifix until their king was slain; and in Sicily men know that if a black cat serves seven masters in turn he carries the soul of the seventh into hell. In Russia black cats become devils at the end of seven years, and in southern Europe they are merely serving their apprenticeship as witches. Norwegian folk-lore is rich in ghastly stories like that of the wealthy miller whose mill has been twice burned down on Whitsun night, and for whom a traveling tailor offers to keep watch. The tailor chalks a circle on the floor, writes the Lord's prayer around it, and waits until midnight, when a troop of cats rush in, and hang a great pot of pitch over the fireplace. Again and again they try to overturn this pitch, but every time the tailor frightens them away; and when their leader endeavors stealthily to draw him outside of his magic circle, he cuts off her paw with his knife. Then they all fly howling into the night, and the next morning the miller sees with joy his mill standing whole and unharmed. But the miller's wife cowers under the bedclothes, offering her left hand to the tailor, and hiding as best she can her right arm's bleeding stump.

Finer even than this tale is the well-known story which "Monk" Lewis told to Shelley of a gentleman who, late one night, went to visit a friend living on the outskirts of a forest in east Germany. He lost his path, and, after wandering aimlessly for some time, beheld at last a light streaming from the windows of an old and ruined abbey. Looking in, he saw a procession of cats lowering into the grave a small coffin with a crown upon it. The sight filled him with horror, and, spurring his horse, he rode away as fast as he could, never stopping until he reached his destination, long after midnight. His friend was still awaiting him, and at once he recounted what had happened; whereupon a cat that lay sleeping by the fire sprang to its feet, cried out, "Then I am the King of the Cats!" and disappeared like a flash up the chimney.

For my part, I consider this the best cat story in all literature, full of suggestiveness and terror, yet picturesque withal, and leaving ample room in the mind for speculation. Why was not the heir apparent bidden to the royal funeral? Was there a disputed succession, and how are such points settled in the mysterious domain of cat-land? The notion that these animals

gather in ghost-haunted churches and castles for their noctur-
nal revels is one common to all parts of Europe. We remember how the little maiden of the "Mountain Idyl" confides to
Heine that the innocent-looking cat in the chimney-corner is
really a witch, and that at midnight, when the storm is high,
she steals away to the ruined keep, where the spirits of the
dead wait spellbound for the word that shall waken them.
In all scenes of impish revelry cats play a prominent part,
although occasionally, by virtue of their dual natures, they
serve as barriers against the powers of evil. There is the old
story of the witch's cat that was grateful to the good girl who
gave it some ham to eat—I may observe here, parenthetically,
that I have never known a cat that would touch ham—and
there is the fine bit of Italian folk-lore about the servant maid
who, with no other protector than a black cat, ventures to
disturb a procession of ghosts on the dreadful Night of the
Dead. "It is well for you that the cat lies in your arms," the
angry spirit says to her; "otherwise what I am, you also would
be." The last pale reflex of a universal tradition I found three
years ago in London, where the bad behavior of the Westminster cats—proverbially the most dissolute and profligate
specimens of their race—has given rise to the pleasant legend
of a country house whither these rakish animals retire for
nights of gay festivity, and whence they return in the early
morning, jaded, repentant, and forlorn.

Of late years there has been a rapid and promising growth
of what disaffected and alliterative critics calls the "cat cult,"
and poets and painters vie with one another in celebrating
the charms of this long-neglected pet. Mr. M. H. Spielmann's
beautiful volume in praise of Madame Henriette Ronner and
her pictures, is a treasure upon which many an ardent lover
of cats will cast wandering and wistful glances. It is impossible for even the most disciplined spirit not to yearn over
these little furry darlings, these gentle, mischievous, lazy,
irresistible things. As for Banjo, that dear and sentimental
kitten, with his head on one side like Lydia Languish, and a

AMENITIES   147

decorous melancholy suffusing his splendid eyes, let any ob-
durate scorner of the race look at his loveliness and be converted. Mrs. Graham R. Tomson's pretty anthology, *Concerning Cats,* is another step in the right direction; a dainty
volume of selections from French and English verse, where
we may find old favorites like Cowper's "Retired Cat" and
Calverly's "Sad Memories," graceful epitaphs on departed
pussies, some delightful poems from Baudelaire, and three,
no less delightful, from the pen of Mrs. Tomson herself,
whose preface, or "foreword," is enough to win for her at
once the friendship and sympathy of the elect. The book,
while it contains a good deal that might well have been
omitted, is necessarily a small one; for poets, English poets
especially, have just begun to sing the praises of the cat, as
they have for generations sung the praises of the horse
and dog. Nevertheless, all English literature, and all the
literatures of every land, are full of charming allusions to this
friendly animal—allusions the brevity of which only enhances
their value. Those two delicious lines of Herrick's, for example:—

> *And the brisk mouse may feast herself with crumbs,*
> *Till that green-eyed kitling comes,*

are worth the whole of Wordsworth's solemn poem, "The
Kitten and the Falling Leaves." What did Wordsworth
know of the innate vanity, the affectation and coquetry, of
kitten-hood? He saw the little beast gamboling on the wall,
and he fancied her as innocent as she looked—as though any
living creature *could* be as innocent as a kitten looks! With
touching simplicity, he believed her all unconscious of the
admiration she was exciting:—

> *What would little Tabby care*
> *For the plaudits of the crowd?*
> *Over happy to be proud,*
> *Over wealthy in the treasure*
> *Of her own exceeding pleasure!*

Ah, the arrant knavery of that kitten! The tiny impostor, showing off her best tricks, and feigning to be occupied exclusively with her own infantile diversion! We can see her now, prancing and paddling after the leaves, and all the while peeping out of "the tail o' her ee" at the serene poet and philosopher, and waving her naughty tail in glee over his confidence and condescension.

Heine's pretty lines:—

> And close beside me the cat sits purring,
>   Warming her paws at the cheery gleam;
> The flames keep flitting, and flicking, and whirring;
>   My mind is wrapped in a realm of dream,

find their English echo in the letter Shelley writes to Peacock, describing, half wistfully, the shrines of the Penates, "whose hymns are the purring of kittens, the hissing of kettles, the long talks over the past and dead, the laugh of children, the warm wind of summer filling the quiet house, and the pelting storm of winter struggling in vain for entrance." How incomplete would these pictures be, how incomplete is any fireside sketch, without the purring kitten or drowsy cat!

> The queen I am o' that cozy place;
> As wi' ilka paw I dicht my face,
> I sing an' purr wi' mickle grace.

This is the sphinx of the hearthstone, the little god of domesticity, whose presence turns a house into a home. Even the chilly desolation of a hotel may be rendered endurable by these affable and discriminating creatures; for one of them, as we know, once welcomed Sir Walter Scott, and softened for him the unfamiliar and unloved surroundings. "There are no dogs in the hotel where I lodge," he writes to Abbotsford from London, "but a tolerably conversable cat *who* eats a mess of cream with me in the morning." Of course it did, the wise and lynx-eyed beast! I make no doubt that, day after day and week after week, that cat had wandered superbly amid the common throng of lodgers, showing favor to none, and growing cynical and disillusioned by constant contact with a crowd. Then, one morning, it spied the noble, rugged face which neither man nor beast could look upon without loving, and forthwith tendered its allegiance on the spot. Only "tolerably conversable" it was, this reserved and town-bred animal; less urbane because less happy than the much-respected retainer at Abbotsford, Master Hinse of Hinsefeld, whom Sir Walter called his friend. "Ah, mon grand ami, vous avez tué mon autre grand ami!" he sighed, when the huge hound Nimrod ended poor Hinse's placid career. And if Scott sometimes seems to disparage cats, as when he unkindly compares Oliver-le-Dain to one, in *Quentin Durward*, he atones for such indignity by the use of the little pronoun "who" when writing of the London puss. My own habit is to say "who" on similar occasions, and I am glad to have so excellent an authority.

It were an endless though a pleasant task to recount all that has been said, and well said, in praise of the cat by those who have rightly valued her companionship. M. Loti's Moumoutte Blanche and Moumoutte Chinoise are well known and widely beloved, and M. Théophile Gautier's charming pages are too familiar for comment. Who has not read with delight of the Black and White Dynasties that for so long ruled with gentle sway over his hearth and heart; of Madame Théophile, who thought the parrot was a green chicken; of Don Pierrot de Navarre, who deeply resented his master's staying out late at night; of the graceful and fastidious Séraphita; the gluttonous Enjolras; the acute Bohemian, Gavroche; the courteous and well-mannered Eponine, who received M. Gautier's guests in the drawing-room and dined at his table, taking each course as it was served, and restraining any rude distaste for food not to her fancy. "Her place was laid without a knife and fork, indeed, but with a glass, and she went regularly through dinner, from soup to dessert, awaiting her turn to be helped, and behaving with a quiet propriety which most children might imitate with advantage. At the first stroke of the bell she would appear, and when I came into the dining-room she would be at her post, upright on her chair, her forepaws on the edge of the tablecloth; and she would present her smooth forehead to be kissed, like a well-bred little girl who was affectionately polite to relatives and old people."

I have read this pretty description several times to Agrippina, who is extremely wayward and capricious about her food, rejecting plaintively one day the viands which she has eaten with apparent enjoyment the day before. In fact, the difficulty of catering to her is so well understood by tradesmen that recently, when the housemaid carried her on an errand to the grocery—Agrippina is very fond of these jaunts and of the admiration she excites—the grocer, a fatherly man, with cats of his own, said briskly, "Is this the little lady who eats the biscuits?" and presented her on the spot with several choice varieties from which to choose. She is fastidious, too, about the way in which her meals are served; disliking any other dishes than her own, which are of blue-and-white china; requiring that her meat should be cut up fine and all the fat removed, and that her morning oatmeal should be well sugared and creamed. Milk she holds in scorn. My friends tell me sometimes that it is not the common custom of cats to receive so much attention at table, and that it is my fault Agrippina is so exacting; but such grumblers fail to take into consideration the marked individuality that is the charm of every kindly treated puss. She differs from her sisters as widely as one woman differs from another, and reveals varying characteristics of good and evil, varying powers of intelligence and adaptation. She scales splendid heights of virtue, and, unlike Sir Thomas Browne, is "singular in offenses." Even those primitive instincts which we believe all animals hold in common are lost in acquired ethics and depravity. No heroism could surpass that of the London cat who crawled back five times under the stage of the burning theatre to rescue her litter of kittens, and, having carried four of them to safety, perished devotedly with the fifth. On the other hand, I know

of a cat who drowned her three kittens in a water-butt, for
no reason, apparently, save to be rid of them, and that she
might lie in peace on the hearth rug—a murder well planned,
deliberate, and cruel.

> So Tiberius might have sat,
> Had Tiberius been a cat.

Only in her grace and beauty, her love of comfort, her
dignity of bearing, her courteous reserve, and her independence of character does puss remain immutable and unchanged.
These are the traits which win for her the warmest corner by
the fire, and the unshaken regard of those who value her
friendship and aspire to her affection. These are the traits
so subtly suggested by Mrs. Tomson in a sonnet which every
true lover of cats feels in his heart *must* have been addressed
to his own particular pet:—

> Half gentle kindliness, and half disdain,
> Thou comest to my call, serenely suave,
> With humming speech and gracious gestures grave,
> In salutation courtly and urbane;
> Yet must I humble me thy grace to gain,
> For wiles may win thee, but no arts enslave;
> And nowhere gladly thou abidest, save
> Where naught disturbs the concord of thy reign.
>
> Sphinx of my quiet hearth! who deign'st to dwell
> Friend of my toil, companion of mine ease,
> Thine is the lore of Ra and Rameses;
> That men forget dost thou remember well,
> Beholden still in blinking reveries,
> With sombre sea-green gaze inscrutable.

Of Pleasant Noises

BY

D. B. WYNDHAM LEWIS

ABOUT THE END of the fourteenth century there lived in the grassy Norman valley called the Vaux de Vire, on the edge of the Cotentin, a fulling-miller named Olivier Basselin, whose nose was ruddier than the cherry, whose laugh could be heard on a clear day as far away as St. Lô, and who wrote some of the best drinking-songs in the world; of which I have a large number in a book.

This roaring miller was the chief of a little band, cluster, or gaggle of country poets, nearly all peasants; for if the Norman, according to Octave Mirabeau and Maupassant, is hard, avaricious, gluttonous, and rooted to his soil (he also gave us government and reopened for us islanders a window on the rest of Europe, greatly to the annoyance of a super-cilious gentleman in a bowler hat with whom I had an argument the other day), he could once both make up and sing good songs. Now among the songs of Olivier Basselin there is one which he made one day on passing the village cooper's and hearing him hammering at a cask. It begins:

> O tintamarre plaisant
> Et doulcement resonnant
> Des tonneaulx que l'on relie!

"O the delicious sweetly-resounding racket of wine-casks being coopered!" And he continues: "Faith, a sign that we shall be drinking soon! By Gosh, the lovely clamour! It has saved me from dying of melancholy this very day!"

From *On Straw and Other Conceits,* by D. B. Wyndham Lewis. Reprinted by permission of the publishers, Edwin V. Mitchell, Hartford, Conn., and Coward-McCann, Inc., New York, and the author.

Now Heaven and my Patron forbid that I should fall into the disgraceful error of praising a wine-bibber, and a medieval at that! I dare say the same quick gush of joy informs a totally abstaining and modern breast on passing a cocoa factory and hearing the bean-polishers singing at their work; and I dare say Mr. Eustace Miles feels the same on hearing the rattle of the nuts pouring into the Mock-Steak machine. *O tintamarre plaisant!* And this brings me to my point, namely, that there are thousands of noises so pleasant and gladsome, whether of themselves or through their associations, that they make the heart fly and twitter like a bird. Did not the clink of bottles please the infant Gargantua so that "at the sound of Pintes and Flaggons he would on a sudden fall into an Extasie, as if he had been tasted of the Joyes of Paradise"? Hey?

Another bibber, I fear. But not (please Heaven) medieval.

The war horse in Holy Writ loved the sound of the trumpet, and would say, Ha! Trumpets are always a pleasant noise (provided they are not sounding you to rise early and combat) : and their brazen uproar is particularly heartening at a Coronation, or in the forest scene in "Boris Godounov," or even in that massy Requiem of Berlioz—though in this they put one in mind of Death : another medieval superstition.

The squeals of a bumptious critic threatened with the State punishment called *peine forte et dure*, now alas! abolished, I would walk a long way to hear; at the same time lightly criticising the key and timbre of his yells.

The noise made by nightingales in the full moon has been commented on at enormous length by a mort of poets.

> *How thick the bursts come crowding through the leaves!*
> *Again—thou hearest!*
> *Eternal Passion!*
> *Eternal Pain!*

That was written by an Inspector of Schools under the Government of Queen Victoria. The noise of water boiling in a kettle, the noise of a great wood thrashed by a storm, the noise of bees bumbling in a summer afternoon, of horses galloping, of a fiddle playing Couperin, of ducks quacking on green English ponds, of little waves guggling round a boat's bows, of strong masterful men utterly discomfited, of bacon sputtering in a pan in the cool of morning, of knaves foaming against Providence, of bells heard at sea, of adulterators of honest liquor unmasked and objurgating, of—

Shall I tell you, by the way, what the old French poet said in a Ballade about this last kind of scoundrel? He said: "May the swabs have their giblets tickled with a Turkish arrow and a sharp sword; may Greek fire scorch their thatch and a great tempest scatter their brains; may their carrion bodies hang from a high gibbet, and may they die very swiftly in agony from the gout; I demand and request also that they be prodded with red-hot iron bars and flayed alive by ten hangmen, boiled in oil in the morning, and torn apart by four ramping great horses—the taverners who hocus our good wine." I call that a Wish. There are two more stanzas like that.

—of girls laughing on an April day, of the crackling and whispering of a beech-log fire in February, of a hunting-horn heard in the green depths of the forest (though óne poet I know esteems this a melancholy noise), of Andalusian voices lisping at nightfall, of drums throbbing far off to the tramp of infantry, of groaning farm-wagons heavy with harvest, of stockbrokers howling after a market crash, of ice tinkling in a jug under the Dog-Star, of grasshoppers chirping in August hayfields, of high tides swishing regularly on shingle beaches, of distant scythes being honed, of anchor-chains rattling down in haven: all these are lovely and pleasant noises, enlarging and uplifting human hearts.

I would add, also, the bawling of Mr. ******, a Leading Thinker, when menaced with punishment by the State for endeavouring to befuddle and incornifistigropilibustulate honest men's minds. I would not have him dealt with in the stern old way, that is by

a) The Question Ordinary.

b) The Boot, the favourite pastime of James the First, whom the Scots gave us: a great booby and dribbler, and half-mad even by Northern standards.

c) The punishment awarded Gossouin de Louet, a citizen of Paris, in the year 1435, for plotting to throw the English out of Paris; he was *par gehine et question tresdurement traveillié de son corps,* which is something most uncomfortable, but was pardoned by Bedford, acting for Henry VI. I have just been reading his case.

These were punishments for men. I would have the Leading Thinker merely slapped and exposed to the derision of all true citizens. His screams, I think, would be in the Mixo-Lydian Mode, on the dominant F sharp: a very pleasing noise.

There is one noise, a Master Noise, which to some may be hackneyed, to others harsh, to others meaningless, to others dull, to others tuneless, but to me exquisite, soothing, rare, and never-too-often-to-be-repeated: the noise (forgive my quaint frenzy) of great fat cheques being ripped violently from their moorings and presented unawares to poor men. Match me (as the Don sang, but referring to a rose-red city of the East)—

> *Match me such marvel, whether East or West,*
> *So full of blooming ecstasy and zest.*

I have done.

PART TWO

5

CULTURE AND EDUCATION

Knowledge and Learning

BY

JOHN HENRY NEWMAN

I HAVE BEEN insisting (in my two preceding Discourses) first, on the cultivation of the intellect, as an end which may reasonably be pursued for its own sake; and next, on the nature of that cultivation, or what that cultivation consists in. Truth of whatever kind is the proper object of the intellect; its cultivation then lies in fitting it to apprehend and contemplate truth. Now the intellect in its present state, with exceptions which need not here be specified, does not discern truth intuitively, or as a whole. We know, not by a direct and simple vision, not at a glance, but, as it were, by piecemeal and accumulation, by a mental process, by going round an object, by the comparison, the combination, the mutual correction, the continual adaptation, of many partial notions, by the employment, concentration, and joint action of many faculties and exercises of mind. Such a union and concert of the intellectual powers, such an enlargement and development, such a comprehensiveness, is necessarily a matter of training. And again, such a training is a matter of rule; it is not mere application, however exemplary, which introduces the mind to truth, nor

From *The Idea of a University,* by John Henry Newman. Reprinted by permission of the publisher, Longmans, Green & Co., Inc., New York.

the reading many books, nor the getting up many subjects, nor the witnessing many experiments, nor the attending many lectures. All this is short of enough; a man may have done it all, yet be lingering in the vestibule of knowledge:—he may not realize what his mouth utters; he may not see with his mental eye what confronts him; he may have no grasp of things as they are; or at least he may have no power at all of advancing one step forward of himself, in consequence of what he has already acquired, no power of discriminating between truth and falsehood, of sifting out the grains of truth from the mass, of arranging things according to their real value, and, if I may use the phrase, of building up ideas. Such a power is the result of a scientific formation of mind; it is an acquired faculty of judgment, of clear-sightedness, of sagacity, of wisdom, of philosophical reach of mind, and of intellectual self-possession and repose—qualities which do not come of mere acquirement. The bodily eye, the organ for apprehending material objects, is provided by nature; the eye of the mind, of which the object is truth, is the work of discipline and habit.

This process of training, by which the intellect, instead of being formed or sacrificed to some particular or accidental purpose, some specific trade or profession, or study or science, is disciplined for its own sake, for the perception of its own proper object, and for its own highest culture, is called Liberal Education; and though there is no one in whom it is carried as far as is conceivable, or whose intellect would be a pattern of what intellects should be made, yet there is scarcely any one but may gain an idea of what real training is, and at least look towards it, and make its true scope and result, not something else, his standard of excellence; and numbers there are who may submit themselves to it, and secure it to themselves in good measure. And to set forth the right standard, and to train according to it, and to help forward all students towards it according to their various capacities, this I conceive to be the business of a University.

Now this is what some great men are very slow to allow; they insist that Education should be confined to some particular and narrow end, and should issue in some definite work, which can be weighed and measured. They argue as if every thing, as well as every person, had its price; and that where there has been a great outlay, they have a right to expect a return in kind. This they call making Education and Instruction "useful," and "Utility" becomes their watchword. With a fundamental principle of this nature, they very naturally go on to ask, what there is to show for the expense of a University; what is the real worth in the market of the article called "a Liberal Education," on the supposition that it does not teach us definitely how to advance our manufactures, or to improve our lands, or to better our civil economy; or again, if it does not at once make this man a lawyer, that an engineer, and that a surgeon; or at least if it does not lead to discoveries in chemistry, astronomy, geology, magnetism, and science of every kind. . . .

Let us take "useful," as Locke takes it, in its proper and popular sense, and then we enter upon a large field of thought, to which I cannot do justice in one Discourse, though today's is all the space that I can give to it. I say, let us take "useful" to mean, not what is simply good, but what *tends* to good, or is the *instrument* of good; and in this sense also, Gentlemen, I will show you how a liberal education is truly and fully a useful, though it be not a professional, education. "Good" indeed means one thing, and "useful" means another; but I lay it down as a principle, which will save us a great deal of anxiety, that, though the useful is not always good, the good is always useful. Good is not only good, but reproductive of good; this is one of its attributes; nothing is excellent, beautiful, perfect, desirable for its own sake, but it overflows, and spreads the likeness of itself all around it. Good is prolific; it is not only good to the eye, but to the taste; it not only attracts us, but it communicates itself; it excites first our admiration and love, then our desire and our gratitude, and that, in proportion to its intenseness and fulness in particular instances. A great good will impart great good. If then the intellect is so excellent a portion of us, and its cultivation so excellent, it is not only beautiful, perfect, admirable, and noble in itself, but in a true and high sense it must be useful to the possessor and to all around him; not useful in any low, mechanical, mercantile sense, but as diffusing good, or as a blessing, or a gift, or power, or a treasure, first to the owner, then through him to the world. I say then, if a liberal education be good, it must necessarily be useful too.

You will see what I mean by the parallel of bodily health. Health is a good in itself, though nothing came of it, and is especially worth seeking and cherishing; yet, after all, the blessings which attend its presence are so great, while they are so close to it and so redound back upon it and encircle it, that we never think of it except as useful as well as good, and praise and prize it for what it does, as well as for what it is, though at the same time we cannot point out any definite and distinct work or production which it can be said to effect. And so as regards intellectual culture, I am far from denying utility in this large sense as the end of Education, when I lay it down, that the culture of the intellect is a good in itself and its own end; I do not exclude from the idea of intellectual culture what it cannot but be, from the very nature of things; I only deny that we must be able to point out, before we have any right to call it useful, some art, or business, or profession, or trade, or work, as resulting from it, and as its real and complete end. The parallel is exact:— As the body may be sacrificed to some manual or other toil, whether moderate or oppressive, so may the intellect be devoted to some specific profession; and I do not call *this* the culture of the intellect. Again, as some member or organ of the body may be inordinately used and developed, so may memory, or imagination, or the reasoning faculty; and *this* again is not intellectual culture. On the other hand, as the body may be tended, cherished, and exercised with a simple view to its general

health, so may the intellect also be generally exercised in order
to its perfect state; and this *is* its cultivation.

Again, as health ought to precede labour of the body, and
as a man in health can do what an unhealthy man cannot do,
and as of this health the properties are strength, energy,
agility, graceful carriage and action, manual dexterity, and
endurance of fatigue, so in like manner general culture of
mind is the best aid to professional and scientific study, and
educated men can do what illiterate cannot; and the man who
has learned to think and to reason and to compare and to
discriminate and to analyze, who has refined his taste, and
formed his judgment, and sharpened his mental vision, will
not indeed at once be a lawyer, or a pleader, or an orator, or
a statesman, or a physician, or a good landlord, or a man of
business, or a soldier, or an engineer, or a chemist, or a geologist, or an antiquarian, but he will be placed in that state
of intellect in which he can take up any one of the sciences
or callings I have referred to, or any other for which he has
a taste or special talent, with an ease, a grace, a versatility,
and a success, to which another is a stranger. In this sense
then, and as yet I have said but a very few words on a large
subject, mental culture is emphatically *useful*.

If then I am arguing, and shall argue, against Professional
or Scientific knowledge as the sufficient end of a University
Education, let me not be supposed, Gentlemen, to be disre-
spectful towards particular studies, or arts, or vocations, and
those who are engaged in them. In saying that Law or Medicine is not the end of a University course, I do not mean
to imply that the University does not teach Law or Medicine.
What indeed can it teach at all, if it does not teach something
particular? It teaches *all* knowledge by teaching all *branches*
of knowledge, and in no other way. I do but say that there
will be this distinction as regards a professor of Law, or of
Medicine, or of Geology, or of Political Economy, in a University and out of it, that out of a University he is in danger
of being absorbed and narrowed by his pursuit, and of giving

Lectures which are the Lectures of nothing more than a lawyer, physician, geologist, or political economist; whereas in a University he will just know where he and his science stand, he has come to it, as it were, from a height, he has taken a survey of all knowledge, he is kept from extravagance by the very rivalry of other studies, he has gained from them a special illumination and largeness of mind and freedom and self-possession, and he treats his own in consequence with a philosophy and a resource, which belongs not to the study itself, but to his liberal education.

This then is how I should solve the fallacy, for so I must call it, by which Locke and his disciples would frighten us from cultivating the intellect, under the notion that no education is useful which does not teach us some temporal calling, or some mechanical art, or some physical secret. I say that a cultivated intellect, because it is a good in itself, brings with it a power and a grace to every work and occupation which it undertakes, and enables us to be more useful, and to a greater number. There is a duty we owe to human society as such, to the state to which we belong, to the sphere in which we move, to the individuals towards whom we are variously related, and whom we successively encounter in life; and that philosophical or liberal education, as I have called it, which is the proper function of a University, if it refuses the foremost place to professional interests, does but postpone them to the formation of the citizen, and, while it subserves the larger interests of philanthropy, prepares also for the successful prosecution of those merely personal objects, which at ·first sight it seems to disparage. . . .

Today I have confined myself to saying that that training of the intellect, which is best for the individual himself, best enables him to discharge his duties to society. The Philosopher, indeed, and the man of the world differ in their very notion, but the methods, by which they are respectively formed, are pretty much the same. The Philosopher has the same command of matters of thought, which the true citizen and gentleman has of matters of business and conduct. If then a practical end must be assigned to a University course, I say it is that of training good members of society. Its art is the art of social life, and its end is fitness for the world. It neither confines its views to particular professions on the one hand, nor creates heroes or inspires genius on the other. Works indeed of genius fall under no art; heroic minds come under no rule; a University is not a birthplace of poets or of immortal authors, of founders of schools, leaders of colonies, or conquerors of nations. It does not promise a generation of Aristotles or Newtons, or Napoleons or Washingtons, of Raphaels or Shakespeares, though such miracles of nature it has before now contained within its precincts. Nor is it content on the other hand with forming the critic or the experimentalist, the economist or the engineer, though such too it includes within its scope. But a University training is the great ordinary means to a great but ordinary end; it aims at raising the intellectual tone of society, at cultivating the public mind, at purifying the national taste, at supplying true principles to popular enthusiasm and fixed aims to popular aspiration, at giving enlargement and sobriety to the ideas of the age, at facilitating the exercise of political power, and refining the intercourse of private life. It is the education which gives a man a clear conscious view of his own opinions and judgments, a truth in developing them, an eloquence in expressing them, and a force in urging them. It teaches him to see things as they are, to go right to the point, to disentangle a skein of thought, to detect what is sophistical, and to discard what is irrelevant. It prepares him to fill any post with credit, and to master any subject with facility. It shows him how to accommodate himself to others, how to throw himself into their state of mind, how to bring before them his own, how to influence them, how to come to an understanding with them, how to bear with them. He is at home in any society, he has common ground with every class; he knows when to speak and when to be silent; he is able to converse, he is able to listen; he can ask a question pertinently, and gain a lesson seasonably, when he has nothing to impart himself; he is ever ready, yet never in the way; he is a pleasant companion, and a comrade you can depend upon; he knows when to be serious and when to trifle, and he has a sure tact which enables him to trifle with gracefulness and to be serious with effect. He has the repose of a mind which lives in itself, while it lives in the world, and which has resources for its happiness at home when it cannot go abroad. He has a gift which serves him in public, and supports him in retirement, without which good fortune is but vulgar, and with which failure and disappointment have a charm. The art which tends to make a man all this, is in the object which it pursues as useful as the art of wealth or the art of health, though it is less susceptible of method, and less tangible, less certain, less complete in its result.

Mr. Dooley on the Education of the Young

BY

FINLEY PETER DUNNE

"If ye had a boy wud ye sind him to colledge?" asked Mr. Hennessy. "Well," said Mr. Dooley, "at th' age whin a boy is fit to be in colledge I wudden't have him around th' house."

THE TROUBLED Mr. Hennessy had been telling Mr. Dooley about the difficulty of making a choice of schools for Packy Hennessy, who at the age of six was at the point where the family must decide his career.

" 'Tis a big question," said Mr. Dooley, "an' wan that

From *Mr. Dooley at His Best*, edited by Elmer Ellis. Reprinted by arrangement with the publisher, Charles Scribner's Sons, New York.

seems to be worryin' th' people more thin it used to whin ivry
boy was designed f'r th' priesthood, with a full undherstandin'
be his parents that th' chances was in favor iv a brick yard.
Nowadays they talk about th' edycation iv th' child befure
they choose th' name. 'Tis: 'Th' kid talks in his sleep. 'Tis
th' fine lawyer he'll make.' Or, 'Did ye notice him admirin'
that photygraph? He'll be a gr-reat journalist.' Or, 'Look
at him fishin' in Uncle Tim's watch pocket. We must thrain
him f'r a banker.' Or, 'I'm afraid he'll niver be sthrong enough
to wurrk. He must go into th' church.' Befure he's baptized
too, d'ye mind. 'Twill not be long befure th' time comes whin
th' soggarth'll christen th' infant: 'Judge Pathrick Aloysius
Hinnissy, iv th' Northern District iv Illinye,' or 'Profissor P.
Aloysius Hinnissy, LL.D., S.T.D., P.G.N., iv th' faculty iv
Northre Dame.' Th' innocent child in his cradle, wondherin'
what ails th' mist iv him an' where he got such funny lookin'
parents fr'm, has thim to blame that brought him into the
wurruld if he dayvilops into a sicond story man befure he's
twinty-wan an' is took up be th' polis. Why don't you lade
Packy down to th' occylist an' have him fitted with a pair
iv eye-glasses? Why don't ye put goloshes on him, give him a
blue umbrelly an' call him a doctor at wanst an' be done with
it?

"To my mind, Hinnissy, we're wastin' too much time
thinkin' iv th' future iv our young, an' thryin' to larn thim
early what they oughtn't to know till they've growed up. We
sind th' childher to school as if 'twas a summer garden where
they go to be amused instead iv a pinitinchry where they're
sint f'r th' original sin. Whin I was a la-ad I was put at me
ah-bee abs, th' first day I set fut in th' school behind th' hedge
an' me head was sore inside an' out befure I wint home. Now
th' first thing we larn th' future Mark Hannas an' Jawn D.
Gateses iv our nayton is waltzin', singin', an' cuttin' pitchers
out iv a book. We'd be much better teachin' thim th' sthrangle
hold, f'r that's what they need in life.

"I know what'll happen. Ye'll sind Packy to what th' Germans call a Kindygarten, an' 'tis a good thing f'r Germany, because all a German knows is what some wan tells him, and his grajation papers is a certyficate that he don't need to think annymore. But we've inthrajooced it into this country, an' whin I was down seein' if I cud injooce Rafferty, th' Janitor iv th' Isaac Muggs Grammer School, f'r to vote f'r Riordan —an' he's goin' to—I dhropped in on Cassidy's daughter, Mary Ellen, an' see her kindygartnin'. Th' childher was settin' ar-round on th' flure an' some was moldin' dachshunds out iv mud an' wipin' their hands on their hair, an' some was carvin' figures iv a goat out iv paste-board an some was singin' and some was sleepin' an' a few was dancin' an' wan la-ad was pullin' another la-ad's hair. 'Why don't ye take th' coal shovel to that little barbaryn, Mary Ellen?' says I. 'We don't believe in corporeal punishment,' says she. 'School shud be made pleasant f'r th' childher,' she says. 'Th' child who's hair is bein' pulled is larnin' patience,' she says, 'an' the child that's pullin' the hair is discoverin' th' footility iv human endeavor,' says she. 'Well, oh, well,' says I, 'times has changed since I was a boy,' I says. 'Put thim through their exercises,' says I. 'Tommy,' says I, 'spell cat,' I says. 'Go to th' divvle,' says th' cheerub. 'Very smartly answered,' says Mary Ellen. 'Ye shud not ask thim to spell,' she says. 'They don't larn that till they get to colledge,' she says, 'an',' she says, 'sometimes not even thin,' she says. 'An' what do they larn?' says I. 'Rompin',' she says, 'an' dancin',' she says, 'an' indepindance iv speech, an' beauty songs, an' sweet thoughts, an' how to make home home-like,' she says. 'Well,' says I, 'I didn't take anny iv thim things at colledge, so ye needn't unblanket thim,' I says. 'I won't put thim through anny exercise today,' I says. 'But whisper, Mary Ellen,' says I, 'don't ye niver feel like bastin' the seeraphims?' 'Th' teachin's iv Freebull and Pitzotly is conthrary to that,' she says. 'But I'm goin' to be married an' lave th' school on Choosdah, th' twinty-sicond iv Janooary,' she says, 'an' on Mondah, th' twinty-first, I'm goin' to ask a few iv th' little darlin's to th' house an',' she says, 'stew thim over a slow fire,' she says. Mary Ellen is not a German, Hinnissy.

"Well, afther they have larned in school what they ar're licked f'r larnin' in th' back yard—that is squashin' mud with their hands—they're conducted up through a channel iv free an' beautiful thought till they're r-ready f'r colledge. Mamma packs a few doylies an' tidies into son's bag, an' some silver to be used in case iv throuble with th' landlord, an' th' la-ad throts off to th' siminary. If he's not sthrong enough to look f'r high honours as a middleweight pugilist he goes into th' thought department. Th' prisident takes him into a Turkish room, gives him a cigareet an' says: 'Me dear boy, what special branch iv larnin' wud ye like to have studied f'r ye be our compitint profissors? We have a chair iv Beauty, an' wan iv Puns an' wan iv Pothry on th' Changin' Hues iv th' Settin' Sun, an' wan on Platonic Love, an' wan on Non-sense Rhymes, an' wan on Sweet Thoughts, an' wan on How Green Grows th' Grass, an' wan on th' Relation iv Ice to th' Greek Idee iv God,' he says. 'This is all ye'll need to equip ye f'r th' perfect life, onless,' he says, 'ye intind bein' a dintist, in which case,' he says, 'we won't think much iv ye, but we have a good school where ye can larn that disgraceful thrade,' he says. 'An' th' la-ad makes his choice, an' ivry mornin' whin he's up in time he takes a whiff iv hasheesh an' goes off to hear Profissor Maryanna tell him that 'if th' dates iv human knowledge must be rejicted as subjictive, how much more must they be subjicted as rejictive if, as I think, we keep our thoughts fixed upon th' inanity iv th' finite in comparison with th' onthinkable truth with th' ondivided an' inimaginable reality. Boys, ar-re ye with me?' . . ."

"I don't undherstand a wurrud iv what ye'r sayin'," said Mr. Hennessy.

"No more do I," said Mr. Dooley. "But I believe 'tis as Father Kelly says: 'Childher shuddn't be sint to school to larn, but to larn how to larn. I don't care what ye larn thim so long as 'tis onpleasant to thim.' 'Tis thrainin' they need,

Hinnissy. That's all. I niver cud make use iv what I larned in colledge about thrigojoomethry an'—an'—grammar an' th' welts I got on th' skull fr'm th' schoolmasther's cane I have niver been able to turn to any account in th' business, but 'twas th' bein' there an' havin' to get things to heart without askin' th' meanin' iv thim an' goin' to school cold an' comin' home hungry, that made th' man iv me ye see befure ye."

"That's why th' good woman's throubled about Packy," said Hennessy.

"Go home," said Mr. Dooley.

Reading and Education

BY

FRANCIS J. SHEED

DISCUSSION OF EDUCATION is for ever being muddled by two confusions, between Education and Literacy and between Education and Scholarship. The first confusion is gross and easily cleared up; the second is subtle and needs the very closest scrutiny.

There is a kind of superstition about Literacy: you are told that in one country ninety per cent of the people can read and write; while in another ninety per cent cannot. Intellectually the figures mean little. Reading is scarcely an intellectual activity at all; the power to take words off a page is in itself little more than an extra sense. By hearing, for example, what is said reaches the brain through the ear; by reading, what is said reaches the brain through the eye. The whole question is what happens to it when it reaches the brain, and literacy

From *A Ground Plan for Catholic Reading.* Reprinted by permission of the publisher, Sheed and Ward, Inc., New York.

statistics cannot tell you that. Or again, we are delighted that so high a proportion of our fellow-countrymen can read and write; it would be too cruel to ask *what* can they write; but even if you stop short with the question what do they read, the answer is not a matter for great exultation.

The trouble about reading is that it is the name for two totally different activities. Reading—serious reading—the great means of contact with the world about us and our fathers before us, is an educational activity in the fullest sense. Education cannot proceed without it; a defective education can be rectified by it; what a man reads is a surer measure of his education than any number of degrees. But there is a game of the same name, played with similar implements—the pastime called reading. Its genesis is easy to trace. Men hate having anything to do. But men also hate having nothing to do. The human race therefore has always been fertile in the invention of things to do which are equivalent to nothing—things which will pass the time. This accounts for most of our reading; nothing happens in the mind—simply the time passes.

Now obviously everyone wants to pass some time, and the most intellectually active of men will do a certain amount of pastime reading. The question is how much time can one afford merely to pass. The problem is pressing for this reason also, that a man tends to become what he reads; and while real reading may become a passion, this second thing becomes a craving, like smoking, of which the intellectual value is about the same. The trouble is that anyone can read to pass the time, but one has to *learn* how to read in the proper sense.

When Carlyle said that the aim of all education was to teach men to read, he certainly did not mean a mere equipment of alphabets and spelling-books and ink on a page. It is only when all this is mastered, that one can begin to learn to read. That stage reached, the choice lies before every man; either he will make the effort and learn to read, or he will devote his newly acquired technical equipment solely to the passing of the time. In the second case he possibly makes an occasional effort at better things: reads some real book—history, biography, theology, philosophy, poetry; tries to read it at the same pace as the pastime books—not realizing the difference—as though one tried to eat meat as fast as jelly; at that pace makes nothing of it, and gives it up for ever. There is a discipline of reading as of every other good thing. It involves a certain self-conquest. If we are not prepared for that discipline then our universally literate generation will be worse off than the Middle Ages by one more sedative. With this question of reading, the whole of education is bound up, for the greatest thought of mankind is in books and the greatest living teacher can do no higher thing in the intellectual order than teach his pupil to read.

Education fits a man for living. Man exists in a universe: man is: other things are: successful living means a right relation between *man* and *all else that is*. A treatise on education would work this out in relation to all man's faculties and powers—mind, will, imagination, emotions. But this is not a treatise on education, and our only concern here is with education as it affects the mind. Successful living, as we have seen, means a right relation between man and all else that is. The mind's part is to come to the knowledge of that right relation. An educated man is one whose mind is responsive to being, to everything that is. It will be noted that the words 'all' and 'everything' have kept recurring in this paragraph. This is of the very essence of education. You cannot fully know anything until you know everything: less cryptically, the parts get their significance from their place in the totality. If you know only a part but not the whole, you do not even know the part.

Thus we come to the second great distinction, between Education and Scholarship. Scholarship is necessary to education, and an educational system which claims to mould character and neglects learning is charlatanism. Yet a great scholar may fail to achieve that right mental relationship to all that is, which is of the very definition of education. The explanation has already been suggested; he knows an enormous amount about something or other; but he does not see the totality; lacking a view of the whole, he is unbalanced by what he knows of the part. Scholarship is pure gain to the mind that knows the totality: to any other it is, in greater or less degree, an eccentricity. Only the educated mind is at home in the universe. A very crude example will make clear what I am trying to say. The human eye is very beautiful—in the human face. Put that same eye on a plate, and though in one sense it can be investigated more closely and thoroughly, it has lost its beauty and even its significance. A being who knew only eyes and not faces would not even know eyes. A being who knew masses of facts about each feature separately but did not know how the features were arranged in a human face, could imagine only a nightmare and no face.

The process of education thus requires two elements. First, the mind must see the universe of being as a totality, with all its constituents in right relation to one another: it does not know everything but it knows where everything is. Second, there must be the study of individual things. Given such a total view as has been described, then every new piece of knowledge is an enrichment. Indeed the value of this individual knowledge is immense. If it is true that the part lacks significance to one who does not see the whole, it is also true that the whole lacks reality to a person of small knowledge. After all the *totality* is a totality of *being* and we must study not only totality (which as seen by the mind is a matter of shape and arrangement) but also being (which is the stuff thus shaped and arranged); being comes to us in the individual thing learnt and there is no limit to our progress in the realization of it. Everything that is, has something to contribute to our knowledge of being in its immeasurable richness and variety.

But here again a careful distinction must be made: the new knowledge is of educational value *not simply* as an item known, adding one to the total of items remembered. Nothing is more instructive than to dig out the question-papers of old examinations—the examinations we passed in our youth. Usually we find that we do not know the answers—often enough we do not so much as know what the questions mean. Yet we knew once; we spent long years in acquiring the knowledge; education could not have proceeded without it. Education, then, is arrived at by learning things most of which we are destined ineluctably to forget; and this is not as wasteful as it might seem. Even the thing forgotten may be of high educational value.

The object of the mind is to know what is—that is, to know being. Being comes to it through fact, or event, or another man's thought. The mind takes in the fact (of science, say) or event (of history) or thought (of this or that philosopher or poet). This is the mechanics of the educational process—this pushing into the mind of facts and events and the rest of it. All this is simply something done to the mind. Therefore in itself it is not education. Education is something that happens *in* the mind. What does happen in the mind? Often enough nothing. The fact learnt may lie there —not acting, not acted upon, quite useless—long enough to be written down in an examination; after which it can with impunity be forgotten, leaving the mind as unaffected by its passing as by its entry. In the better case the mind takes hold of it, thinks about it, extracts the kernel of being from it, enriches itself with that. Even if the individual fact or event or set of words in which that speck of being was clothed be forgotten, it is a great thing that the mind should thus have fed upon it. Fortunately we do not forget everything. Our minds hold on to certain truths, and the store of these increases. New relations of things are seen and new depths, carrying the mind further towards that right relation to all that is, which is its own special perfection.

What happens in the mind is educational. The really valuable knowledge is not that of which we can say—'On such a day, in such a book, I learnt this.' Facts can be shoved into the mind like books into a bag: and as usefully. Push in as many books as you please and the bag has still gained nothing. All that happens is that it bulges. A bag is no better for all that it has carried. Heads can similarly bulge from the mere mass of facts known but not assimilated into the mind's substance. A phenomenon the student will have noticed, at first incredulously but with a growing callousness as the years pass, is that very learned people are often utter fools. And far from this being a paradox, one sees how it happens; so far from learning and foolishness being incompatible, they are comfortable bedfellows. There is no fool like the learned fool: a mind which merely takes in facts without assimilating them can obviously take in far more of them, since it can devote to learning new facts that time which better minds devote to nourishing themselves upon the old. The mind's feeding upon being is education; examinations, alas, are mainly a test of what remains in the memory: the best kind of examination may go further and discover what has happened to the surface of the mind; but the educational reality—what has happened in the very depths of the mind—no examination has been devised to discover that.

To return to the totality: it will be clear that this is the indispensable element. The man who rightly sees the whole will gain an enormous amount from a mere handful of individual things known. It cannot too often be repeated that the man who knows only the individual things, will not know even them: for he will not know their context.

What then is this knowledge of the totality, and who can impart it? I was once talking on these matters at a Teachers' College; and, arrived at this point, I said that for the total view which education demands one must know God; the air chilled instantly; plainly the educators I was addressing were disappointed in me. What, they felt, had God to do with education? Education was a matter for specialists. Yet two things seem to me clear: that unless we rightly see God, we have no true view of the totality; and that one who does not believe in God is by that very fact stating the sheer impossibility of a total view and so of education itself.

For the theist, the matter hardly needs stating. God is not simply the supreme Being, enthroned at the apex of all that is in such wise that the universe may be conceived as so many strata of being from the lowest to the highest and God over all: if that were so, one might conceive of a true study of the lower strata which should take no account of God. But the truth is that God is at the very centre of all things whatsoever. They come into existence only because He creates them; they remain in existence only because He sustains them. To omit God, therefore, from your study of things is to omit the one being that explains them: you begin your study of things by making them inexplicable! Further, all things are made not only by God but for God; in that lies their purpose and the relation of each thing to all others. For the believer in God, therefore, a view of the universe unrelated to God is a chaos far worse than a vision of features unrelated to a face.

This truth, which to the theist is a positive reason for knowing God that education may be a possibility, is for the atheist a sad condition making education impossible. If there be no mind directing the whole universe of being, then there is no universe, no totality. There is only a constantly fluctuating sum of individual things, accidental in their very origin (since no mind brought them into being), purposeless (since no mind meant them for anything and accidents have no purpose), a drift of things drifting nowhere. Nothing can be known save out of its context, for there is no context.

But the place of God in our view of the totality of things —and so of education—is not simply a matter of recognizing Him as first cause and last end and sustainer in being more intimate to each being than it is to itself; there is also His revelation of the purpose for which He made man—not simply that He made man for Himself but just what this involves in terms of man's being and action. This question of purpose is a point overlooked in most educational discussion, yet it is quite primary. How can you fit a man's mind for living if you do not know what the purpose of man's life is? You can have no reasonable understanding of any activity —living as a totality or any of its departments—if you do not know its purpose. You do not even know what is good or bad for a man till you know the purpose of his existence, for this is the only test of goodness or badness—if a thing helps a man in the achievement of the purpose for which he exists, then it is good for him; if not, it is bad. And the one quite certain way to find out the purpose of anything is to ask its maker. Otherwise you can only guess. The Catholic knows that man has a Maker and that the Maker has said what He made man for. Therefore—not of himself but by the revelation of God—the Catholic knows the purpose of human life and if he be an educator he has the answer to this primary question. He may be a thoroughly bad educator—perhaps through being like so many of us a born fool—but he has the first requirement. For the life of me I cannot see how anyone else can have it or can even think he has it.

Beyond these elementary truths about God, there is His further revelation of His own nature, and of the means by which man may achieve fulfilment. There are refinements here which belong only to the theologian, but there is also a mass of truth necessary for all men in the sense that without it their view of the whole will be falsified and for that very reason they will know nothing properly. That there is a God; what He is; that man's destiny is to do something which by nature he cannot do, so that he must receive from God powers to act above his nature; that his own dependence upon God is literally that of nothingness since apart from God's will there is in man only nothingness; yet that man is *not* nothing but a being of eternal significance; that his dependence, absolute as it is, is not that of a machine upon a mad mechanic or a slave upon a mad king but of a child upon a father whose power and love are one single thing; that God's incomprehensibility, the root of what we call mystery, is a matter of exultation since it assures us that the universe is controlled by a being infinite in perfection; that all things in life—suffering and failure included—are incidents in a universe directed by God and so can be for his own richest advantage—all these and a mass of truths beside are necessary to be known by man, and education is impossible without them.

And not only to be known in the sense that if we were asked about any of them we could think of the correct answer; but so known that they enter as a matter of course into every judgment that the mind forms. The test of maturity in a mind is precisely this: how much of what a man knows enters as a matter of course into all his judgments. Normally, if a man has to come to a decision, he will without effort take certain things into account—his own inclination, for instance, his bodily needs, the effect upon his wife and children, the reaction of his employer, the run of public opinion; a man may do so much who has never received any education at all. If he as naturally takes into account the will of God, the purpose of his own life, the relation of the temporal to the eternal, the relation of his own partial knowledge to God's total knowledge, the fact of Calvary, his relationship to other men in God, his relationship to other members of the Mystical Body—then, and only then, has he the first essential of an educated mind.

The upshot of all this is that education has as its one indispensable requisite something that only a Catholic can give. This is the strictly educational argument for Catholic education. There are other arguments of a moral and theological order, but the two sets of arguments must be sharply distinguished. A non-Catholic institution may be dangerous to Catholic faith and practice and that is the most serious consideration of all. But my point here is that *a non-Catholic institution cannot give an education;* it can give a magnificent mass of scholarship and a rich mental training; but in the intellectual order there is one thing necessary, a comprehensive view of the totality of being, and this it cannot give. This does not mean that a Catholic institution will inevitably succeed. It may fail on the side of scholarship and the minds of its students, not fed on truth to the measure of their power, will emerge all feeble—even if the total view has been given to them, they will have it only as a skeleton; or it may fail in the communication of the total view, teaching religion as simply one subject in the curriculum and a rather dull subject at that.

But whether he goes to a non-Catholic college or not, the Catholic will find himself soon enough in the largest non-Catholic institution of all—the world of real life. This precisely is the problem for all of us. In papers, movies, novels, in daily conversation, in normal practice we are constantly under the pressure of a different view from our own; no need to particularize; the plain truth is that the Church teaches us one universe and we live in another. If the superiority of the world's view were treated in the world as matter of argument, it would be a help; but it is simply assumed. Argument might stimulate us to defence; indifference soothes us into apathy. The temptation is to accept one set of values by faith but to live by another set in daily practice. This temptation must be resisted with all our might. Yet to throw all the burden of resistance upon the will is sheer cruelty: the mind too must be fortified. The best fortification of the mind is the total possession of the true view—a possession fundamental and operating as a matter of course in every judgment; to a mind thus fortified, everything serves; falsehood is seen to be false and not given hospitality. Yet every falsehood may contain truth or suggest it; and this truth, too, the minds makes its own.

Billy Sanders Discusses Fathers and Sons

BY

JOEL CHANDLER HARRIS

MR. SANDERS WAS beaming when he walked into the editorial rooms. To use his own comparison, his face was as full of smiles as a keg of fresh beer, and he was especially polite to the young lady stenographers. His countenance resembled that of a baby who is watching the antics of a playful kitten. He held a letter in his hand and waved it over his head with a triumphant air. Holding it some distance from his eyes, he read the address—"Mr. Billy Sanders, of Shady Dale." His smile broadened. "Now, what do you think of that? Don't a man's name look purty when it's writ out by a smart 'oman that knows precisely how for to take her pen in hand? It looks that-a-way to me. Now here's the letter. She takes a text, same as a preacher. Read it an' take it to yourself, same as I did." He handed the letter to the poet, who read as follows: "Thar never was a boy ruined in the world that his mammy an' daddy didn't have a han' in the ruinin'." This was what Mr. Sanders called the text. The letter went on:

Dear Mr. Sanders: In all your philosophizing you never said a truer thing. Can't you say more of it in your inimitable way? There is nothing more needed in this country than a stronger, firmer home life. After fourteen years of teaching boys and girls, good and bad, many of the latter, I have found the words of your text absolutely true. I want to thank you for them; and I want to thank you for all your Shady Dale philosophy.

Sincerely yours,

A.C.

From *Joel Chandler Harris: Editor and Essayist,* by Mrs. Julia Collier Harris. Reprinted by arrangement with the publisher, The University of North Carolina Press, Chapel Hill, N. C.

"The 'oman that writ this letter has got hoss-sense," remarked Mr. Sanders, "an' ef you'll teach a passel of boys fourteen years old, you'll have some on it, too. I kin go into any school-house or college in this broad land, an' pick out the boys that has had home trainin'. They'll show it at study, at play, on the street an' at church. You'll see the signs wharsomever you turn your eyes.

"Natchally, whar a boy aint got no daddy or mammy, he's bound for to run wild ef the State don't take him in hand, or ef he aint holp by some of our numerous orphan asylums. Thar never was a boy born into the world that don't have to have the hickory put to him more than once, an' the oftener the better. You may think my talk is harsh, but the more I love a boy, the more I wanter see him come under some strong an' heavy hand, bekaze I know it's his only salvation. You may look back on all the youngsters you've know'd, an' you'll find that we ain't got any more wisdom than Solomon, ef as much. He tore the bottom out of the basket in a mighty few words. 'Spar' the rod an' spile the child.' Ef he'd 'a' never said nothin' else, them seven words would 'a' made him the wisest man the world ever seed. No newspaper paragrapher has ever beat it yit. Ef brevity's the sole of whiteleather, your Uncle Solomon has got it down mighty fine; ef he aint, you may call me Mabel, an' print in the paper that I've done gone an' eloped wi' a college fiddler named Clarence Raymond. When you hear man or 'oman say they can't control the'r boys, you can put it down for a fact that thar's somethin' in that home that calls for the sanitary inspector, the preacher an' the doctor, though I don't know how uther one on 'em can give the mammy an' daddy moral fibre. You can patch a pa'r of jeans britches but you can't patch a weak mind; the thing's been tried too much an' too long. It looks like the whole country has been took down wi' the same epidemic, an' now the State is called on for to pertect the youngsters that could better pertect themselves ef they had 'a' been raised right. But I want to tell you one thing, the wanderin' boy tonight will wander tomorrow night an' the night arter, onless his mammy or daddy gives him a dose of cow-rope an' barrel-stave. It's the natur' on 'em; the more you indulge 'em the more they want to be indulged, an' bimeby, they take the bit in the'r teeth, an' right then my wanderin' boy tonight gits good an' ripe.

"An' then, when ma comes home from her club an' pa gits in fresh from his'n, or sets behind his paper readin' the gamblin' market reports, a great hue an' cry is set up about our wanderin' boy tonight, warranted to smoke a package of cigarettes ever' fifteen minnits. What's to be done? Why, pa heaves a sigh like a bellowsed hoss' an' ma hums a tune betwixt her sniffles. Now, what's to hender pa from gwine out arter the youngster wi' a rawhide, an' yankin' him home, an' teachin' him a lesson that he'll never forgit as long as he lives? Mention it to 'em, an' you're a cruel monster. What! raise whales on the beautiful an' tender skin of our darlin' boy! Why, you're too old-fashioned for to live. What's the State for but to be a parient to our darlin' child? Can't it pass laws to pertect him from whiskey an' tobacco? An' then it's hooray for ever'thing but the right thing!

"Now, I ain't got nothin' in the world ag'in prohibition or the anti-cigarette law; when the State has a law on its books, I'm for it ef it's good, bad or indifferent. But what I say is that sech laws don't go to the root of the matter; they don't kill what you might call the family boll-weevil. The trouble, when thar's any, is to be found right in the home that the wanderin' boy strays from, an' I say that thar oughter be a law pertectin' children from weak-minded parients. Ever' man an' 'oman that's got a boy child should be made to toe the mark an' raise the'r children right. It may be a hard thing to do, but thar aint no secret about it; it may take up a good deal of the'r time an' attention, but what are they here for? That's what I want to know.

"Give a boy a half a chance, an' he'll be all right. No human bein' was ever born for to be a vagabond an' a drunkard, though you'd think so from the way some people raise the'r boys. Some are too hard on 'em, an' some are too leenient, an' them two extremes meet an' shake hands in a bar-room, or in the neighborhood of a blind-tiger. Ef ma understood her business, she'd soon see that nary two boys is precisely alike. Each one is hisself, an' you can't make him somebody else, but by treatin' him right you can make him a good man. An' pa oughter open his weather eye an' take notice, an not leave ever'thing to a tender-hearted 'oman. He oughter take a hour off from his business ever'day for to make the acquaintance of his children; he oughter be made to do it.

"I know a man, an' you fellers know him, too, that tried his best for to raise his boys right; he didn't tell 'em that healthy fun is sinful, or that whiskey is rank pisen. They had the'r frolics, same as kittens do, an' they've all grow'd up to be good men. When they was growin' up, they had jest as many liberties as was good for 'em, an' they had a good time gener'lly. Thar wa'n't no innocent fun they missed, not even the circus; but they know'd right whar the line was —it had been p'inted out to 'em—an' ef they crossed it they know'd right what the'd git. The beauty about it was that they allers got it when it was due—cow-rope or barrel-stave. Ef they come in at night feelin' bad, they know'd whar the dram-bottle was, an' they know'd they could go an' mix up a toddy, or git the'r mammy to do it for 'em. An' what's the result? You could guess it ef you had any sense. Not one of 'em has ever been drunk, an' the whole bunch is as straight as a yardstick. Now, to begin with, they wa'n't a whit better than any other boys; they had a high pulse an' a longin' for things forbidden, but as fur as they went was to let the'r mouth water a little, bekaze they know'd that dad was waitin' for 'em at home wi' a big stick ef they went wrong. They had somebody for to be afear'd on, an' they know'd it, an' so they let the other fellers taste of evil things, while they rolled up the'r britches an' went polin' home.

"An' that word home puts me in mind of another big thing, maybe the biggest of all. The mammy an' daddy that makes home so nice that a boy'll ruther stay thar than to sneak out in the alley-ways, will never have much occasion to complain of the'r children. They'll stay at home an' be happy thar. I've watched this kinder thing for fifty year, an' I'm not a-doin' of any guess-work; what I've seed, I've seed, an' I aint been blind sence I was born. What one man kin do, all men kin do, an' ef they don't do it, it's bekaze they want to shirk the duties that Heaven has laid on 'em. I jest give you the example of one man's way of raisin' boys, but I know hundreds that have done jest as well. The trouble is that the great majority of folks want the State government for to take the'r places, an' legislate temptation out'n the way; they want policemen for to go hand in hand wi' 'em a good part of the'r journey through this vale of tears. But I wouldn't give you a thrip for a boy that aint never had temptations flung in his way; it's a part of his reel eddication, an' he'll never be a man ontell he's l'arned how to resist 'em.

"Now, don't go an' fool yourself by thinkin' that I'm atalkin' ag'in prohibition, bekaze I aint. The law'll do good even ef it don't wipe out whiskey altogether. As the ol' 'oman said, when she was about to die, 'I may never git right well, but I certainly hope I'll git a good deal better,' an', shore enough, she rallied an' lived many a long year. Prohibition mayn't be perfect, but it'll keep some folks sober longer than they think it will, an' it'll drive some of our big problems into the swamps. For myself, I firmly believe that ever' man should be his own special an' private prohibitionist, but, as I've told you before, we've all consented to bury the principles of ginnywine Democracy so deep that they'll never be dug up ag'in, an' we've got things in hand that Tom Jefferson never so much as guessed at. An' they're things that we'll have for to settle wi'out dependin' on the way our forefathers settled the'r little troubles. This is as much as to say that we've traveled a consider'ble way from the fellers that framed the Constitution, maybe not bekaze we wanted to, but bekaze we had to. Maybe we're on the wrong road, but we'll find it out in due time, an' then we'll have to come polin' back, might'ly fretted at the weight of the wallets on our backs. Thar's one thing about it, ef we do have to take the back track, we kin do it wi'out sheddin' any tears. I see Tom Watson is for prohibition, an' ef that's the case, any Jeffersonian kin foller suit wi'out havin' too many dry grins.

"Now, you think that I've got clean away from the mammy an' daddy business, but I aint. Some on 'em think that they can have a quiet night's rest bekaze prohibition is wi' us, but that's whar they make a mistake. E'en about the wust white man I ever laid eyes on never tuck a drink of whiskey in his life, an' never used tobacco in any shape. He had lots wuss habits than them. He was a gambler from the word go, an' he swindled his way to the grave, all bekaze his mammy and daddy thought he was a piece of perfection. They thought that a boy that didn't drink, ner chaw, ner smoke, was the next thing to bein' a angel, but ef I was to tell you the things that model boy done, includin' one or two murders, you wouldn't sleep good tonight. I know'd a man, an' some on you would know him, too, ef I was to blab his name, that had three as likely boys as you'd wish to see. He was tender-hearted an' affectionate, an' as sentimental as a romantic 'oman. Well, he started to raisin' his boys right by the time they could talk. He never had a hickory in the house; his idee was that moral persuasion would do the work. He kept 'em out'n temptation; they couldn't play wi' no bad boys, an' on Sundays they had to stay close in the house, an' read the right kind of books—books suited to the day an' hour. Well, they grow'd up to whar they just couldn't be kep' in an' treated like hothouse plants; they had to git out an' shake theirselves, an' see what was to be seed. They thought they found out that ever'thing was a leetle diffunt from what they had been told, an' then the Satan in their bones begun for to grow, an' he grow'd an' grow'd ontell he got big enough to take complete possession of 'em.

"The last one on 'em went to the bad. Why? They was the healthiest an' most promisin' youngsters you ever laid eyes on, but they was kep' in an' coddled too much; they never knocked about wi' boys of the'r own age, an' they wa'n't allowed for to live the lives of boys. So when they did git out, Satan swooped down on 'em like a hawk on a young chicken.

"Thar aint much of a problem in raisin' boys ef you'll have a little common-sense about it. Don't let 'em run wild like pigs in the woods, an' don't keep the lines too tight, an' when things go wrong don't be afear'd of usin' a raw-hide. But don't forgit that the mammies an' daddies of the land are twice responsible when one of the'r boys goes wrong. Ef the legislatur' wants to do a good work, an' make better citizens out'n the risin' generation, let it put a heavy penalty on the dear parients of the boys that go wrong. Take this as my last call for reform on this subject, an' le' me slip you a So-long as I sneak out' the door."

The Love of Excellence

BY

JOHN LANCASTER SPALDING

Why is this glorious creature to be found
One only in ten thousand? what one is,
Why may not millions be? what bars are thrown
By Nature in the way of such a hope?

Wordsworth.

HE TEACHES TO good purpose who inspires the love of excellence, and who sends his pupils forth from the school's narrow walls with such desire for self-improvement that the whole world becomes to them a God-appointed university. And why shall not every youth hope to enter the narrow circle of those for whom to live, is to think, who behold "the bright countenance of truth in the quiet and still air of delightful studies."

From *Opportunity and Other Essays,* by John Lancaster Spalding. Reprinted by permission of the copyright owner, His Excellency, the Bishop of Peoria, Illinois.

An enlightened mind is like a fair and pleasant friend who comes to cheer us in every hour of loneliness and gloom; it is like noble birth which admits to all best company; it is like wealth which surrounds us with whatever is rarest and most precious; it is like virtue which lives in an atmosphere of light and serenity, and is itself enough for itself. Whatever our labors, our cares, our disappointments, a free and open mind, by holding us in communion with the highest and the fairest, will fill the soul with strength and joy. The artist, day by day, year in and year out, hangs over his work, and finds enough delight in the beauty he creates; and shall not the friend of the soul be glad in striving ceaselessly to make his knowledge and his love less unlike the knowledge and the love of God? Seldom is opportunity of victory offered to great captains, the orator rarely finds fit theme and audience, hardly shall the hero meet with occasions worthy of the sacrifice of life; but he who labors to shape his mind to the heavenly forms of truth and beauty beholds them ever present and appealing. Life without thought and love is worthless; and to the best men and women belong only those who cultivate with earnestness and perseverance their spiritual faculties, who strive daily to know more, to love more, to be more beautiful. They are the chosen ones, and all others, even though they sit on thrones, are but the crowd.

Without a free and open mind there is no high and glad human life. You may as well point to the savage drowsing in his tent, or to cattle knee-deep in clover, and bid me think them high, as to ask me to admire where I can behold neither intelligence nor love. All that we possess is qualified by what we are. Gold makes not the miser rich, nor its lack a true man poor; and he who has gained insight into the fair truth that he is a part of all he sees and loves, is richer than kings, and lives like a god in his universe. Possibilities for us are measured by the kind of work in which we put our hearts. If a man's thoughts are wholly busy with carpentering do not expect him to become anything else than a carpenter; but if his aim is to build up his own being, to make his mind luminous, his heart tender and pure, his will steadfast, who but God shall fix a limit beyond which he may not hope to go. Education, indeed, cannot confer organic power; but it alone gives us the faculty to perceive how infinitely wonderful and fair are man's endowments, how boundless his inheritance, how full of deathless hope is that to which he may aspire. Religion, philosophy, poetry, science—all bring us into the presence of an ideal of ceaseless growth toward an all-perfect Infinite, dimly discerned and unapproachable, but which fascinates the soul and haunts the imagination with its deep mystery, until what we long for becomes more real than all that we possess, and yearning is our highest happiness. Ah! who would throw a veil over the vision on which young eyes rest when young hearts feel that ideal things alone are real? Who would rob them of this divine principle of progress which makes growth the best of life?

> *Many are our joys*
> *In youth; but oh, what happiness to live*
> *When every hour brings palpable access*
> *Of knowledge, when all knowledge is delight!*

In all ages, we know those made wise by experience, which teaches us to expect little, whether of ourselves or others, have made the thoughts and hopes of youth a jest, even as men have made religion a jest, having nothing to offer us in compensation for its loss, but witticisms and despair. This is the fatal fault of life, that when we have obtained what is good—as wealth, position, wife, and friends—we lose all hope of the best, and with our mockery discourage those who have ideal aims; who, remembering how the soul felt in life's dawn, retain a sense of God's presence in the world, to whom with growing faculties they aspire, feeling that whatsoever point they reach, they still have something to pursue. This is the principle of the diviner mind in all high and heroic natures; this is the springhead of deeds that make laws, of "thoughts that enrich the blood of the world"; this is the power which gives to resolve the force of destiny, and clothes the soul with the heavenliest strength and beauty when it stands single and alone, of men abandoned and almost of God.

There is little danger that too many shall ever hearken to the invitation from the fair worlds to which all souls belong, and where alone they can be luminous and free. For centuries, now, what innumberable voices have pleaded with men to make themselves worthy of heaven; while they have moved on heedless of the heaven that lies about us here, placing their hopes and aims in material and perishable elements, athirst neither for truth, nor beauty, nor aught that is divinely good! They sleep, they wake, they eat, they drink; they tread the beaten path with ceaseless iteration, and so they die. If one come appealing for culture of intellect, not because they who know, are stronger than the ignorant and make them their servants, but because an open, free, and flexible mind is good and fair, better than birth, position, and wealth, they turn away as though he trifled with their common-sense. Life, they say, is not for knowledge, but knowledge for life; and they neither truly know, nor live. And if here and there some nobler soul stand forth, he degrades himself to an aspirant to fame, forgetting truth and love.

> Enough there are on earth who reap and sow,
> Enough who give their lives to common gain,
> Enough who toil with spade and axe and plane,
> Enough who sail the seas where rude winds blow;
>
> Enough who make their life unmeaning show,
> Enough who plead in courts, who physic pain;
> Enough who follow in the lover's train,
> And taste of wedded hearts the bliss and woe.
>
> A few at least may love the poet's song,
> May walk with him, their visionary guide,
> Far from the crowd, nor do the world a wrong;
> Or on his wings through deep blue skies may glide
> And float, by light transfused, like clouds along
> Above the earth and over oceans wide.

With unresting, wearing thought and labor we are striving to make earth more habitable. We drag forth from its inner parts whatever treasures are hidden there; with steam's mighty force we mould brute matter into every fair and serviceable form; we build great cities, we spread the fabric of our trade; the engine's iron heart goes throbbing through tunnelled mountains and over storm-swept seas to bear us and our wealth to all regions of the globe; we talk to one another from city to city, and from continent to continent along ocean's oozy depths the lightning flashes our words, spreading beneath our eyes each morning the whole world's gossip—but in the midst of this miraculous transformation, we ourselves remain small, hard and narrow, without great thoughts or great loves or immortal hopes. We are a crowd where the highest and the best lose individuality, and are swept along as though democracy were a tyranny of the average man under which superiority of whatever kind is criminal. Our population increases, our cities grow, our roads are lengthened, our machinery is made more perfect, the number of our schools is multiplied, our newspapers are read in ever-widening circles, the spirit of humanity and of freedom breathes through our life; but the individual remains common-place and uninteresting. He lacks intelligence, has no perception of what is excellent, no faith in ideals, no reverence for genius, no belief in any highest sort of man who has not shown his worth in winning wealth, position, or notoriety. We have a thousand poets and no poetry, a thousand orators and no eloquence, a thousand philosophers and no philosophy. Every city points to its successful men who have millions, but are themselves poor and unintelligent; to its writers who, having sold their talent to newspapers and magazines, sink to the level of those they address, dealing only with what is of momentary interest, or if the question be deep, they move on the surface, lest the many-eyed crowd lose sight of them. The preacher gets an audience and pay on condition that he stoop to the gossip which centres around new theories, startling events, and mechanical schemes for the improvement of the country. If to get money be the end of writing and preaching, then must we seek to please the multitude who are willing to pay those who entertain and amuse them. Will not our friends, even, conceive a mean opinion of our ability, if we fail to gain public recognition?

So we make ourselves "motleys to the view, and sell cheap what is most dear." We must, perforce, show the endowment which can be brought to perfection only if it be permitted to grow in secrecy and solitude. The worst foe of excellence is the desire to appear; for when once we have made men talk of us, we seem to be doing nothing if they are silent, and thus the love of notoriety becomes the bane of true work and right living. To be one of a crowd is not to be at all; and if we are resolved to put our thoughts and acts to the test of reason, and to live for what is permanently true and great, we must consent, like the best of all ages, to be lonely in the world. All life, except the life of thought and love, is dull and superficial. The young love for a while, and are happy; a few think; and for the rest existence is but the treadmill of monotonous sensation. There are but few, who, through work and knowledge, through faith and hope and love, seek to escape from the narrowness and misery of life to the summits of thought where the soul breathes a purer air, and whence is seen the fairer world the multitude forebodes. There are but few whose life is

> *Effort and expectation and desire,*
> *And something evermore about to be;*

but few who understand how much the destiny of Man hangs upon single persons; but few who feel that what they love and teach, millions must know and love

> *A people is but the attempt of many*
> *To rise to the completer life of one;*
> *And those who live as models for the mass*
> *Are singly of more value than them all.*

Only the noblest souls awaken within us divine aspirations.

They are the music, the poetry, which warms and illumines whole generations; they are the few who, born with rich endowments, by ceaseless labor develop their powers until they become capable of work which, were it not for them, could not be done at all. History is the biography of aristocrats, of the chosen ones with whom all improvement originates, who found States, establish civilizations, create literatures, and teach wisdom. They work not for themselves; for in spite of human selfishness and the personal aims of the ambitious, the poet, the scholar, and the statesman bless the world. They lead us through happy isles; they clothe our thoughts and hopes with beauty and with strength; they dissipate the general gloom; they widen the sphere of life; they bring the multitude beneath the sway of the law.

Now, here in America, once for all, whatever the thoughtless may imagine, we have lost faith in the worth of artificial distinctions. Indeed plausible arguments may be found to prove that the kind of man democracy tends to form, has no reverence for distinctions of whatever kind, and is without ideals, and that as he is envious of men made by money, so he looks with the contempt of unenlightened common-sense upon those whom character and intellect raise above him. This is not truth. The higher you lift the mass, the more will they acknowledge and appreciate worth, the clearer will they see that what makes man human, beautiful, and beneficent is conduct and intelligence; and so increasing enlightenment will turn thought and admiration from position and wealth, from the pomp and show of life to what makes a man's self, his character, his mind, his manners even—for the source of manners lies within us. In a society like ours the chosen ones, the best, the models of life, and the leaders of thought will be distinguished from the crowd not by accident or circumstance, but by inner strength and beauty, by finer knowledge, by purer love, by a deeper faith in God, by a more steadfast trust that it must, and shall be, well with a world which God makes and rules, and which to the fairest mind is fairest, and to the holiest soul most sacred.

Here and now, if ever anywhere at any time, there is need of men, there is appeal to what is godlike in man, calling upon us to rise above our prosperities, our politics, our mechanical aims and implements, and to turn the courage, energy, and practical sense which have wrought with miraculous power in developing the material resources of America, to the cultivation of our spiritual faculties. We alone of the great modern nations are without classical writers of our own, without a national literature. The thought and love of this people, its philosophy, poetry, and art lies yet in the bud; and our tens of thousands of books, even the better sort, must perish to enrich, the soil that nourishes a life of heavenly promise. Hitherto we have been sad imitators of the English, but not the best the English have done will satisfy America. Their language indeed will remain ours, and their men of genius, above all their poets, will enrich our minds with great thoughts nobly expressed. But a literature is a national growth; it is the expression of a people's life and character, the more or less perfect utterance of what it loves, aims at, believes in, hopes for; it has the qualities and the defects of the national spirit; it bears the marks of the thousand influences that help to make that spirit what it is—and English literature cannot be American literature, for the simple reason that Americans are not Englishmen, any more than they are Germans or Frenchmen. We must be ourselves in our thinking and writing, as in our living, or be insignificant, for it is a man's life that gives meaning to his thought; and to write as a disciple is to write in an inferior way, since the mind at its best is illumined by truth itself and not taught by the words of another. It is not to be believed that this great, intelligent, yearning American world will content itself with the trick and mannerism of foreign accent and style, or that those who build on any other than the broad foundation of our own national life shall be accepted as teachers and guides. There is, of course, no method known to man by which a great author may be formed; no science which teaches how a literature may be created. The men who have written what the world will not

permit to die have written generally without any clear knowledge of the worth of their work, just as great discoverers and
inventors seem to stumble on what they seek; nevertheless
one may hope by right endeavor to make himself capable of
uttering true thoughts so that they shall become intelligible
and attractive to others; he may educate himself to know and
love the best that has been spoken and written by men of
genius, and so become a power to lift the aims and enlarge
the views of his fellow-men. If many strive in this way to
unfold their gifts and to cultivate their faculties, their influence will finally pervade the life and thought of thousands,
and it may be of the whole people.

I do not at all forget Aristotle's saying that "life is practice
and not theory"; that men are born to do and suffer, and
not to dream and weave systems; that conduct and not culture
is the basis of character and the source of strength; that a
knowledge of Nature is of vastly more importance to our
material comfort and progress than philosophy, poetry, and
art. This is not to be called in question; but in this country
and age it seems hardly necessary that it be emphasized, for
what is the whole world insisting upon but the necessity of
scientific instruction, the importance of practical education,
the cultivation of the money-getting faculty and habit, and the
futility of philosophy, poetry, and art? Who is there that
denies the worth of what is useful? Where is there one who
does not approve and encourage whatever brings increase of
wealth? Are we not all ready to applaud projects which give
promise of providing more abundant food, better clothing,
and more healthful surrounding for the poor? Does not our
national genius seem to lie altogether in the line of what
is practically useful? Is it not our boast and our great achievement that we have in a single century made the wilderness of a
vast continent habitable, have so ploughed and drained and
planted and built that it can now easily maintain hundreds of
millions in gluttonous plenty? Is not our whole social and
political organization of a kind which fits us to deal with questions and affairs that concern our temporal and material

welfare? What innumerable individuals among us are con-
gressmen, legislators, supervisors, bank and school directors,
presidents of boards and companies, committee-men, council-
men, heads of lodges and societies, lawyers, professors, teachers, editors, colonels, generals, judges, party-leaders, so that the
sovereign people seems to have life and being only in its titled
representatives! What does this universal reign of title and
office mean but the practical education which responsibility
gives? If from the midst of this paradise of utility, materialism, and business, a voice is raised to plead for culture, for
intelligence, for beauty, for philosophy, poetry, and art, why
need any one take alarm? While human nature remains what
it is, can there be danger that the many will be drawn away
from what appeals to the senses, to what the soul loves and
yearns for? If the Almighty God does not win the multitude
to the love of righteousness and wisdom, how shall the words
of man prevail?

It is a mistake to oppose use to beauty, the serviceable to
the excellent, since they belong together. Beauty is the blossom
that makes the fruit-tree fair and fragrant. Life means more
than meat and drink, house and clothing. To live is also to
admire, to love, to lose one's self in the contemplation of the
splendor with which Nature is clothed. Human life is the
marriage of souls with things of light. Its basis, aim, and end
is love, and love makes its object beautiful. Man may not
even consent to eat, except with decency and grace; he must
have light and flowers and the rippling music of kindly speech,
that as far as possible he may forget that his act is merely
animal and useful. He will lose sight of the fact that clothing
is intended for protection and comfort, rather than not dress
to make himself beautiful. To speak merely to be understood, and not to speak also with ease and elegance, is not to
be a gentleman. How easily words find the way to the heart
when uttered in melodious cadence by the lips of the fair and
young. Home is the centre and seat of whatever is most useful
to us; and yet to think of home is to think of springtime and

flowers, of the songs of birds and flowing waters, of the voices of children, of floating clouds and sunsets that linger as though heaven were loath to bid adieu to earth. The warmth, the color, and the light of their boyish days still glow in the hearts and imagination of noble men, and redeem the busy trafficking world of their daily life from utter vulgarity. What hues has not God painted on the air, the water, the fruit, and the grain that are the very substance and nutriment of our bodies? Beauty is nobly useful. It illumines the mind, raises the imagination, and warms the heart. It is not an added quality, but grows from the inner nature of things; it is the thought of God working outward. Only from drunken eyes can you with paint and tinsel hide inward deformity. The beauty of hills and waves, of flowers and clouds, of children at play, of reapers at work, of heroes in battle, of poets inspired, of saints rapt in adoration—rises from central depths of being, and is concealed from frivolous minds. Even in the presence of death, the hallowing spirit of beauty is felt. The full-ripe fruit that gently falls in the quiet air of long summer days, the yellow sheaves glinting in the rays of autumn's sun, the leaf which the kiss of the hoar frost has made blood-red and loosened from the parent stem—are images of death but they suggest only calm and pleasant thoughts. The Bedouin, who, sitting amid the ruins of Ephesus, thinks but of his goats and pigs, heedless of Diana's temple, Alexander's glory, and the words of Saint Paul, is the type of those who place the useful above the excellent and the fair; and as men who in their boards of trade buy and sell cattle and corn, dream not of green fields and of grain turning to gold in the sun of June, so we all, in the business and worry of life, lose sight of beauty which makes the heart glad and keeps it young.

The mind of man is the earthly home of beauty, and if any real thing were fair as the tender thought of imaginative youth, heaven were not far. All we love is but our thought of what only thought makes known and makes beautiful, and for what we know love's thought may be the essence of all things.

Fairer than waters where soft moonlight lies,
Than flowers that slumber on the breast of Spring,
Than leafy trees in June when glad birds sing,
Than a cool summer dawn, than sunset skies;

Than love, gleaming through Beauty's deep blue eyes,
Than laughing child, than orchards blossoming;
Than girls whose voices make the woodland ring,
Than ruby lips that utter sweet replies—

Fairer than these, than all that may be seen,
Is the poetic mind, which sheds the light
Of heaven on earthly things, as Night's young Queen
Forth-looking from some jagged mountain height
Clothes the whole earth with her soft silvery sheen
And makes the beauty whereof eyes have sight.

Nature is neither sad nor joyful. We but see in her the reflection of our own minds. Gay scenes depress the melancholy, and gloomy prospects have not the power to rob the happy of their contentment. The spring may fill us with fresh and fragrant thoughts, or may but remind us of all the hopes and joys we have lost; and autumn will speak to one of decay and death, to another of sleep and rest, after toil, to prepare for a new and brighter awakening. All the glory of dawn and sunset is but etheric waves thrilling the vapory air and impinging on the optic nerve; but behind it all is the magician who sees and knows, who thinks and loves. "It is the mind that makes the body rich." Thoughts take shape and coloring from souls through which they pass; and a free and open mind looks upon the world in the mood in which a fair woman beholds herself in a mirror. The world is his as much as the face is hers. If we could live in the fairest spot of earth, and in the company of those who are dear, the source of our happiness would still be our own thought and love; and if they are great and noble, we cannot be miserable however meanly surrounded. What is reality but a state of soul, finite in man, infinite in God? Theory underlies fact, and to the divine mind all things are godlike and beautiful. The chemical elements are as sweet and pure in the buried corpse as in the blooming body of youth; and it is defective intellect, the warp of ignorance and sin, which hides from human eyes the perfect beauty of the world.

> *Earth's crammed with heaven,*
> *And every common bush afire with God;*
> *But only he who sees, takes off his shoes.*

What we all need is not so much greater knowledge, as a luminous and symmetrical mind which, whatsoever way it turn, shall reflect the things that are, not in isolation and abstraction, but in the living unity and harmony wherein they have their being.

The worth of religion is infinite, the value of conduct is paramount; but he who lacks intellectual culture, whatever else he may be, is narrow, awkward, unintelligent. The mirror of his soul is dim, the motions of his spirit are sluggish, and the divine image which is himself is blurred.

But let no one imagine that this life of the soul in the mind is easy; for it is only less difficult than the life of the soul in God. To learn many things; to master this or that science; to have skill in law or medicine; to acquaint one's self with the facts of history, with opinions of philosophers or the teachings of theologians—is comparatively not a difficult task; and there are hundreds who are learned, who are skilful, who are able, who have acuteness and depth and information, for one who has an open, free, and flexible mind—which is alive and active in many directions, touching the world of God and Nature at many points, and beholding truth and beauty from many sides; which is serious, sober, and reasonable, but also fresh, gentle, and sympathetic; which enters with equal ease into the philosopher's thought, the poet's vision, and the ecstasy of the saint; which excludes no truth, is indifferent to no beauty, refuses homage to no goodness. The ideal of culture indeed, like that of religion, like that of art, lies beyond our reach, since the truth and beauty which lure us on, and flee the farther the longer we pursue, are nothing less than the eternal and infinite God.

And culture, if it is not to end in mere frivolity and gloss, must be pursued, like religion and art, with earnestness and reverence. If the spirit in which we work is not deep and holy, we may become accomplished but we shall not gain wisdom, power, and love. The beginner seeks to convert his belief into knowledge; but the trained thinker knows that knowledge ends in belief, since beyond our little islets of intellectual vision, lies the boundless, fathomless expanse of unknown worlds where faith and hope alone can be our guides. Once individual man was insignificant; but now the earth itself is become so—a mere dot in infinite space, where, for a moment, men wriggle like animalcules in a drop of water. And if at times a flash of light suddenly gleam athwart the mind, and it seem as though we were about to get a glimpse into the inner heart of being, the brightness quickly dies, and only the surfaces of things remain visible. Oh, the unimaginable length of ages when on the earth there was no living thing! then life's ugly, slimy beginnings; then the conscious soul's fitful dream stretching forth to endless time and space; then the final sleep in abysmal night with its one star of hope twinkling before the all-hidden throne of God, in the shadow of whose too great light faith kneels and waits!

Why shall he whose mind is free, symmetrical, and open, be tempted to vain glory, to frivolous boasting? Shall not life be more solemn and sacred to him than to another? Shall he indulge scorn for any being whom God has made, for any thought which has strengthened and consoled the human heart? Shall he not perceive, more clearly than others, that the unseen Power by whom all things are, is akin to thought and love, and that they alone bring help to man who make him feel that faith and hope mean good, and are fountains of larger and more enduring life? The highest mind, like the purest heart, is a witness of the soul and of God.

6

LITERATURE AND ART

The Unrecognised Air

BY

ALFRED NOYES

THERE IS ONE great influence in European literature, even in modern European literature, which is as vital and all-permeating as that of the air on the creatures that breathe it. Even where the makers of that literature are unconscious of it, or even unwilling to recognise it, they are dependent upon it for the very colour of the corpuscles in their veins.

It need hardly be said that the word "modern" is used here in its proper sense to mark the latest of the three great divisions of history (the other two being the ancient and the mediæval) and not, as it is so commonly used in the Press to-day, to signify merely the conventions of the last publishing season. If we include Dante as the supreme figure of mediæval literature, the singer in whom, at once, the Middle Ages culminated and the modern period began; and if we survey those works of literature, from his day to our own, which seem to possess qualities of permanent value; it is impossible to dissociate them from certain elements that have been contributed to human thought and emotion by the Christian religion, even though these elements may be seized and transmuted as the oxygen of the atmosphere is transmuted by those who breathe it. It

From *The Opalescent Parrot,* by Alfred Noyes. Reprinted by permission of the publisher, Sheed and Ward, Inc., New York.

is not carrying the analogy too far to say that in many cases
the distinctly anti-Christian literature in many respects corresponds only to what is breathed out again after the breather
has extracted—consciously or unconsciously—what he needed
for his own life; and that Voltaire himself was able to breathe
out a destructive atmosphere only because he had unconsciously drawn in, and made use of, its more vital constituents.
For the influence of Christianity is not limited to those who
acknowledge it, or are aware of it.

> If the Red Slayer thinks he slays,
>   Or if the slain thinks he is slain,
> They know not well the subtle ways
>   I keep and pass and turn again.

And so, to strike at once the very centre of the enemy's
shield, it may be pointed out that Voltaire (who may be
regarded as the typical anti-Christian of modern world literature) has only one weapon of attack that still retains its
weight and can still be respected in the higher regions of the
intellect to-day. This is his contention that the God of the
theologians is lacking in the higher attributes of his own
"Supreme Being." In other words, it was impossible for
Voltaire to think as the pagan Lucretius. Confronted by the
Lisbon earthquake, he could feel none of the pagan satisfaction of the man who from a secure shore watches the death-
agonies of another; and the higher attributes which he insists
are necessary to his own Supreme Being are precisely those
upon which the spirit of Christianity, transcending all the
theologies, had taught him to insist:—

> Ignorer ton être suprême,
> Grand Dieu! c'est un moindre blasphème,
> Et moins digne de ton courroux
> Que de te croire impitoyable,
> De nos malheurs insatiable,
> Jaloux, injuste comme nous.

So he wrote in his "Ode sur le Fanatisme"; what is this but
an insistence on the very attributes of the Deity which it has

been the glory and the power of the Christian religion to find in its own Founder, and to give as the central explanation of its own mystery, "God so loved the world." Creeds and systems, theologies and theologians may have failed again and again and to the uttermost; but nothing can alter the fact that the strength of Christianity, the wisdom that was hidden from the wise and revealed to the simplicity and love of little children, the infinite justice at one with infinite mercy and divine compassion had so wrought upon the minds of men that Voltaire himself was intellectually compelled to judge its own priests by the standards which they had forgotten. Nor is this conclusion affected in the least by Voltaire's own blindness and thrice-proven intellectual dishonesty, as when in his haste to condemn what he thought might be one of the evidences of the Old Testament legend of the Flood he attacked the real discoveries of the early geologists, and in the very irony of which he was so proud became himself a lasting subject for the irony of history.

This incorporation of the elements of Christianity in the works of writers who are professedly anti-Christian is one of the most striking characteristics revealed by a careful analysis of modern literature. It occurs in poets like Shelley and Swinburne, the first of whom attacked the lifeless creeds of his own day, and described himself as an "atheist" only to make one of the most burning confessions of faith that has ever been made in poetry; faith, not in any sectarian system, but in

> *That Light whose smile kindles the universe*
> *That Beauty in which all things work and move.*

Shelley's vision of that Light and world-sustaining Love is at one with the vision of St. John; and the music in which it is expressed is a continuation of the music of Dante, in the opening and close of the "Paradiso" :—

> *La gloria di colui che tutto move*
> *Per l'universo penetra, e risplende*
> *In una parte più, e meno altrove.*

and

L'amor che move il sole e l'altre stelle.

In the later poet, Swinburne, there are even more striking illustrations of the debt of anti-Christian writers to Christianity, both in thought and feeling. Tennyson, while praising the splendour and strength of one of Swinburne's early works once asked him the significant question whether it was *fair* to abuse the Deity in the language and imagery of the Hebrew prophets. But Swinburne goes farther than this. In "Songs before Sunrise" he expresses his own highest thoughts and emotions in the language of the Bible; and, in poems like "Quia Multum Amavit," the validity of those thoughts and emotions depends upon the validity of the figures and the imagery that he is using. His poem "Before a Crucifix," for instance, in the fury of its attack on the Christianity of the churches, seemed to many of the orthodox to be merely a piece of fanatical blasphemy. But its real content is something more than this; and, when he is confronted by the realities of suffering, and grief in the world around him, it is not to the Greek vision of Aphrodite or any pagan imagery that he turns, to express his highest thoughts about it. Step by dark step, this so-called anti-Christian is blindly led on, as a musician is led on by a surrounding orchestra, to postulate the very principles which he was supposed, possibly even by himself, to be denying.

> *O sacred head, O desecrate,*
> *O labour-wounded feet and hands,*
> *O blood poured forth in pledge to fate*
> *Of nameless lives in divers lands,*
> *O slain and spent and sacrificed*
> *People, the grey-grown speechless Christ.*

Though he is turning the imagery to a new purpose, its validity here depends upon the truth of the central idea of Christianity, the God who became man, and the ultimate object of the poet's worship is indistinguishable from that of the saints of the Middle Ages.

And the blood blots his holy hair
And white brows over hungering eyes
That plead against us, . . .

There is indeed a sense in which some of the greatest of the
anti-Christian writers may be said to be fulfilling rather than
destroying the law which they seemed to others (and sometimes to themselves) to be attacking. Their spirit, though
weakened by perversities or warped by intellectual pride, or
reacting against its own environment in a way that has no
meaning for others, has often, burning at its core, the anger
of Christ in the temple against those who have made it into
a den of thieves. The really valuable part of the modern
literature of "rebellion," whether it be in a Christian like
Tolstoi or in professedly anti-Christian writers, has this, and
this alone, as the foundation of whatever greatness it possesses. At the same time it must be remembered that seeing
the motes in the eyes of others, and seeing them with anger,
is an occupation that, in literature, as in life, may obscure
many other matters of importance; and the literature of "rebellion" and destructive thought, as such, has never risen to
the heights of the great creative world-poets. The two great
epics that literature can oppose to those of antiquity during
the last nineteen hundred years are both attempts to unfold
the system of the universe, and in both cases the intellectual
groundwork and the spiritual vision that gives them their
permanent value were the direct result of the Christian
religion. The world-ranging mind of Dante could never have
achieved the great musical consummation of thought in the
line

E la sua volontade e nostra pace,

if the seed had not been sown in his mind by the earlier simplicity of the prayer "Thy will be done on earth as it is in
heaven." It was the Bible that enabled Milton to rise to the
height of his great argument in "Paradise Lost"—a poem
compared with which even the music of Homer seemed to
Landor like that of a tinkling cymbal on the shores of the

ocean—and it is never to be forgotten that the values of that music are not to be sought or discovered merely in the story he tells, or in what the logician can extract from the surface-meaning of the words. Attempts to interpret the Bible allegorically have been regarded with a just suspicion, for they have sometimes been mere evasions of questions that deserve a direct answer, and they have been pressed into the service of intellectual dishonesty. But Milton affirmed directly that his own art is a "process of speech" without which it would be impossible to tell of the acts of God. His meaning is to be sought in the symbolical values of great art and great poetry —as we seek it in the works of the great painters, or in a symphony of Beethoven. The very movement of the words has a meaning that transcends their literal meaning as far as a great cathedral transcends that of the separate stones of which it is built.

> Hail, holy Light, off-spring of heaven first-born
> Or of the Eternal, co-eternal beam
> May I express thee unblamed, since God is light
> And never but in unapproached light
> Dwelt from Eternity, dwelt then in thee . . .

Such passages as these in the great blind poet are transfigured by the spirit of holiness that he invoked. They are the mountain-peaks of the world's literature, making the heaven of heavens their dwelling-place.

II

But the influence of Christianity upon literature is not limited to those writers who have either opposed it or, as in the two supreme masters of epic during the last nineteen hundred years, drawn their inspiration directly from its fountain-head. It is impossible here to cover the whole field, but one may indicate briefly that the literature of mediæval chivalry, in ballad and romance, as well as in the statelier poems of the Crusades by Ariosto and Tasso, derived its nobility and beauty from ideas that had been sown and fostered by Christianity.

The new compassion for the weak, the new reverence for womanhood, the truth and honour of Chaucer's "perfect gentle knight"; and, everywhere, those gleams of the beauty of holiness, even though it were praised as a remote star in a heaven beyond the reach of our sin-stained earth; all these things were derived from the religion of which the wandering knight in the greatest of all the poems of chivalry —Spenser's "Faerie Queene"—bore the emblem upon his shield:

> And on his breast a bloody cross he bore
> The dear remembrance of his dying Lord.

But in the wider fields of later literature, where the cross was no longer worn upon the breast, the influence is no less potent. The Elizabethan drama, dealing with all sorts and conditions of men and women, may be traced back by the curious to its origin in the old morality plays; but the debt is a wider and a deeper one than that. Hazlitt has pointed out how much the Elizabethan drama owes to a religion which had taught us the love of good for the sake of good, and, answering the question, "Who is our neighbour?" by the words "one whose wounds we can bind up," has done more to humanise the thoughts and tame the unruly passions than all who have tried to reform or benefit mankind. The very idea of the desire to do good, or regarding the human race as one family, is hardly to be found in any other code. The Greeks and Romans never thought of considering others. . . . But in the Christian religion the heart of a nation becomes malleable, capable of pity, of forgiveness, of relaxing in its claims and remitting its power. And so, in Shakespeare, though his works are dramatic and can give no direct expression of his own personal creed, we can trace everywhere the prints of

> . . . those blessed feet
> Which fourteen hundred years ago were nailed
> For our advantage on the bitter cross.

We trace it in his deep sense of the moral law, and still more

in his humanity, which echoes the Sermon on the Mount, and
adds a second benediction to it.

> *The quality of mercy is not strained,*
> *It droppeth as the gentle rain from heaven*
> *Upon the place beneath. It is twice blessed.*
> *It blesseth him that gives and him that takes.*

Just as Dante owed one of his most consummate passages
of intellectual music to a sentence in the Lord's Prayer, so
Shakespeare owes this passage to the spirit that breathed upon
a tortured world the divine sentence, "Blessed are the merciful, for they shall obtain mercy." To say that there is much
in Shakespeare (as in Dante also) that conflicts with the teaching of Christ is merely to say that he was human, and that
only a God could reveal the perfect harmony. The fact remains that the poetry of Shakespeare has a capacity of thought
and emotion, a breadth of charity and humanity that were not
possible to Greece and Rome. He owes these characteristics
to the Christian religion and to that figure of whom another
Elizabethan dramatist—Dekker—wrote

> *The best of men*
> *That e'er wore earth about him was a sufferer;*
> *A soft, meek, patient, humble tranquil spirit;*
> *The first true gentleman that ever breathed.*

These influences are so widely and so subtly spread that it is
impossible to examine them in detail. It is only possible to
say that they have coloured the whole fabric of European
thought, even where it is least conscious of the fact, and even
where it has apparently discarded the last shadow of a religious creed. But in later poets, like Wordsworth, Tennyson
and Browning in England; Victor Hugo in France; and
Goethe in Germany, the debt is far clearer than in the Elizabethan period. It is not that these poets all definitely profess
a Christian creed (Goethe certainly did not, even though in
"Faust" he uses the Catholic symbolism), but their highest
thought and emotion are of an order that belongs as definitely

to Christendom, and to Christendom alone, as the use of light
and fire belongs to man alone among the creatures on this
planet. When Wordsworth writes:

> *One lesson, shepherd, let us two divide,*
>   *Taught both by what she shows, and what conceals;*
> *Never to blend our pleasure or our pride*
>   *With sorrow of the meanest thing that feels,*

he is only expressing in set terms a spirit that is far more
deeply interfused through all the literature of his period. For
the subtler spiritual elements which literature derived from
the Christian religion, we must turn to the mystics and the
idealistic philosophers. But here again it should not be forgotten that it is not merely in the "mystics" or in the devotional poets like Herbert and Crashaw and Christina Rossetti
that these elements are to be found. They leaven the whole
of the higher literature of modern Europe, and exert a
mysterious quickening power, not only upon philosophical
critics like Carlyle and Tolstoi but on the "religion of beauty"
of the poets of the romantic revival, with its aspirations into
the unseen; and on the "religion of humanity" (with its desire
to set the crooked straight), which, even where it was un-
avowed and unconscious, so strongly characterises the work of
the greatest modern novelists. Of these last, in England, the
best example is Dickens, who never writes as one making
what are called religious professions, and yet perhaps has done
more than any other writer in modern times to hasten the
kingdom of heaven on earth. The sense of pity, the charity,
the human kindness that suffuse the vast world of his creation
continue the work of the Master whom he seldom directly
invokes. One of these rare occasions when, like a long-sup-
pressed cry, the direct appeal breaks from his lips, is in that
marvellous scene—not surpassed by Shakespeare or any other
—where a foolish and mean woman, far too commonplace to
interest the modern exponents of intellectual pride, is brutally
treated by the man to whom she was bearing a child.

He answered with an imprecation and a blow.
No angry cries; no loud reproaches. Even her weeping
  and her sobs were stifled by her clinging round him . . .
O woman, God-beloved in old Jerusalem! . . .

It is the cry of the Master himself over the unremembering
City of God.

Art and Prudence

BY

ERIC GILL

ART IS SKILL—skill in doing or skill in making.
Whatever else art may be it is always that.
     Skill is the body of art.
     Deliberation is its soul or "form." [1]
Art is deliberate skill—skill with mind behind it.
     "Art abides always on the side of the mind."
There is a thing called the mind of God.
     Hence there is a thing called the art of God.
There is a thing called the mind of man.
     Hence there is a thing called the art of man.
     Only by metaphor do we speak of the art of the spider;
     The spider, having no mind, cannot use deliberate skill.
     The skill of the spider is directly dependent upon the
          mind of God.
     The art of the spider is the art of God.
The art of the spider is like that of a factory "hand"—di-

From *Beauty Looks After Herself,* by Eric Gill. Reprinted by permission
of the publisher, Sheed and Ward, Inc., New York.

[1] Deliberation—the act of the mind in choosing. It does not necessarily
require a process of ratiocination.
     Form—the principle which determines a thing in its species.

rected from outside. As the owner of a jam factory
said to a visitor: "I am God almighty in this place."
But man has a mind of his own and therefore free will.
A rational soul necessarily connotes free will.
Hence there is strictly speaking an art of man as well as an
art of God.
But, unlike God, man cannot make out of nothing.
Man's mind, his intelligence and will, can only know the
truth that God knows and desire the good that God
wills.
Imbecility and ill will are privations.

Skill in making and skill in doing are both loosely called art.
Doing is an activity directed to an end in view—the end in
view being man's good, his last good, Heaven.
But when a man's deeds are directed not to his own good
simply but to the good of a *thing,* then doing becomes
making.
An act that is good, or thought to be good, with regard to
oneself is called a *prudent* act.
An act that is good, or thought to be good, with regard to a
thing to be made is called *art.*
A man whose acts are conformed to his own good is called
a *prudent man.*
A man whose acts are conformed to the good of things is
called an *artist.*
In both cases skill in doing is required.
Skill in doing good to oneself is called *prudence.*
Skill in doing good to things is called *art.*
Prudence is the means to happiness in oneself.
Art is the means to pleasure in what is not oneself.
To have happiness is the object of prudence.
Happiness in oneself is a good and is the object of the
will.
Happiness is subjective.
To have pleasure in things is the object of art.

Pleasure in things is a good and is the object of the intelligence.

Pleasure is objective.

Great intelligence is not necessary for prudence (happiness).

Great prudence is not necessary for intelligence (pleasure).

A fool may be a saint.

A villain may be an artist.

A fool may be a villain.

A saint may be an artist.

But a fool cannot be an artist, nor a villain a saint.

Ethics is the science of happiness in oneself.

Æsthetics is the science of pleasure in things.

Both are departments of philosophy.

Prudence is the application of ethics to practice.

Art is the application of æsthetics to practice.

The practice of prudence is called morals.

The practice of art is called craft or craftsmanship.

Happiness being man's goal, his final goal, it behoves a man to be a prudent man; for prudence has man's final happiness for its object.

But happiness is a state of mind.

It is that state of mind in which what is desired is known.

Final happiness is the state of mind in which the desired good is the known good—

In which the desired God is the known God.

When what is desired is known it is said to be *seen*.

Final happiness is to see God.

This is called "the Beatific Vision."

Happiness is, therefore, not a state of bliss merely;

It is a state of bliss in knowledge.

But knowledge is necessarily knowledge of something—not of *no* thing.

Happiness is in a knowledge of that thing or those things that are pleasing.

Happiness is in knowledge of those things that are pleasing to the mind.

Those things are pleasing to the mind which are in themselves good.

God alone is good.

So those things are pleasing to the mind which are of God or in God.

Here below we may see God in all things (that is earthly happiness).

We may see through all things to God.

The state of Heaven is that in which we see all things in God.
We see through God to all things.

The prudent man acts so that he may achieve the blissful state of heavenly happiness.

But that state is one in which he has knowledge of all things in God—*Gaudium de veritate.*

Happiness is therefore not separable from pleasure in things.

Prudence is therefore not separable from art.

As making has need of doing—so prudence has need of art.

The achieving of happiness in oneself is the business of prudence.

The supplying of pleasure in things is the business of art.

Art and prudence are, as it were, one flesh.

There is a marriage between them.
There is also a lovers' quarrel between them.
Each seeks the perfection of its own.

Now man taken abstractly as the bride of God is female.

Hence the Church is the bride of Christ.
Man and the Church are one.
The clergy alone are not the Church.
The laity alone are not the Church.
Man united to God is the Church.

Man taken abstractly in his collaboration with God, *i.e.* as maker, is male.

Man the artist is male.

But, unlike God, he is not creator of things out of noth-
    ing.
He is creator in the second degree.
He is a channel, a vehicle for God's creative power.
Through man God brings creation to a greater and more
    poignant degree of beauty.
Art improves on Nature.
That is what it is for.
Beauty is the splendour of Being.
The beautiful thing is that which being seen pleases.
The beautiful is therefore the object of art, for only beautiful
    things give pleasure to the mind, and the pleasure of
    the mind is the object of art.
The skill of the artist has for its end the production of things
    which shall give pleasure being seen.
Being seen means being desired and known.
    But this pleasure is not the pleasure of knowing.
    It is the pleasure of knowing the thing seen.

The Church is man in his aim of achieving happiness
She is therefore the guardian of faith and morals.
    She is the mouthpiece of Prudence.
    The Church is Prudent Man.
    The Church is man knowing and acting in accordance
        with his end—happiness in Heaven—the Beatific
        Vision.
The artist is man in his aim of making what shall give pleasure.
    Happiness feeds on pleasure.
    Pleasant things are the meat and drink of happiness.
The ultimate happiness is heaven; for union with God is
    union with the source of all good and therefore with
    all things that are pleasing.

Now the perfectly prudent man is a man of perfectly good will.
The perfect artist is a man of perfectly good sense.
Perfectly good will is, it seems, possible to man.
Perfectly good sense is, it seems, not possible to man.

His finite condition deprives him of the possibility of perfect knowledge.

Moreover, the perfection of good will is passive:—

"Grant that I may love thee always; then do with me what thou wilt," and again: "Be it done to me according to thy word."

But perfectly good sense is active.

(The words of God effect what they signify.)

Man can be perfectly passive.

Man cannot be perfectly active.

He can do nothing of himself.

"We are not able to please thee by our own acts."

Man can only be a perfectly willing agent.

His free will does not give him creative power.

It gives him simply perfect power to will what God wills.

A finite intelligence does not give him perfect knowledge of what God knows.

Hence prudence is superior to art with regard to man, but "art . . . metaphysically is superior to prudence."

Man *taken abstractly* is both female and male.

He is both man of prudence and artist.

He is both churchman and statesman.

In the concrete, man is divided.

Church and State are separated.

Prudence and art are opposed—not as enemies but as lovers.

In the concrete, Church and prudence take precedence of government over State and art.

And each seeks the perfection of its own.

But in the modern world this right and proper opposition is obscured.

It is obscured by the tyranny of commerce—by the tyranny of the middleman, conveniently so called because he stands in the middle obstructing everything and obstructing particularly the marriage of art and prudence.

The servant has become the master.

The go-between has become the boss.

In the welter the Church, in the order of doing, seeks to salvage what she can for prudence.

In the order of making, the State salvages what it can for art.

Under these circumstances the prudent man often becomes a prig and the artist often becomes merely a purveyor of sentimental trifles.

Under a régime of commercial insubordination the mass of men are neither men of prudence nor artists.

But a semblance of prudence is more in evidence than even a semblance of art.

Worldly prudence makes a better show of virtue than worldly art.

To make money, to achieve material security and prosperity, looks more virtuous than to make what is merely pleasing.

Stock-broking morality and the morality of manufacturers and bankers stinks less in the nostrils of the prudent man, with his eye on Heaven, than does the art of music halls or of dancing places.

Such morality seems to be directed to the indubitably legitimate end of making money for the support of families.

There seems no doubt that men must live and must support their families.

On the other hand, music-hall art and such like seems to be directed to no known end but worldly pleasure.

The prudent man looks askance at it.

St. Augustine said: "Love God and do what you will."

Dilige Deum et fac quod vis.

The artist says: "Love and make what you like."

This is the highest prudence.

But the prudent man thinks them dangerous sayings: for

though most men know what they like doing or making, few men know certainly they love God.

Nevertheless, these rules are the only really safe rules.

It is the business of the prudent man to inculcate the love of God.

The love of God involves acceptance of what God has revealed and obedience to His law.

But "the service of God is perfect freedom."

This is not because love makes the law of no effect but because he who loves God loves what God loves.

"As the eyes of servants are upon the hands of their masters, as the eyes of a maidservant are upon the hands of her mistress, so are our eyes upon the Lord our God."

So also the obedience of a wife to her husband spells neither sin nor servility.

But in the modern world prudence is rare—though seemingly less rare than art.

Our governors, the men of business, our rich men, are struggling for power.

Our workmen, we poor men, are struggling for worldly pleasure.

The Church is powerless.

Statesmen are at the mercy of financiers.

Saints and artists are but hot-house plants—eccentrics.

But though sanctity be peculiar, prudence has the lip-service of rich men.

Honesty still remains the best policy.

"Safety first" becomes the best catch-word.

Happiness is still desirable.

And though it be a hot-house plant, art also has the lip-service of rich men.

The appetite for pleasure still requires satisfaction.

But, in a world in which man's last end has been forgotten or denied, the pursuit of worldly happiness seems less dangerous than the pursuit of worldly pleasure.

Therefore worldly happiness seems less an enemy than worldly pleasure.

The man who seeks happiness here below is looked upon more kindly than he who seeks pleasure.

The man of business is looked upon more kindly by the man of prudence than is the artist.

For the man of business ministers to happiness, though only worldly happiness.

But the artist ministers to pleasure, and often the pleasure of the sense merely.

Avarice seems less hideous to the prudent man than *Idolatry*.

Selfishness seems less damnable to him than *Sensuality*.

There is therefore some ill-feeling between the prudent man and the artist.

The lovers' quarrel between art and prudence has become an unloving "scrap."

The opposition has become a conflict.

The man of prudence is shocked by the artist's inclination to value things as ends in themselves—

Worth *making* for their own sakes—

Loved for their beauty.

He sees *idolatry* at the end of that road.

He is also shocked by the artist's acceptance of all things of sense as beautiful and therefore pleasing in themselves—

Worth *having* for their own sakes—

Loved for their pleasantness.

He sees sensuality at the end of that road.

Upon the other hand, the artist is shocked by the prudent man's inclination to see things merely as means to ends—

Not worth anything for their own sakes—

Their beauty neither seen nor loved.

He sees Manchester at the end of that road.

He is also shocked by the prudent man's inclination to see in the pleasures of sense mere filthiness.

To him that is a kind of blasphemy.

The prudent man accuses the artist of sin.
The artist cries "blasphemer" in reply.
    They see no good in one another.

It is not for me to speak as a man of prudence—
        though the artist is a man and should be a prudent man.
I can only speak as artist.
As artists it is for us to see all things as ends in themselves—
    To see all things in God and God is the end—
    To see all things as beautiful in themselves.
    "The beauty of God," says St. Thomas Aquinas, quoting
        Denis, "is the cause of the being of all that is."
It is for us to see things as worth making for their own sakes,
        and not merely as means to ends.
    We are not "welfare workers."
    We do not even seek "to leave the world better than we
        found it."
    We are as children making toys for men and God to play
        with, and "playing before Him at all times."
But this serious view is not taken by many men of prudence.
    Theirs is the frivolous view that things are not worth
        anything in themselves.
Clothes, for instance, are not for us as they seem to be for the
        prudent man, merely useful protections against cold or
        unchastity.
Clothes are primarily for dignity and adornment.
    Whether men and women go naked, or whether they go
        clothed as monks and nuns, or whether they go half-
        naked or half-clothed like our mothers and sisters—
        it is all one to us.
    It is for them to decide—and their pastors.
    We merely ask that they be beautiful—that they be things
        which give pleasure being seen.
    What else should anyone ask?
Trains, for instance: suppose two trains go from Manchester
        to London; one through a stinking and noisy tunnel all

the way, the other silently through green valleys. Which train would a sensible person take?

Your prudent man, it seems, having regard merely to the end of the journey, would ask simply which was the quicker route.

Your artist, your practical man (for art is a virtue of the practical intelligence) would ask which would make the journey better in itself—as a journey.

Let us return to the beginning.
Prudence is concerned with the man.
Art is concerned with the thing.
Man is more important than things.
Prudence is more important than art.
Man's end is happiness.
The end of art is pleasure.
But happiness consists in pleasure.

> Happiness is the state of being *pleased* with things, of being pleased with *things*.

Making pleasing things is the business of art.

The pleasure of the senses is good.
Art which aims at pleasing the mind through the sense is good.
The pleasure of the mind is good.
Art which aims at pleasing the mind and in regard to which the senses are disinterested is good.
But man is matter and spirit—

> Both are real and both good.

An art which pleases the senses only and does not make its appeal to the whole man is necessarily bad art.
An art which makes its appeal to the mind only and does not please the whole man is necessarily bad art.
That is good art which pleases the senses as they ought to be pleased and mind as it ought to be pleased.

With good art prudence should have no quarrel;

> God gave man senses that man should have pleasant feelings.

The reasonable pleasure of the senses is the God-designed reward of those acts, such as eating and "sleeping," which God wills men to do.

With good art prudence should have no quarrel;
God gave men minds wherewith to have pleasant thoughts.
The reasonable pleasure of the mind is the reward of those acts which are called contemplative: that is to say: the vision of Being, the vision of things as ends.
But many prudent men quarrel with art, however good, because many prudent men are prudes.
The prude is afraid of the pleasure of the senses.
And many prudent men quarrel with art, however good, because many prudent men are proud.
The proud man scorns anything not in imitation of himself: that is to say: he scorns anything which has not himself for its end.
These quarrels can never be settled until most men of prudence are also artists and most artists have become men of prudence.
This pleasing state of affairs will not come about until the present civilisation has passed away.

Preface to *The Nigger of the Narcissus*

BY

JOSEPH CONRAD

A WORK THAT aspires, however humbly, to the condition of art should carry its justification in every line. And art itself may be defined as a single-minded attempt to render the highest kind of justice to the visible universe, by bringing to light the truth, manifold and one, underlying its every aspect. It is an attempt to find in its forms, in its colours, in its light, in its shadows, in the aspects of matter and in the facts of life what of each is fundamental, what is enduring and essential— their one illuminating and convincing quality—the very truth of their existence. The artist, then, like the thinker or the scientist, seeks the truth and makes his appeal. Impressed by the aspect of the world the thinker plunges into ideas, the scientist into facts—whence, presently, emerging they make their appeal to those qualities of our being that fit us best for the hazardous enterprise of living. They speak authoritatively to our common-sense, to our intelligence, to our desire of peace or to our desire of unrest; not seldom to our prejudices, sometimes to our fears, often to our egoism—but always to our credulity. And their words are heard with reverence, for their concern is with weighty matters: with the cultivation of our minds and the proper care of our bodies, with the attainment of our ambitions, with the perfection of the means and the glorification of our precious aims.

It is otherwise with the artist.

Confronted by the same enigmatical spectacle the artist descends within himself, and in that lonely region of stress

and strife, if he be deserving and fortunate, he finds the terms
of his appeal. His appeal is made to our less obvious capacities: to that part of our nature which, because of the warlike
conditions of existence, is necessarily kept out of sight within
the more resisting and hard qualities—like the vulnerable
body within a steel armour. His appeal is less loud, more
profound, less distinct, more stirring—and sooner forgotten.
Yet its effect endures forever. The changing wisdom of successive generations discards ideas, questions facts, demolishes
theories. But the artist appeals to that part of our being which
is not dependent on wisdom: to that in us which is a gift and
not an acquisition—and, therefore, more permanently enduring. He speaks to our capacity for delight and wonder, to the
sense of mystery surrounding our lives; to our sense of pity,
and beauty, and pain; to the latent feeling of fellowship with
all creation—and to the subtle but invincible conviction of
solidarity that knits together the loneliness of innumerable
hearts, to the solidarity in dreams, in joy, in sorrow, in aspirations, in illusions, in hope, in fear, which binds men to each
other, which binds together all humanity—the dead to the
living and the living to the unborn.

It is only some such train of thought, or rather of feeling,
that can in a measure explain the aim of the attempt, made in
the tale which follows, to present an unrestful episode in the
obscure lives of a few individuals out of all the disregarded
multitude of the bewildered, the simple and the voiceless.
For, if any part of truth dwells in the belief confessed above,
it becomes evident that there is not a place of splendour or a
dark corner of the earth that does not deserve, if only a passing glance of wonder and pity. The motive then, may be held
to justify the matter of the work; but this preface, which is
simply an avowal of endeavour, cannot end here—for the
avowal is not yet complete.

Fiction—if it at all aspires to be art—appeals to temperament. And in truth it must be, like painting, like music, like all
art, the appeal of one temperament to all the other innumerable temperaments whose subtle and resistless power endows

passing events with their true meaning, and creates the moral, the emotional atmosphere of the place and time. Such an appeal to be effective must be an impression conveyed through the senses; and, in fact, it cannot be made in any other way, because temperament, whether individual or collective, is not amenable to persuasion. All art, therefore, appeals primarily to the senses, and the artistic aim when expressing itself in written words must also make its appeal through the senses, if its high desire is to reach the secret spring of responsive emotions. It must strenuously aspire to the plasticity of sculpture, to the colour of painting, and to the magic suggestiveness of music—which is the art of arts. And it is only through complete, unswerving devotion to the perfect blending of form and substance; it is only through an unremitting never-discouraged care for the shape and ring of sentences that an approach can be made to plasticity, to colour, and that the light of magic suggestiveness may be brought to play for an evanescent instant over the commonplace surface of words: of the old, old words, worn thin, defaced by ages of careless usage.

The sincere endeavour to accomplish that creative task, to go as far on that road as his strength will carry him, to go undeterred by faltering, weariness or reproach, is the only valid justification for the worker in prose. And if his conscience is clear, his answer to those who in the fulness of a wisdom which looks for immediate profit, demand specifically to be edified, consoled, amused; who demand to be promptly improved, or encouraged, or frightened, or shocked, or charmed, must run thus:—My task which I am trying to achieve is, by the power of the written word to make you hear, to make you feel—it is, before all, to make you *see*. That— and no more, and it is everything. If I succeed, you shall find there according to your deserts: encouragement, consolation, fear, charm—all you demand—and, perhaps, also that glimpse of truth for which you have forgotten to ask.

To snatch in a moment of courage, from the remorseless rush of time, a passing phase of life, is only the beginning of the task. The task approached in tenderness and faith is to hold up unquestioningly, without choice and without fear, the rescued fragment before all eyes in the light of a sincere mood. It is to show its vibration, its colour, its form; and through its movement, its form, and its colour, reveal the substance of its truth—disclose its inspiring secret: the stress and passion within the core of each convincing moment. In a single-minded attempt of that kind, if one be deserving and fortunate, one may perchance attain to such clearness of sincerity that at last the presented vision of regret or pity, of terror or mirth, shall awaken in the hearts of the beholders that feeling of unavoidable solidarity; of the solidarity in mysterious origin, in toil, in joy, in hope, in uncertain fate, which binds men to each other and all mankind to the visible world.

It is evident that he who, rightly or wrongly, holds by the convictions expressed above cannot be faithful to any one of the temporary formulas of his craft. The enduring part of them—the truth which each only imperfectly veils—should abide with him as the most precious of his possessions, but they all: Realism, Romanticism, Naturalism, even the unofficial sentimentalism (which like the poor, is exceedingly difficult to get rid of,) all of these gods, after a short period of fellowship, abandon him—even on the very threshold of the temple—to the stammerings of his conscience and to the outspoken consciousness of the difficulties of his work. In that uneasy solitude the supreme cry of Art for Art itself, loses the exciting ring of its apparent immorality. It sounds far off. It has ceased to be a cry, and is heard only as a whisper, often incomprehensible, but at times and faintly encouraging.

Sometimes, stretched at ease in the shade of a roadside tree, we watch the motions of a labourer in a distant field, and after a time, begin to wonder languidly as to what the fellow may be at. We watch the movements of his body, the waving of his arms, we see him bend down, stand up, hesitate, begin again. It may add to the charm of an idle hour to be told the purpose of his exertions. If we know he is trying to lift a stone, to dig a ditch, to uproot a stump, we look with a more real interest at his efforts; we are disposed to condone the jar of his agitation upon the restfulness of the landscape; and even, if in a brotherly frame of mind, we may bring ourselves to forgive his failure. We understood his object, and, after all, the fellow has tried, and perhaps he had not the strength —and perhaps he had not the knowledge. We forgive, go on our way—and forget.

And so it is with the workman of art. Art is long and life is short, and success is very far off. And thus, doubtful of strength to travel so far, we talk a little about the aim—the aim of art, which, like life itself, is inspiring, difficult—obscured by mists. It is not in the clear logic of a triumphant conclusion; it is not in the unveiling of one of those heartless secrets which are called the Laws of Nature. It is not less great, but only more difficult.

To arrest, for the space of a breath, the hands busy about the work of the earth, and compel men entranced by the sight of distant goals to glance for a moment at the surrounding vision of form and colour, of sunshine and shadows; to make them pause for a look, for a sigh, for a smile—such is the aim, difficult and evanescent, and reserved only for a very few to achieve. But sometimes, by the deserving and the fortunate, even that task is accomplished. And when it is accomplished —behold!—all the truth of life is there: a moment of vision, a sigh, a smile—and the return to an eternal rest.

On Humour and Satire

BY

RONALD KNOX

WHAT, THEN, IS the relation between humour and satire? Which is the parent, and which the child? Which is the normal organ, and which the morbid growth? I said just now that satire borrows its weapons from the humorist, and that is certainly the account most of us would be prepared to give of the matter off-hand. Most things in life, we reflect, have their comic side as well as their serious side; and the good-humoured man is he who is content to see the humorous side of things even when the joke is against himself. The comic author, by persistently abstracting from the serious side of things, contrives to build up a world of his own, whose figures are all grotesque, whose adventures are the happy adventures of farce. Men fight, but only with foils; men suffer, but only suffer indignities; it is all a pleasant nursery tale, a relief to be able to turn to it when your mind is jaded with the sour facts of real life. Such, we fancy, is the true province of the Comic Muse; and satire is an abuse of the function. The satirist is like one who should steal his little boy's water-pistol and load it with vitriol, and so walk abroad flourishing it in men's faces. A treacherous fellow, your satirist. He will beguile the leisure of an Athenian audience, needing some rest, Heaven knows, from the myriad problems of a relentless war with powerful neighbours, by putting on a little play called *The Birds*. Capital; we shall enjoy that. Two citizens of Athens, so the plot runs, take wings to themselves and set out to build a bird city, remote from the daily instance of this subnubilar world.

Excellent! That is just what we wanted, a relief for tired brains! And then, the fellow has tricked us, it proves, after all! His city in the clouds is, after all, only a parody of an Athenian colony, and the ceremonies which attend its inauguration are a burlesque, in the worst possible taste, of Athenian colonial policy. We came here for a holiday, and we are being treated to a sermon instead! No wonder the Athenian audiences often refused the first prize to Aristophanes. Skip twenty-one centuries, and find yourself in the times of the early Georges. There has been a great vogue, of late, for descriptions of travel in strange countries; and now (they are saying in the coffee-houses) the Dean of St. Patrick's, Dublin, has written a burlesque of these travel narratives, about countries that never existed at all—the ingenious dog! And then, as we read, it dawns upon us suddenly that Lilliput and Brobdingnag are not, after all, so distant, so imaginary; in fact, we have never really got away from the England of the Georges at all. The spirit of satire has overlooked us, like a wicked fairy, and turned the milk of human kindness sour as we churned it.

My present thesis, not dogmatically asserted but rather thrown out as if for discussion, is that this way of viewing the relations between humour and satire is a perversion of history. To think of satire as a particular direction which humour may happen to take, a particular channel into which humour may be diverted, is to neglect, surely, the broad facts as we have stated them above. Humour is of an age, satire of all ages; humour is of one particular civilization, satire of all countries. Is it not, then, more reasonable to suppose that satire is a normal function of the human genius, and humour that has no satire in it a perversion of the function, a growth away from the normal? That our sense of the ridiculous is not, in its original application, a child's toy at all, but a weapon, deadly in its efficacy, entrusted to us for exposing the shams and hypocrisies of the world? The tyrant may arm himself in triple mail, may surround himself with bodyguards, may sow his kingdom with a hedge of spies, so that free speech is crushed and criticism muzzled. Nay, worse, he may so debauch the consciences of his subjects with false history and with sophistical argument that they come to believe him the thing he gives himself out for, a creature half-divine, a heaven-sent deliverer. One thing there is that he still fears; one anxiety still bids him turn this way and that to scan the faces of his slaves. He is afraid of laughter. The satirist stands there, like the little child in the procession when the Emperor walked through the capital in his famous new clothes; his is the tiny voice that interprets the consciousness of a thousand onlookers: "But, Mother, he has no clothes on at all!"

Satire has a wider scope, too. It is born to scourge the persistent and ever-recurrent follies of the human creature as such. And, for anybody who has the humility to realize that it is aimed at him, and not merely at his neighbours, satire has an intensely remedial effect; it purifies the spiritual system of man as nothing else that is human can possibly do. Thus, every young man who is in love should certainly read *The Egoist* (there would be far less unhappiness in marriage if they all did), and no schoolmaster should ever begin the scholastic year without re-reading Mr. Bradby's *Lanchester Tradition,* to remind him that he is but dust. Satire is thus an excellent discipline for the satirized: whether it is a good thing for the satirist is more open to question. *Facit indignatio versum;* it is seldom that the impetus to write satire comes to a man except as the result of a disappointment. Since disappointment so often springs from love, it is not to be wondered at that satirists have ever dealt unkindly with woman, from the days of Simonides of Amorgos, who compared woman with more than thirty different kinds of animals, in every case to her disadvantage. A pinched, warped fellow, as a rule, your satirist. It is misery that drives men to laughter. It is bad humour that encourages men first to be humorous. And it is, I think, when good-humoured men pick up this weapon of laughter, and, having no vendettas to work off with it, begin tossing it idly at a mark, that humour without satire takes its origin.

In a word, humour without satire is, strictly speaking, a perversion, the misuse of a sense. Laughter is a deadly explosive which was meant to be wrapped up in the cartridge of satire, and so, aimed unerringly at its appointed target, deal its salutary wound; humour without satire is a flash in the pan; it may be pretty to look at, but it is, in truth, a waste of ammunition. Or, if you will, humour is satire that has run to seed; trained no longer by an artificial process, it has lost the virility of its stock. It is port from the wood, without the depth and mystery of its vintage rivals. It is a burning-glass that has lost its focus; a passenger, pulling no weight in the up-stream journey of life; meat that has had the vitamins boiled out of it; a clock without hands. The humourist, in short, is a satirist out of a job; he does not fit into the scheme of things; the world passes him by.

The pure humourist is a man without a message. He can preach no gospel, unless it be the gospel that nothing matters; and that in itself is a foolish theme, for if nothing matters, what does it matter whether it matters or not? Mr. Wodehouse is an instance in point, Mr. Leacock nearly so, though there is a story in *Arcadian Adventures with the Idle Rich* about the amalgamation of two religious bodies on strictly commercial lines, which comes very close to pure satire. Barry Pain is a humorist who is seldom at his best when he attempts satire; the same fate dogged Mark Twain, though I think he would have liked to be a satirist. Mr. A. A. Milne is in a similar case, and so indeed are all the modern *Punch* writers by the terms (you might say) of their contract. No contrast is more surprising than the contrast in atmosphere between the letterpress of *Punch* before 1890 and its letterpress since. The old *Punches* are full of very bad satire; there is hardly anything else in them! it is all on the same sort of level as *John Bull* in its Bottomley days—anti-aristocratic, anti-foreign, anti-clerical, very much like some rag of the Boulevards. Today, it is the home of superbly finished humour—humour cultivated as a fine art. But satire is absent.

Some of the greatest humourists have halted between two

destinies, and as a rule have been lost to satire. Sir W. S. Gilbert, a rather unsuccessful satirist in his early days, inherited the dilemma from his master, Aristophanes. *Patience* is supreme satire, and there is satire in all the operas; but in their general effect they do not tell: the author has given up to mankind what was meant for a party. Mr. Chesterton is in the same difficulty; he is like Johnson's friend who tried to be a philosopher, but cheerfulness would keep on coming in. The net effect of his works is serious, as it is meant to be, but his fairy-like imagination is for ever defeating its own object in matters of detail. But indeed, Mr. Chesterton is beyond our present scope; for he is rash enough to combine humour not merely with satire but with serious writing; and that, it is well known, is a thing the public will not stand. A few modern authors have succeeded, in spite of our latter-day demand for pure humour, in being satirists first and last: Samuel Butler of *Erewhon,* and W. H. Mallock, and Mr. Belloc, I think, in his political novels. The very poor reception given to these last by the public proves that there is more vinegar in them than oil.

Humour, if we may adopt for a moment the loathsome phraseology of journalism, has "come to stay." It is, if our analysis be true, a by-product and in a sense a waste-product; that does not mean that it has no significance. A pearl is a by-product, and from the fishmonger's point of view a waste-product; but it has value so long as people want it. And there is at present a public demand for humour which implies that humour should take its place among the arts, an art for the art's sake, not depending on any fruits of practical utility for its estimation. There is art in O. Henry, though he does not scourge our vices like Juvenal; there is art in Heath Robinson, though he does not purge our consciences like Hogarth. What rank humour is to take as compared with serious writing is, perhaps, an unanswerable problem; our histories of nineteenth century literature have not yet been bold enough to tackle it. It is probable, I think, that humour is relatively ephemeral; by force of words humour means caprice, and the caprice of yesterday is apt to leave us cold. There is a generation not yet quite dead which says that nothing was ever so funny as the *Bongaultier Ballads*. The popularity of the *Ingoldsby Legends* is now, to say the least, precarious; and I doubt if the modern youth smacks its lips as we did over the *Bab Ballads* themselves. Read a book of A. A. Milnes', and then turn to an old volume of *Voces Populi,* and you will realize that even in our memory humour has progressed and become rarefied. What reputations will be left unassailable when the tide has receded, it would be rash to prophesy. For myself, I like to believe that one name will be immortal at least, that of Mr. Max Beerbohm. Incomparably equipped for satire, as his cartoons and his parodies show, he has yet preferred in most of his work to give rein to a gloriously fantastic imagination, a humourist in satirist's clothing. One is tempted to say with the prophet: May I die the death of the righteous, and may my last end be like his!

Meanwhile, a pertinent question may be raised, What will be the effect of all this modern vogue for pure humour upon the prospects of satiric writing? We are in danger, it seems to me, of debauching our sense of the ridiculous to such an extent as to leave no room for the disciplinary effect of satire. I remember seeing Mr. Shaw's *Press Cuttings* first produced in Manchester. I remember a remark, in answer to the objection that women ought not to vote because they do not fight, that a woman risks her life every time a man is born, being received (in Manchester!) with shouts of happy laughter. In that laughter I read the tragedy of Mr. Bernard Shaw. He lashes us with virulent abuse, and we find it exquisitely amusing. Other ages have stoned the prophets; ours pelts them instead with the cauliflower bouquets of the heavy comedian. No country, I suppose, has greater need of a satirist today than the United States of America; no country has a greater output of humour, good and bad, which is wholly devoid of any satirical quality. If a great American satirist should arise, would his voice be heard among the hearty guffaws which are dismally and eternally provoked by Mutt,

Jeff, Felix, and other kindred abominations? And have we, on this side of the Atlantic, any organ in which pure satire could find a natural home? I believe the danger which I am indicating to be a perfectly real one, however fantastic it may sound—the danger, I mean, that we have lost, or are losing, the power to take ridicule seriously. That our habituation to humorous reading has inoculated our systems against the beneficent poison of satire. Unhappy the Juvenal whom Rome greets with amusement; unhappier still the Rome, that can be amused by a Juvenal!

I am not sure, in reading through this essay again, that there is any truth in its suggestions. But I do not see that there can be any harm in having said what I thought even if I am no longer certain that I think it.

Imagination

BY

COVENTRY PATMORE

THERE ARE THINGS which can never be more than approximately defined, and which, even when so defined, are to be rightly understood only in proportion to the degrees in which they are possessed by those who would attempt to comprehend them. Such are, for example, "imagination" and "genius"; which, being faculties that are possessed in a very low degree by nearly all and in a very high degree by extremely few, are matters of the most general interest and the most variable apprehension. That such faculties should, however, as far as possible, be understood is of great practical importance to all persons; inasmuch as it greatly concerns all to

From *The Rod, the Root and the Flower,* by Coventry Patmore. Reprinted by permission of the publisher, G. Bell & Sons, Ltd., London.

know something of the signs, sanctions, and claims of those powers by which they are inevitably more or less ruled externally and internally.

It is nothing against a definition of an entity which cannot be fully defined, to say that such definition is "new." It was objected against an interpretation by St. Augustine of some Old Testament history or parable, that other authorities have given other interpretations. "The more interpretations the better," was the saint's reply. In such cases various definitions and interpretations are merely apprehensions of various sides of a matter not wholly to be embraced or comprehended by any single definition or interpretation. In recent times genius and imagination have come to be widely regarded as one and the same thing. They are not so, however, though they are perhaps indissolubly connected. The most peculiar and characteristic mark of genius is insight into subjects which are dark to ordinary vision and for which ordinary language has no adequate expression. Imagination is rather the language of genius: the power which traverses at a single glance the whole external universe, and their combinations, which are best able to embody ideas and feelings otherwise inexpressible; so that the "things which are unseen are known by the things which are seen." Imagination, in its higher developments, is so quick and subtle a power that the most delicate analysis can scarcely follow its shortest flights. Coleridge said that it would take a whole volume to analyse the effect of a certain passage of only a few syllables in length. In dealing with such a work as *The Tempest* criticism is absolutely helpless, and its noblest function is to declare its own helplessness by directing attention to beauty beyond beauty which defies analysis. *The Tempest,* like all very great works of art, is the shortest and simplest, and indeed the only possible expression of its "idea." The idea is the product of genius proper; the expression is the work of imagination. There are cases, however, in which it is hard to distinguish at all between these inseparable qualities. The initiation of a scientific theory seems often to have been due to the action of the imagination working independently of any peculiar direct insight; the analogy-discovering faculty—that is, the imagination—finding a law for a whole sphere of unexplained phenomena in the likeness of such phenomena to others of a different sphere of which the law is known. Hence the real discoverers of such theories are scarcely ever those who have obtained the credit of them; for nothing is usually more abhorrent to men of extraordinary imagination than "fact-grinding." Such men, after having flung out their discoveries to the contempt or neglect of their contemporaries, leave the future proof of them to mental mechanics: religiously avoiding such work themselves, lest, as Goethe said of himself, they should find themselves imprisoned in "the charnel-house of science." Genius and imagination of a very high kind are not at all uncommon in children under twelve years of age, especially when their education has been "neglected." The writer can guarantee the following facts from personal witness: A clever child of seven, who could not read, and had certainly never heard of the Newtonian theory of gravitation, said to his mother suddenly, "What makes this ball drop when I leave hold of it?—Oh, I know: the ground pulls it." Another child, a year or two older, lay stretched on a gravel path, staring intently on the pebbles. "They are alive," he cried, in the writer's hearing; "they are always wanting to burst, but something draws them in." This infantine rediscovery of the doctrine of the co-inherence of attraction and repulsion in matter seems to have been an effort of direct insight. The repetition of the Newtonian apple revelation seems rather to have been the work of the imagination, tracking likeness in difference; but to discern such likeness is, again, an effort of direct insight, and justifies Aristotle's saying that this power of finding similitude in things diverse is a proof of the highest human faculty. The poet's eye glances from heaven to earth, from earth to heaven; and his faculty of discerning likeness in difference enables him to express the unknown in the terms of the known, so as to confer upon the former a *sensible* credibility, and to give the latter a truly sacramental dignity. The

soul contains world upon world of the most real of realities
of which it has no consciousness until it is awakened to their
existence by some parable or metaphor, some strain of rhythm
or music, some combination of form or colour, some scene of
beauty or sublimity, which suddenly expresses the inexpressible
by a lower likeness. The vulgar cynic, blessing when he only
means to bray, declares that love between the sexes is "all
imagination." What can be truer? What baser thing is there
than such love, when it is not of imagination all compact? or
what more nearly divine, when it is? Why? Because the imagination deals with the spiritual realities to which the material realities correspond, and of which they are only, as it
were, the ultimate and sensible expressions. And here it may
be noted, by the way, that Nature supplies the ultimate
analogue of every divine mystery with some vulgar use or
circumstance, in order, as it would seem, to enable the stupid
and the gross to deny the divine without actual blasphemy.

Profligacy and "fact-grinding" destroy the imagination by
habitually dwelling in ultimate expressions while denying or
forgetting the primary realities of which they are properly
only the vessels. Purity ends by finding a goddess where im-
purity concludes by confessing carrion. Which of these is the
reality let each man judge according to his taste. "Fact-
grinding"—which Darwin confessed and lamented had destroyed his imagination and caused him to "nauseate Shakespeare"—commonly ends in destroying the religious faculty,
as profligacy destroys the faculty of love; for neither love
nor religion can survive without imagination, which Shelley, in
one of his prefaces, identifying genius with imagination, declares to be the power of discerning spiritual facts. Those
who have no imagination regard it as all one with "fancy,"
which is only a playful mockery of imagination, bringing together things in which there is nothing but an accidental simi-
larity in externals.

Literature in Its Social Aspects

BY

AUBREY DE VERE

IN AN AGE in which literature aspires to become universal, it is impossible for even the trifling not to perceive that nothing else connected with it is so momentous as the moral relations which it establishes with man. A serious tone of mind is forced upon any one who reflects on this great moral problem. There are many who look upon the subject with despondency. Knowing the manifold temptations connected with books—temptations from which, till lately, the great mass of mankind have been preserved by the urgency of daily toil and the absence of literary culture—they ask what is to be the consequence when the snares that assail the palace beset the cottage no less? Hitherto, they remark, the lot of the many has been one of physical toil, but of intellectual rest. It has lain in a valley thickset with fair households. On the one side has risen the great mountain range of inductive science, and on the other that of Christian Theology; but the poor man's foot has tarried by the stream that turns his mill, and no one has challenged him to scale the crags. Is all this to be changed? Among books the supply of good and bad will depend on the demand. Which class will the many prefer? Will literature, on the whole, be a nurse of the virtues or a pander to vice? There is neither a rural village nor a mighty city the peace of which will not one day depend upon the answer which time must make to such questions. I can but offer a few suggestions on the subject. Let us begin with the more hopeful.

There are, then, virtues as well as vices which we commonly associate with the few, and which, notwithstanding, sound literature tends to impart to all men of good will. Let us

From *Essays, Chiefly Ethical and Literary*, by Aubrey De Vere.

name, for instance, magnanimity. One who ranges among the great men of all ages, and recognizes that far-reaching influence by which, silently, unostentatiously, and grasping at no power, they have built up the empire of thought, is less likely than another to join in the stress and strain of petty emulations. He does not need the lordship over a narrow circle. To him there are sceptres not made of iron or gold, and spiritual thrones, to rest at the foot of which is better than vulgar rule. The remote power, he knows, is the more permanent. The senate amid which he may, if he deserves it, sit as assessor, includes all the great men who have ever lived; yet within it there is no clamour and no pressure at the gate.

Nor should sound literature be less a promoter of unworldliness and self-sacrifice. It is the noble bequest of men who gathered up intellectual treasures while those around them snatched at gewgaws, or lay passive in listlessness. It denounces self-indulgence. "Who is he," says the great Tuscan bard,

So pale with musing in Pierian groves?

Those whose ears were open to "the whispers of the lonely Muse" were supposed of old to have closed them against the "Lydian airs" of the frivolous or sensual. Literature was thus regarded as a manly art, the foe of luxury, and the inspirer of heroism; while in some languages the very term that denoted a life given to the imaginative arts was that word which meant "virtue." If, in later times, literature has been cultivated but as a means to a selfish end—if vanity has been the student's stimulus, if an intellectual voluptuousness, more insidious than coarse sensuality, has turned the haunt of the Muses into a garden of epicurean delights—the loss sustained by literature has punished the wrong. She possesses a healing power; but, like other physicians, she may catch the malady while she bends over the sickbed. Men of letters have often, and not always unjustly, charged the clergy with learning wordliness from the world they were sent to reform. Their own order bears no talisman against a similar infection. What sense of her genuine functions belongs to a literature which flatters where it should instruct, and flings itself in fawning dedications at the feet of a public more adulated than ever was Oriental despot? For excuse it can but take refuge in wit like Aristippus, who, on being reproved for falling at the feet of Dionysius while presenting a petition to him, replied, "That it was not his fault if Dionysius had ears in his feet."

Servile men of letters are reproved by the very name of the "liberal arts." Such arts are liberal, because, drawing us out from the false centre of self, and the narrow circle of merely conventional interests, they dilate our individual being to the dimensions of a world-wide humanity, imparting to us thus the freedom of "no mean city." In this respect, as in some others, the loftiest literature is a shadow of religion, though the difference between the substance and the shadow is of course infinite, and though the shadow is often distorted by the inequalities of the surface along which it is projected. Contented ignorance is bounded by the senses: Literature breaks down that limit. A shelf stored with books of travel enables the artisan at his daily toil to send forth his thoughts through all lands. A few volumes of history, and Time is to him a grave that has given up its dead. Add a few volumes of poetry to a few of history, and the present catches all the radiance of the past. They remind us that if the things round us seem to us but little, so seemed to those who lived at an earlier day those things the fame of which has lasted for centuries. They tell us that in the present, too, virtue and genius retain that immortalising touch which changes dust into gems. It is through landscape-paintings that we learn best to appreciate nature, and perceive that weather-stain has its beauty as well as mountain and lake. Thus it is through a Homer or a Herodotus that we learn to understand life. In every parish there is a whole Iliad of action and of passion, if we have been taught to trace their workings by one of those men whom Nature has chosen for her expositors. Everywhere around us there spreads the Infinite, but we need the optic glass to bring it out. A true book is such a glass: and such a book is now a

telescope, drawing the distant close—now a microscope, mag-
nifying what is near. It is thus that nature's largeness is made
to break through the limits of our littleness; and that matter,
subjecting itself to the interpretation of mind, becomes elevated, as it were, into spirit.

Influences such as these must ever be diffused in proportion
as education—an education not based upon vanity—extends
its sphere. They work for the many, because they work
through those sympathies that exist in all. For the poor and
the rich alike there is but one mode of being delivered from
the thraldom of self: it is that of taking interest in things un-
connected with self: the negative evil can only be obviated by
the positive good. Can any one doubt that a cultivated Imagination helps a moral purpose? It is the ideal power that alone
enables us to realise what belongs to the remote and the unseen, and by realising, to love it. If from the far distance of
past time objects flash out as with a magic distinctness, like
that which, in the evening of a rainy day, draws near to us the
mountain-range till bush and scar leap forward to catch the
"discriminating touch" of a setting sun, it is not wonderful
that our affections too should attach themselves to beings thus
suddenly made known to us—beings in whom we descry at
once all that we are and all that we fain would be! Which
of the virtues is not fostered by this noble emulation? Soph-
ocles, it has been generally thought, can belong but to the few:
but it was to the many that he addressed himself. In his most
touching tragedy, Antigone is warned that whosoever buries
the dead bodies of her brothers shall share their fate. She
replies that this mandate is but the law of a tyrant, and that it
has never issued from Jove nor from that sceptred Justice
which reigns among the Shades—that she will be true to the
dead, and bear her fate. Is her resolve more a lesson of
fidelity to the nursling of the palace than to the son of the
shepherd, the fisherman, or the artisan? Heroic arms of old
cut down the Pelian pines, and dragged the oar all night long
through the foam of an unknown sea. Is this more a lesson of
courage and perseverance to the Arctic discoverer than to the

village boy who finds a brave resolution checked by a trivial obstacle? Men read these things, and their physical aspect itself, mien, and step, are altered. A breath from far summits sends strength into their souls. Experience not their own is imparted to them; the heart is made more single; but the mind is made many-sided; and the faculties of the individual are multiplied into those of his kind.

The arts that do these things impart to man the noblest freedom, that of just dependence and true service. In conferring freedom on responsive minds, they confer empire also. We are told that "the meek inherit the earth." They do so doubtless because humble hearts are large hearts, and possess, through love and through absence of pride and fear, the reality of those serene enjoyments which belong to our universal nature, and which are grasped but in shadow by those who make the world their prey. The enlarging influence of an imagination developed by the higher class of literature does for the intellect of man something analogous to that which a holier power does for him at the depths of his being. It creates a communion of intelligences; it abolishes isolation; it bestows on each what belongs to all: it cannot therefore but abate prejudice, break through narrowness, destroy littleness. All this, we are sometimes told, may yet but create a good the enemy of some higher good. Doubtless it not only may, but must do so if the gift be perverted; but the very adage, *Corruptio optimi res pessima est,* includes the confession that the gift is good, though the corruption of it be fatal. Fatal indeed is the influence of a literature, however able, which forgets its true vocation, and seeks its reward in what is below, not in what is above it. An allegiance broken is commonly an allegiance transferred. When literature ceases to be the servant of Truth, it becomes the slave of the world, and ministers but to bondage. A touch from the breath of vanity changes what was a "palace of the Humanities" into a splendid prison, and the pictures with which the walls of that palace were once hung are replaced by mirrors reflecting but self-love.

7

BIOGRAPHY AND CRITICISM

Alfred the Great
(849-901)

BY

G. K. CHESTERTON

ALFRED OF WESSEX, one of the first four or five great men of the Dark Ages, was born in Wantage about the middle of the ninth century, probably in 849. He comes on the field of history, then almost continuously a field of battle, from under the shadow of the shield of Ethelred, his elder brother, already at war with the invading Danes; and there is always something about him indescribably humble and handy, like one who unpretentiously hammers away at an inherited task; a quality not at all inconsistent, but rather specially consistent, with his strong twist of personal originality. All his house was devoted to the Catholic faith; but Alfred was a sort of accident, who added to that devotion a dexterity and military instinct which saved it, apparently against all the chances of war. Thus it was he, while still a cadet, who really won the Battle of Ashdown against the barbarians, while his royal brother was praying in his tent; and it is supremely typical of the time that the chronicler records the victory and says that it was doubtless due to the prayers of Ethelred. Various victories and defeats followed; until the whole barbarian invasion

From *The English Way,* edited by Maisie Ward. Reprinted by permission of the publisher, Sheed and Ward, New York and London; and the executrix of the estate of the late Gilbert Keith Chesterton.

gathered itself into one vast wave under Guthrum out of East Anglia and swept the West Country from end to end like a sea, leaving Alfred clinging, as it were, to an islet in the pool of Athelney, and waiting for better times. He gradually gathered round him the remnants of the Christian population, and in the spring of 878 appeared suddenly with an army before the Danish camp at Ethandune, possibly Edington; smashed in their palisades, captured their royal leader and his raven banner, and imposed on him the famous treaty of Wedmore, by which he and his people were baptised and withdrew their forces from Wessex, retaining only lands farther to the north and east. The rest of the story is sufficiently familiar; fresh outbreaks among the barbarians led to his extending his power over London and establishing a small navy in the Channel; and even obtaining a certain indefinite suzerainty over the north. But his best work was internal rather than external; and perhaps the best of all was the part that was purely educational. He clarified and codified the best laws of the West Saxon traditions; but he became a more important sort of legislator in the moral sphere when he translated Boethius for his people, with very characteristic additions of his own; and so brought into England the full tradition of Europe; the tradition of the Christian Creed resting upon the Pagan culture. He had been troubled all his life with a recurrent and rather mysterious disease; and he died at the early age of fifty-two, in the first year of the new century. The night of the barbarian peril was already over, and he died in the dawn.

A thousand years of thanks and praise have rightly concentrated upon Alfred a light of unique and universal admiration. From the first words of the Anglo-Saxon Chronicle to the last wireless messages of the Anglo-Saxon clubs and dinners in Boston or Philadelphia, there has been a chiming unanimity, a chain of polite or popular compliment, in which there is actually no break at all. A Scottish rationalist like Hume, a romantic Tory like Scott, a Voltairean sceptic like Gibbon, a prudent Catholic like Lingard, an imprudent pro-Catholic like Cobbett, a practical and (spiritually) rather stupid Protestant like Macaulay, would all at any moment have testified to the solid and unquestioned moral reputation of Alfred. Men by the modern time had come to call him The Great; which was perhaps the only really true thing they knew about him. Everybody agreed to call him Great; and nothing perhaps has so completely obscured his greatness. He is one of two or three men who have been nearly obliterated by praise.

It would have been better for him, in the long run, or at least for his significance, if he had happened to be a cleric like Dunstan, that other maker of England in the Dark Ages; and so become, for a few foolish centuries, the butt of all the ravings of the anti-clerical superstition. Then there would have been subsequently, or eventually, a sort of excitement in digging him up from among the dead, and proving that he was not so unmistakably among the damned; the sort of pleasure felt by Ruskin or Rossetti in rediscovering mediæval beauty in what had always been counted mediæval ugliness. There would have been a thrill for the first Victorian thinker who maintained the paradox that a saint could be a good man. His real personality would probably be more vivid to us if he had been denounced by Hume and derided by Gibbon, and his real virtues dramatically rediscovered by Maitland or by Gasquet. It would have been better for him, in the same sense if he had lived a few centuries earlier, when the night of barbarism was denser, as did the mysterious Arthur; so that sceptics might turn him into a myth and romancers into a romance. Then he, too, might have lingered in florid old French love stories merely as a jealous husband; until modern research re-established him for the first time as a just ruler. In that case, again, the good might have been interred with his bones in the ninth century and never dug up again till the nineteenth. The disclosing and cleansing of such sacred relics might almost have awakened a part of the interest accorded to the chips off the skeleton of a hypothetical ape. Or again, it might have been better for him in this sense if he had been a foreigner, even a great foreigner like Charlemagne; who from the first, however much he was admired, aroused that insular subconscious suspicion of any attempt to reunite Europe; hating it if it excluded England; hating it more if it included England. So, when our national mood was narrowest, we hated in Austria even the flat and fading shadow of the Holy Roman Empire; and in Napoleon hated more vividly the return of the Romans. Then, once more, there might have been a belated understanding after a long misunderstanding; just as many are doing justice to the Austrian system after it has been destroyed; and there are even signs of a faint effort to be fair to Napoleon. But Alfred was picked out from the first by converging and unwavering beams of the limelight of conventional laudation; he stands in a dazzling light that hides him like darkness; he is covered with a sort of white radiance that has all the effect of whitewash, and which has hidden from generations of the readers of our history the least notion of the twilight in which he really wandered and the light by which he was really led.

Perhaps the best stage of the story was that of the old chronicles, which duly and dully recorded good and bad kings; and very correctly recorded Alfred among the good. After that came a more narrow national motive, natural enough, but not exactly impartial, which presented Alfred as the inventor of the British Navy and the University of Oxford; and for twopence would have presented him as the inventor of the Union Jack and the Boat Race. But the patriotic partisanship which expressed the natural pride of a nation was a far finer and healthier thing than that queer and pedantic fashion which proclaimed only the pride of a race. Alfred really was in many ways extremely English, as we shall observe later; but, anyhow, he certainly was born in the British Isles and might be said to stand at the beginning of the British Empire. But, from the way the Victorian historians talked about Teutons and Saxons and the Germanic institutions, one might really suppose that Alfred was standing at the beginning of the German Empire. The whole thing was founded on a false conception of history; which supposed such a period to be the beginning of a glorious German or Germanic expansion, instead of the end and ebb of the old Roman expansion. Because it happens to be the beginning of our particular national history it is treated as if it were the morning of the world. The men who lived in that time felt it as the evening of the world; not to say the end of the world. And the greatest of the men who lived in that time certainly cannot be understood if that fact is not understood. But in the familiar picture everything is accentuated that suggests only the new Nordic adventure. King Alfred confronts us, blonde and bland, with the battle-axe and helmet of a Viking, but the face of a rather sleepy Quaker; ready to found Christianity, cricket, the Anglo-Saxon race, the Anglo-American alliance, the Boy Scouts or anything else that may require a friendly person in the ninth century to found it. Now, nobody in the ninth century, however friendly, felt in the least like that. It was not even anything so bright as the beginning of barbarism; it was, to all appearance, simply the end of civilisation. In some ways, and especially in some places, it was even the end of over-civilisation. The importance of Boethius is symbolic; the last of the old sages; the scholarly servant who already has a savage master. But Alfred was not himself of the type that indicates merely a lusty or even a normal time. He was as brave as a lion and as wary as a wild fox; but he had nothing whatever of the serenity and solidity that makes up the perfect ideal of the Blonde Beast. He was an original as well as an origin. There is something even of the eccentric about him, evidently catching the memories of men when they speak of his speeches and actions; his abrupt and casual confession of mortal sins in his youth, long after they had doubtless been normally absolved; his abstractions and absences, due probably to the unknown disease that struck him on his wedding-day; presumably something convulsive or epileptic; anyhow, something isolating him from mere social routine. His outlook also was individual rather than racial or national; his additions to Boethius show how vividly he understood the vital issue of his age. "I say, as do all Christian men, that it is a Divine Providence that rules, and not Fate." Then, even more than at most times, the fight with heathenism was the fight with fatalism. It was all the more so because all the Fates seemed to be on the side of all the heathens. In Christian psychology, if there were nothing else, Alfred is the type of a wiry and tenacious will, that wears down even Fate; for what we call Fate is only the fashion of this world that passes away, if any man can wait for it to pass. But Alfred had no clear notion of what civilisation he was founding; but only of what civilisation his enemies were destroying. The real moral of his story is a moral for moderns. He himself lived in a world very like the modern world; that is, a world that had become much too ancient. Intelligent men like Alfred looked at that time on barbarism very much as many now look on Bolshevism: believing it to be wrong, but very much doubting whether it would be practically proved wrong, so far as anything can be proved by mere success. The Christian system was already coming within a century of its first thousand years; and many doubted whether it was not dying, as they do now, within a century of its two thousand years. The encouraging quality in the story of Alfred is the testimony to Christian tenacity in the face of such recurrent threats of decline. The final triumph of heathenism is not so near to us now as it was to him then. As he weathered the storm then, we have every reason to hope that we shall weather it now. But it was a very weather-beaten seaman who weathered it; and one wrinkled with the old age of the old civilisation; a man not without subtlety and quite without optimism; a true genius of the ninth century.

So much it is necessary to say to wash away the vapid figure of facile virtue which was set up by the theorists of Germanic or Anglo-Saxon progress. But, inside all these things, there is a truth that is true in a much more subtle manner than they could understand. When all is said and confessed and contradicted, Alfred of Wessex *is* very English; not Anglo-Saxon or Saxon, but English; and he is a sort of testimony showing how early something distinctive in our insular culture had begun. It is very difficult to define these things in prose; it would be better to attempt to describe them in poetry. But in all his policy we can see something that is a positive quality, though it might seem to some a negative lack of a quality. Perhaps the shortest description is a lack of the imperial logic. He had very little of that notion of rounding everything and everybody up in the circle of an *orbis terrarum,* which affected most followers of the Roman Empire, even when they dealt with something smaller. There is something in his action that smacks of the opportunist and patchy colonisation of a commercial empire. He calculates how much he can certainly recover from the Danes; how much he can safely leave to them; and cares little for the mathematical unity of the pattern. He is conscious of achieving a broader kingdom, rather than of accepting a narrower empire. He is content to make Wessex wider; and has no appetite to make the world smaller. He would never have failed through a fatal afterthought of rounding off his work, as Napoleon failed by trying to round it off with Russia and Spain. His experiments are English experiments; especially in the fact of remaining experimental. There are many other aspects suggesting the same thing; as in the readiness with which tradition connected his name with legends of lonely adventure or casual human contact. It has truly been said that the story of the cakes would not have been told about a man without humour. But especially was he English in his relation to that great reality which can be real to all Europeans and to all human beings, and which yet realises itself in forms so different and distinguished. He was, if ever there was one, an English Catholic. He was supremely the type that proves to the world what is called a fanatical fixity of faith without fanaticism. He was of the type in which solitary and supernatural conviction expresses itself in energy, but not often in ecstasy. There is a sense in which it is true to say that, when once a man is a Catholic, he has no more need to be a mystic. In that sense, properly limited and understood, Alfred was all the more an English Catholic, because he only knew he was a Catholic and did not know he was an Englishman.

I was walking the other day round his statue that stands at Wantage, and reflecting that but for him not one of the things now standing there would exist at all. In the ninth century it was very doubtful whether there ever would be any Western civilisation at all. It was quite probable that the wild Western lands would be left for dead and Continental culture turn eastward to Byzantium and Asia; with what consequences none can say. And if there had never been any monasteries or camps or cathedrals, there would certainly never have been any shops or hotels or petrol-stations. But I doubt if anybody but myself was at that moment looking at the statue, or even realising the fact. Still, the statues are still standing in Wantage and Winchester; unless they have been since removed for the convenience of motorists.

Clarence Mangan

BY

LIONEL JOHNSON

NO ONE CAN thoroughly realize Mangan's life without some knowledge of Dublin: not knowledge of Ireland at large, for Mangan had practically none, save by reading; but knowledge of that Dublin "dear and dirty," splendid and squalid, fascinating and repulsive, which was Mangan's from the cradle to the grave. There is there an unique piteousness of poverty and decay, a stricken and helpless look, which seem appropriate to the scene of the doomed poet's life. It was a life of dreams and misery and madness, yet of self-pity which does not disgust us, and of a weakness which is innocent; it seems the haunted, enchanted life of one drifting through his days in a dream of other days and other worlds, golden and immortal. He wanders about the rotting alleys and foul streets, a wasted ghost, with the "Dark Rosaleen" on his lips, and a strange light in those mystical blue eyes, which burn for us yet in the

From *Post Liminum*, by Lionel Johnson.

reminiscences of all who ever saw him and wrote of the unforgettable sight. And, with all his remoteness, all his wretchness, there was a certain grimly pathetic and humorous common-sense about him, which saved him from being too angelic a drunkard, too ethereal a vagabond, too saintly a wastrel. Hard as it is to believe at all times, he was an intelligible, an explicable human being, and not some "twy-natured" thing, some city faun. All the accounts and descriptions of him show us a man whom external circumstances, however prosperous and bright, would not have prevailed upon to be as other men are. As has been said of other poets, "he hungered for better bread than can be made of wheat," and would have contrived to lose this way, to be "homesick for eternity," despite all earthly surroundings of happiness and ease. Sensitive in the extreme, he shrank back into the shadows at a breath, not merely of unkindness, but of unpleasantness; he shuddered and winced, blanched and withered away at a touch of the east wind. His miseries, which dictated to him that agonized poem, "The Nameless One," were primarily of his own creation, realities of his own imagination, and, therefore, the more terrible: they were the agonies of a child in the dark, quivering for fear of that nothing which is to him so infinitely real and dread a "something." For Mangan's childhood, boyhood, first youth, though hard and harsh, were not unbearably so; many a poet has borne far worse, and survived it unscathed. A rough and stern, rather than cruel, father; office drudgery with coarse companions; stinted, but not insufficient means; a general absence of congenial sympathy and friendship—these are rude facts to face; but even a poet, all nerves and feeling, need not find life a hell because of them, the world a prison, all things an utter darkness of despair. And even Mangan's failure in love, whatever be the truth of that obscure event, would hardly account, by its own intrinsic sadness, for his abysmal melancholy and sense of doom. Further, when we find him in true deeps of actual woefulness, the bond-slave of opium and alcohol, living in the degradations of poverty, enchained, as St. Augustine has it, *sua ferrea voluntate,* by the iron chain of his unwilling will, yet it is not his fall that haunts him, but that sense of undeserved early torments and tortures, enfolding him as with a black impenetrable cloud. It was not only the lying imaginativeness of the opium-eater or of the drunkard that made him tell stories of fearful things which never happened; nor was it merely his artistic instinct toward presenting his life not quite as it was, but as it might have been, nor yet his elvish turn for a little innocent deception. Beyond a doubt, his temperament, immeasurably delicate and sensitive, received from its early experiences a shock, a shaking, which left him tremulous, impotent, a leaf in the wind, upon the water. His first sufferings in life were but the child's imagined ghosts; but the "shock to the system," to his imaginative sensitive temperament, was lasting, and he lived in a *penumbra* of haunting memories and apprehensions. In Browning's words, it was:

> *The glimmer of twilight,*
> *Never glad confident morning again!*

Life had struck him in his affections and emotions: he could never recover from the blow, could but magnify it in memory and imagination, conceive himself marked by it, go apart from the world to hide it, go astray in the world to forget it. That was Mangan's tragedy.

But he did not suffer it to cloud his poetry with darkness of expression at any time, nor, at its finest times, with darkness of theme or thought. It forced him into writing a deal of unworthy stuff, and a deal of excellent work far below his highest ability and achievement. But not a faint shadow of unhappiness dims the radiance of his "Dark Rosaleen," its adoring, flashing, flying, laughing rapture of patriotic passion. It is among the great lyrics of the world, one of the fairest and fiercest in its perfection of imagery and rhythm; it is the chivalry of a nation's faith struck on a sudden into the immortality of music. And Mangan's next glory, his version of O'Hussey's "Ode to the Maguire," is no less perfect upon its lower, yet lofty, plane. A certain Elizabethan poet has this pleasing stanza upon the Irish of his day, as he viewed them:

> The Irish are as civil, as
> The Russies in their kind;
> Hard choice, which is the best of both,
> Each bloodie, rude, and blind!

The "Ode to the Maguire" gives the noble side to the question, a ferocity that is heroic, in lines of the largest Homeric simplicity and greatness; and as "Dark Rosaleen" sings the devotion of a nation to their country in oppression, so this chants that of a follower to his chief in defeat; but in neither is there the note of despair, in both is the note of glory. Other of Mangan's poems upon Ireland, original and based upon Gaelic originals, have a like lustrous quality: he loved to lose himself in Ireland's past and future, and thereby made poems which will have helped to make the future Ireland. Upon such work as this he left no mark of his mental miseries and physical dishonours; indeed, his poems, though often tragic with sorrow, or trivial with levity, or both at once, are always pure and clear in every sense: in poetry, at least, he lived an innocent life. Besides his own Ireland, there were two chief worlds in which he loved to wander: the moonlit forests of German poetry, often painfully full of "moonshine," and the glowing gardens or glittering deserts of the Eastern, the "Saracenic" world. He wished, half-whimsically and half-seriously, to make his readers believe that he knew some dozen languages; certain it is that he had a strong philological instinct, and much of that aptitude for acquiring a vast half-knowledge of many things not commonly known, which he shares with the very similar, and dissimilar, Poe. But his "translations" from many tongues, even when, as in the case of German, he knew his originals well, were wont to be either frank paraphrases or imitations, often to his original's advantage. Some of his work in this kind is admirable, and of a cunning art: the work of a poet to whom rhythm and metre, with all technical difficulties and allurements, are passionately interesting; yet we regret

the time spent upon most of them, and lost to his own virgin
Muse. He seems to have felt that he was content to earn the
wages upon which he lived from hand to mouth, by such
secondary work, as though he despaired of attempting, or
preferred to keep in sacred silence, his higher song. He has
given us little of that. A selection from his poems can be
bought for sixpence, and one could spare, it may be, a hundred
out of its one hundred and forty-four pages. But what remains
is, in its marvellous moments of entire success, greater than
anything that Ireland has yet produced in English verse, from
Goldsmith to Mr. Yeats. From Mangan's birth in 1803 to
his painful and merciful death in 1849, if there be anything
joyous or pleasant in his record the reader forgets it in the
woes and glooms that precede and follow. He had true
friends, he could talk with them brilliantly, books were ever
a solace and delight to him; little as he cared for fame, he
knew that he deserved it, and he loved his art. His curious
humour, chiefly at his own expense, was sometimes more than
a Heinesque jesting, and shows him with sudden phases or fits
of good spirits. But, for the rest, his life is a record of
phantasmal dejections and cloudings of soul, as though he
were rejected of God and abandoned of man. At almost every
page, a reader fresh to his name and fame might expect the
next to chronicle a suicide's end, like those of Chatterton and
Gerard de Nerval. His story is infinitely sad, but never ab-
jectly or repulsively so. Here is the foredoomed dreamer, of
fragile body and delicate soul, the innocent victim of himself,
about whom we know much that is frail and pitiable, nothing
that is base and mean: the voice, often tremulous in lamentation and broken by weeping, from which rose and rang the
very glory and rapture of Irish song.

> *Him grant a grave to, ye pitying noble,*
> *Deep in your bosoms: there let him dwell!*
> *He, too, had tears for all souls in trouble*
> *Here, and in Hell.*

Charles Waterton: Naturalist

BY

JAMES J. DALY

OUR ENGLISH LITERATURE, as we all know, has passed through its best growing years during an overwhelming Protestant ascendency. For several centuries there were so few Catholic writers that Englishmen might almost be excused for thinking that not only the iron and coal and wealth of old England, but its strong and beautiful language also, were the fitting rewards granted by a bountiful and appreciative Providence to approved national types of Christianity. When Lingard appeared, employing, strange to say, a remarkably pure and idiomatic English, his excellence seemed to be resented, as if he had no right to be as good as he was; and the less said about him, the better. There was an audible gasp of astonishment, accompanied by something like indignation, when Newman arose on a larger stage than Lingard's and proceeded to use the English language as a garment for Catholic thought. The fit was perfect. That the speech of Englishmen should be heard in a Catholic galley was bad enough; that it should seem to be at home there, as if nothing at all had happened in the interval between Sir Thomas More and the Duke of Cumberland, was a mystery and an outrage requiring time and patience to digest.

It is sometimes alleged that Catholics exaggerate the literary excellence of their own writers. The suspicion has been entertained that Patmore and Francis Thompson and Joyce Kilmer, for instances, are the pets of Catholic coteries and have been nursed into a largely factitious prominence. If this be so, the years will tell. But the suspicion seems unwarranted. The

From *A Cheerful Ascetic and Other Essays,* by James J. Daly. Reprinted by permission of the author.

Catholic reading public has neither the numbers nor the influence to initiate popular literary estimates. If it tosses its cap in the air for a coreligionist, it is only after the cheers have been started elsewhere.

Nay, sometimes the cheering finds few or no echoes. Take Charles Waterton. His famous book, *Wanderings in South America,* appeared in 1825. It leaped into immediate popularity. Sydney Smith wrote a long review of it in his best manner for the *Edinburgh.* It was assailed by the stay-at-home naturalists—the "closet-naturalists" as Waterton ironically styled them—and provoked a controversy like that which raged during the consulship of Roosevelt around the so-called nature fakers. And since its appearance a century ago, it has never been allowed to gather dust in the limbo of the top shelf. The original publisher—not a Catholic publisher—issued a sixth edition about the time Waterton died. In 1878, the Rev. J. G. Wood, an Anglican clergyman and distinguished naturalist— he delivered the Lowell lectures in Boston in 1883—edited an edition of the *Wanderings* with a biographical introduction. This useful edition has been reprinted six times. At least two American editions have appeared. In 1909, a New York publishing house (Sturgis and Walton) printed a handsome edition, with an introduction and illustrations by Charles Livingston Bull, and a memoir by Norman Moore, Waterton's biographer in the *Dictionary of National Biography.* The *Wanderings* is one of the latest additions in the "Everyman's Library" series of classics. It is curious to note that Newman and Waterton are the only two Catholic names in that series among the writers of the past hundred years. Not long ago the London *Times* devoted a large part of the leading article of its Literary Supplement to a consideration of Waterton, as the possessor of a permanent place in English literature. And about the same time, an English magazine of the popular kind printed some reminiscences, in which Sir Austen Chamberlain stated that the *Wanderings* was the favorite book of his boyhood. These are straws; but they would indicate that Waterton's work is still raising a little wind.

The element of strangeness about all this is the apparently resolute way in which Catholics have held aloof from all demonstrations in favor of Waterton. He published, besides the *Wanderings*, three volumes of natural-history essays, four volumes in all. Seldom can any one of the four be found in a Catholic library. No Catholic publisher's list contains a Waterton title. Two histories of English literature which have been consulted, both written by Catholics, omit all mention of Waterton. Whenever a reference is made to Waterton in a Catholic periodical, it is done in the manner of one airing his erudition, and is generally inaccurate.

There is so little conceivable reason for the neglect that it actually takes on the lineaments of a mystery. It cannot be because Waterton is a naturalist, and therefore writing outside the circle of common human interest. While he is a naturalist of eminence, he always had impatience, amounting to contempt, for the learned and cumbersome paraphernalia of scientific pedantry. Much to the dismay of the naturalists who recognize his high worth, he never attached the accepted Greek and Latin labels to the objects of his study. He used the popular names, and discussed nature in the large and easy way of a man of the world who knew a thing or two besides the matter in hand. He has far more of the human and the personal in his studies than Gilbert White. These are, after all, superfluous arguments on the side of a book like the *Wanderings*, which, as a matter of fact, is regarded even in the *Cambridge History of English Literature*, as a literary classic. If the book is interesting to the world at large, it ought to be sufficiently interesting to Catholic readers.

While a book of travels is always sure of a certain measure of welcome, it is perhaps right to surmise that it stands a better chance in a country like England than in a self-supporting country like our own. Every second person in England either has a relation beyond the seas, or looks forward to a colonial career. Although the government is alarmed over the

declining interest in the colonial civil service among the under-
graduates of Oxford and Cambridge, the names of Clive,
Hastings, and Rhodes are still potent to stir youthful imagina-
tions. We can understand why Waterton's book of travel
should be more popular in England than in America. But we
do not understand why it should be more popular among non-
Catholic Englishmen than among Catholic Englishmen.

There are three kinds of Catholic writers. Those who find
it impossible, from some limitation in their art or personality,
to make literary material out of their religious experience;
those who learn to play a discreet Catholic accompaniment in
their literary entertainments; and finally those who are boister-
ously Catholic before any and every audience. If Waterton
belonged to the first, or even the second of these three classes,
Catholics might be excused for not paying him special attention. But this, in the language of the penny thriller, is just
where the mystery deepens. Waterton is uproariously Catholic. He scorned concealments. In his clear and simple view
of the matter, it was the other fellow, the child of the Reformation, who ought to practice concealments. He always
blessed himself in public, figuratively speaking and probably
literally speaking also, with the biggest and most deliberate
sign of the cross that he could make. He waved the papal
colors with a joyous delight in the face of early Victorian
England, which was a very Protestant England indeed. How
England came to swallow him, remains as great a mystery as
how Catholics came to forget him.

The first of these two mysteries becomes less insoluble on
a further acquaintance with Charles Waterton. He was a man
of so much transparent honesty and goodness that his most
objectionable enthusiasms wore a convincing air of unselfish
idealism and chivalry. He was a friend of Thackeray, met him
in Rome, and tried to convert him. We nearly all like Thackeray; but just think of anyone trying to make a Catholic out of
that lovable worldling, with all his inherited insular prepos-
sessions strong upon him! The attempt is described in the
Newcomes, where the hero is writing home from Rome: that

the ludicrous side of the incident is not played up as much as it might be, is evidence of goodness of heart in both men.

A friend, who belongs to the old religion, took me, last week, into a church where the Virgin lately appeared in person to a Jewish gentleman, flashed down upon him from heaven in light and splendor celestial, and of course, straightway converted him. My friend bade me look at the picture, and, kneeling down beside me, I know prayed with all his honest heart that the truth might shine down upon me too; but I saw no glimpse of heaven at all; all I saw was a poor picture, an altar with blinking candles, a church hung with tawdry strips of red and white calico. The good kind W. went away humbly saying "that such might have happened again if heaven so willed it." I could not but feel a kindness and admiration for the good man. I know his works are made to square with his faith, that he dines on a crust, lives as chastely as a hermit, and gives his all to the poor.

Alas, the spiritual dispositions of Thackeray were not precisely those of the Abbé Alphonse Ratisbon. If the simple and sanguine temper of Waterton were doomed to disappointment on this occasion, we can still regard the incident as one of the rarest and most touching things in history. It might have won mention in Hazlitt's "Of Persons One Would Wish To Have Seen," if that fine essay had been written some fifty years later.

When Waterton liked a man, he wanted to be sure of liking him for all eternity. Doctor Hobson—Richard Hobson, M. D. Cantab.—was his family physician and close friend. In the year following Waterton's death, Dr. Hobson published a garrulous book entitled: *Charles Waterton: His Home, Habits, and Handiwork. Reminiscences of an Intimate and Most Confiding Personal Association of Nearly Thirty Years.* It testifies to the popularity of Waterton, rather than to the skill of the memoirist, that the book ran into a second edition within five months of its first appearance. The doctor's affection and reverence for his friend are the most noticeable features of the large acreage of verbiage; but the reader's patience is sometimes rewarded. The doctor writes, referring to the apparition of our Lady and her shrine at La Salette, which Waterton had been visiting.

He, of course, on his return, largely expatiated on it, and insisted on my chiming in with him to the full extent of his own self-conviction. He was amazed how I could be so obtuse and bigoted as not to be at once proselytized, expressing the greatest surprise that I was so perverse and hoodwinked as not to go along with him even in his "tolerant belief." After earnestly expostulating with me, "I have," he observed, "often heard it said that none are so deaf as those who won't hear, but I can bear testimony that none are so blind as those who won't see." Although we were both emphatic in our disputation, yet our controversy was invariably maintained with such a thorough conviction of the sincerity of a sacred veneration for the cause we espoused that a word of anger never escaped the lips of either of us. I entertain not the shadow of a doubt but that the squire indulged to the fullest extent in the firm belief of the appearance of the apparition of the Blessed Virgin to the two shepherd children: and that no argument, however sound or lucidly expressed and convincing to Protestants, nor any amount of persuasive powers, however bewitchingly used, could have created an atom of doubt or disbelief in his mind.

The good doctor was a patient and cheerful Boswell. His stanch Protestant ears had to submit to eulogies of the "Romish Church," constantly pledged as the *caput mundi* against the Protestant *caput mortuum*. Nor was the squire without his patience, too. If the doctor obstinately refused to be saved, the zealous apostle, on the other hand, never allowed his temper to be affected. And this is a gentle courtesy not always achievable by zealous apostles.

Waterton, it must be admitted, had certain advantages in his public and private bullying of English prejudices. Much can be forgiven a man whose ancestors fought at Cressy and Agincourt and Marston Moor, and are mentioned by Shakespeare in his *Richard II*. Moreover, he was a landed proprietor and unquestionably belonged to the gentry. Such a man is sure of being allowed considerable leeway on the score of amiable eccentricities. It is extremely doubtful, however, whether the honest and fearless squire was aware of the indulgence his social position could command; but, whether or no, he never appeared nervous about overstraining it. He seized every opportunity of praising the Catholic Church and, in particular, the Jesuits. He always referred to the Reformers of the sixteenth century in terms of gross and most appalling disrespect. The only living thing he did not love and cherish was the rat, and he paid his respects to the reigning royal house by always calling a rat a "Hanoverian rat," because it "always contrives to thrust its nose into every man's house when there is anything to be got."

The Rev. J. G. Wood thinks there were extenuating circumstances for the rudeness.

The Watertons fared but badly in the stormy times of the Reformation, and, preferring conscience to property, they retained their ancient faith, but lost heavily in this world's goods. The many coercive acts against Roman Catholics naturally had their effect, not only on those who actually lived in the time of the Reformation, but upon their successors. A Roman Catholic could not sit in Parliament, he could not hold a commission in the army, he could not be a justice of the peace, he had to pay double land tax, and to think himself fortunate if he had any land left on which taxes could be demanded. He was not allowed to keep a horse worth more than five pounds, and more irritating than all, he had either to attend the parish church or to pay twenty pounds for every month of absence. In fact, a Roman Catholic was looked upon and treated as a wholly inferior being and held much the same relative position to his persecutors as Jews held toward the Normans and Saxons in the times of the Crusades. . . . Waterton was, during some of his best years, a personal sufferer from these acts, and they rankled too deeply in his mind to be forgotten. Hence the repeated and most irrelevant allusions in his writings to Martin Luther, Henry VIII, Queen Bess, Archbishop Cranmer, Oliver Cromwell, Charles Stuart, "Dutch William" (mostly associated with the "Hanoverian rat" and the national debt), and other personages celebrated in history. . . . On principle he refused to qualify as Deputy-Lieutenant and magistrate, because he had been debarred from doing so previously to the Emancipation Act.

Charles Waterton was born on the ancestral domain of Walton in 1782. He was the twenty-seventh Lord of Walton;

and, through his father's mother, ninth in descent from Blessed Thomas More, the martyred Chancellor of Henry VIII. The estate, no longer in the possession of the Watertons, is some three miles outside the village of Wakefield and not far from Leeds. When he was ten, he was sent to Tudhoe, a village near Durham, to a private school conducted by a Catholic priest. This little school had a remote and very slight connection with Ushaw College, on the strength of which Waterton is sometimes erroneously described as having belonged to that college. The article on Ushaw in the *Catholic Encyclopedia* does not include him among its distinguished sons. At the age of fourteen, he entered Stonyhurst where he remained for four years and completed his formal education. The Watertons had given several members to the Society of Jesus: they lie under ancient tombstones in the shadow of the chapel at Stonyhurst. The traditional affection of the Watertons toward the Jesuits was deepened in Charles as a result of his four years with them. Through a long life he eagerly sought every opportunity of testifying in public and private to his affectionate reverence for them. One of his instructors, Father Clifford, a first cousin of Lord Clifford, noting the young naturalist's tendency to range abroad—sometimes beyond bounds—questing for field knowledge in his little private pursuit, thought he saw in him a budding Englishman whose adventurous spirit would probably lead him out of his snug island home into trackless places at the ends of the earth. As a safeguard in such a contingency, he asked young Waterton to promise that he would never touch wine or intoxicating liquor. This promise Charles made and kept to the end of his life.

After leaving Stonyhurst, with accomplishments that included facility in writing Latin verse and a love of English and Latin literature, he spent two years at home with his father, during which time he acquired the reputation of being the most daring rider with the Lord Darlington foxhounds. In 1802, he went to Spain and had a wild year of cholera and earthquakes, ending in a mad dash for home on a sailing vessel. A bold skipper had been found, who was willing to defy a cordon of brigs-of-war, maintaining a strict embargo on the shipping of Malaga. The weakened condition of Waterton's health called for a gentler climate than that of Yorkshire, and in 1804 he voyaged to Demerara, British Guiana, on the sloping forehead of South America. It is close to the equator, and came into American notice prominently some years ago in the famous Venezuela boundary dispute. Here the young naturalist took charge of two estates belonging to his father and uncle. The death of his father two years later required his presence in England, but the new squire returned almost immediately to the tropics, where he continued in the administration of the estates for six years till the death of his uncle, when he was relieved of his double charge and felt free to indulge at leisure his pet hobby.

Then began the series of four journeys which are described in his famous book. Its full title indicates broadly the extent of the journeys and the years in which they were made: *Wanderings in South America, the Northwest of the United States, and the Antilles in the Years 1812, 1816, 1820, and 1824.* The writer in the London *Times* to whom reference has been made, says that Waterton's style is baroque and the least modern part of him, calling attention especially, as Sydney Smith has done already, to the elaborate apostrophes and the classical allusions and quotations. Yet, he is forced to admit that they are oddly in keeping with the general structure, like the statues on the façade or roof of a building. With these outworn little tricks of rhetoric, the style is curiously moldproof and modern. "Many years ago," Mr. Charles Livingston Bull tells us, "when reading this book for the first time, my boyish imagination was so fired that I determined the first opportunity should find me on my way to Waterton's beloved Demerara, and in March of the year 1908, I sailed from New York on a journey in which I covered most of the country which he describes so well and so thoroughly." A dead or superannuated style is not so wonder-working.

While Waterton in his kindly and simple-hearted fashion,

and probably under the influence of Sterne, makes expansive and flourishing gestures, he could be terse enough on occasion, and he possessed no mean mastery of the "difficult art of omission," by means of which, if we believe Stevenson, it is possible to make an Iliad out of the ordinary issue of a daily newspaper. The *Times* critic admits that in one respect Waterton was thoroughly modern in having a journalist's eye for good "copy," and he cites the well-known adventure with a cayman. A cayman, or caiman, is a word one seldom hears now, and is the name of the larger species of alligator.

It would be an easy task to write the headlines with which reporters would diversify the stories they got from him. Indeed, many of them would have been cabled from Para or Georgetown to New York or London, and would have flared through the press of the world. One of his stories survives in its pristine sensationalism. Overnight a caiman had taken a hooked bait attached to a rope, and Waterton wished to catch it alive. His people had the end of the rope and were ordered to pull the reptile toward the shore. Waterton's first idea was to thrust a mast into its mouth, thus making it harmless; but as the creature drew near, lashing the water in rage, he made a sudden plunge, leaped on its back, pulled up its forelegs to "serve as a bridle," and in this heroic posture the pair were dragged out of the water and some forty yards over the sand. There is no reasonable doubt that the story was true, although it lost nothing in the telling.

The writer goes on to give other instances of Waterton's instinctive feeling for whatever would be of lively interest to readers. Among them he quotes the classic description of the sloth, the first accurate description of that strange beast in literature. This was the description which moved Sydney Smith to make a memorable comparison: "The sloth moves suspended, rests suspended, sleeps suspended, and passes his whole life in suspense, like a young clergyman distantly related to a bishop."

It is in this volume that Waterton enters an eloquent defense of the Jesuits against the stereotyped Protestant representations of Southey in his *History of Brazil*. He also showed himself rather careless of a certain phase of English

temper by speaking kindly and sympathetically of Irish endurance under English misrule; and almost equally careless of the
same temper by liking and praising Americans. Of all the
famous English visitors to the United States, he is perhaps the
only writer among them who met us and liked us and did not
regard us from a lofty and superior eminence when telling his
countrymen about us. Wilson's *Ornithology of the United
States* was the book which induced Waterton to go by way of
New York on his fourth and last trip to Demerara. He saw
the Hudson up to Albany, went across the state to Buffalo,
visited Montreal and Quebec, and on his return to New York
stopped at Lake George and Saratoga, "a gay and fashionable
place," where he enjoyed the hotels, the waters, and the
company.

There is a pleasing frankness, and ease and becoming dignity, in the
American ladies; and the good humor, and absence of all haughtiness
and puppyism in the gentlemen, must, no doubt, impress the traveler
with elevated notions of the company who visit this celebrated spa.

Of course he went to Philadelphia, where Wilson's *Ornithology* had been printed. His comment on the city is interesting.

Travelers hesitate whether to give the preference to Philadelphia or to
New York. Philadelphia is certainly a noble city, and its environs
beautiful; but there is a degree of quiet and sedateness in it, which,
though no doubt very agreeable to the man of calm and domestic habits,
is not so attractive to one of speedy movements.

Waterton studied men more than birds while he was here.
We must have been a rather crude nation in 1824, and yet
Waterton has nothing but hearty approval of us, excepting for
our habit of smoking. We still have the habit, but it is no
longer especially characteristic. Waterton's portrait of us may
be flattering beyond our deserts; still it bears a more convincing air of being related to some sort of reality than do the
caricatures and provincial burlesque of Moore and Dickens
and the loose impressionisms of their successors. It took at

least courage, not to mention other virtues, to write and publish the following observation about the American:

> He has certainly hit upon the way (but I could not make out by what means) of speaking a much purer English language than that which is in general spoken on the parent soil. This astonished me much; but it is really the case.

He bids us farewell in a kindly and generous spirit:

> Politicians of other countries imagine that intestine feuds will cause a division in this commonwealth; at present there appears to be no reason for such a conjecture. Heaven forbid that it should happen! The world at large would suffer by it. For ages yet to come, may this great commonwealth continue to be the United States of North America.

It is good to know that, if there are Englishmen like Mr. Kipling and the editor of the *National Review,* there are also Englishmen like Charles Waterton.

After the publication of the *Wanderings,* Waterton settled down and married. His wife died a year after marriage. Her two maiden sisters thereupon yielded to the bereaved husband's wishes and took over the care of his household, which now included an infant son. This arrangement continued in force till Waterton's death forty years later. We see henceforth the country squire instead of the intrepid explorer; though the naturalist still remains uppermost. He is said to have been the first to create a bird sanctuary by building a stone wall three miles in circumference and some eight or nine feet high around his park, besides making other elaborate provisions for protecting animal life and studying its habits. The results of his studies were published in a series of three volumes, interspersed with quaint bits of informal biography. His house stood on an island, approached by a single bridge, where the water birds could be watched from a window. The park was a paradise for all living things except the unfortunate Hanoverian rat. There were frequent excursions to the Continent in the company of the two sisters, and Stonyhurst was regularly a port of call, especially during the Christmas season.

It would be hard to imagine a happier life. But it was not the life of an epicure. The hardy habits of the wilderness persisted. Norman Moore, who lived with him toward the end, gives the squire's morning order: it is substantially the same as that given by Dr. Hobson:

> He went to bed early, and slept upon the bare floor, with a block of wood for his pillow. He rose for the day at half-past three, and spent the hour from four to five at prayer in his chapel. He then read every morning a chapter in a Spanish life of St. Francis Xavier, followed by a chapter of *Don Quixote* in the original, after which he used to stuff birds or write letters till breakfast.

Breakfast was at eight. The Spartan quality of this régime cannot be fully appreciated unless one has experienced the chill of an English winter morning in an unheated house, and has been informed that Waterton's early life in the tropics had made him delicately sensitive to cold. He hardly ever ate meat; his wildest indulgence was a cup of tea; he used to vex the good Doctor Hobson by rigorously observing all the fast days of the Church long after he had passed the age limit set for fasting. He had another habit which appalled the doctor. When Waterton was a young man and about to penetrate alone wild forests far from the medical resources of civilization, he induced a surgeon to teach him how to open and close a vein so that he could bleed himself in an emergency; bleeding, by venesection, or by the application of leeches, was still the universal remedy for nearly every sort of ailment in the early days of the past century. Blood-letting became Waterton's panacea. Even in his eighties he would not hesitate to "take away from twenty to twenty-four ounces of blood, with not merely temporary freedom from all suffering, but with all the permanent benefit that could be desired." So writes Doctor Hobson in amazement. He could open and close a vein with either hand. Sometimes the knife was too much dulled by casual use about the house, and had to be sharpened after a futile attempt (in Waterton's phrase) "to tap the claret." Let modern science shake its incredulous head!

The athlete's joy in overcoming difficulties, which started him on early adventure, was something he never lost. When he was over forty, he climbed to the top of the cross on St. Peter's in Rome, and left his glove on the point of the lightning rod. Pope Pius VII thought the glove impaired the usefulness of the lightning rod and ordered its removal. As no one was eager to assume the task, Waterton had to repeat his feat "to the amusement of his friends and the delight of the populace." He also climbed to the top of the castle of St. Angelo and stood with one foot on the head of the angel. When he was over eighty, he could clamber to the top of the highest oaks in his park. After this, the feats of the young men, who are the "human flies" of the "movies," must appear tame. These well-authenticated accounts lend color to a Stonyhurst legend of Waterton's school days. Once, in that juvenile mood which is the terror of fond parents, he proceeded to prove to some of his schoolboy friends that he could climb the face of the tower at the entrance of the college. The tower, built in the days of James I, rises in four courses of pillars one above another. Waterton had reached the fourth and highest course, and was preparing to negotiate a selected pillar when Father Rector appeared on the scene far below, and, to the disgust of everybody, peremptorily ordered the lad to descend at once. That night a storm blew down the very pillar Waterton was preparing to leg up when the Rector interfered. An examination of the fallen pillar disclosed the fact that there was an old crack straight through it, and it had been in such perilous condition that a slight jar would have overthrown it. The mended pillar has been restored to its place and serves to point a moral for succeeding generations.

Modern science would probably like to know the secret of Waterton's pliability of limb in old age. The years forgot to harden his arteries. "When Mr. Waterton was seventy-seven years of age," says Dr. Hobson, "I was witness to his scratch-

ing the back part of his head with the big toe of his right
foot." And, again the doctor's words must be given, "in the
summer of 1861, when in his seventy-ninth year, Mr. Waterton, in one of his jocose moods, by a run of fifteen yards,
bounded over a stout wire fence, without touching it hand or
foot, and this I carefully measure to three feet six inches in
height." A Stonyhurst tradition—not a loud, boastful tradition: rather a shocked and somewhat politely modulated
tradition—tells how the old naturalist would be as likely as
not to enter a room full of company during the holidays,
walking on his hands. What a terrible old man! Still, with
all his informal ways, no one, we are told, felt like taking
liberties with the squire.

Stonyhurst is a rich field for the lover of Waterton. In its
museum he can see the identical cayman which Waterton rode,
together with the wooden hook and rope used on the famous
occasion. Here, too, is a finely preserved sloth; and indeed, a
large collection of specimens preserved by the naturalist's own
hands and according to a formula of his own, which he claimed
to be superior to every known process of taxidermic art practiced in his day. Latin inscriptions in pentameter verse, of
Waterton's composition, often take the place of the usual
learned labels. One semicircular case is said by Dr. Hobson
to have been the main ornament of the Waterton home. The
general inscription of the exhibit in this case is: "England's
Reformation Zoölogically Illustrated." A beautifully crested
bird rests on a perch above a small fragment of granite inscribed, "The Catholic Church Triumphant: *Tu es Petrus,*
etc." In front and below is a repulsive-looking crab, marked
"Mother Law Church," with eight villainous beetles, denomi-
nated "her dissenting fry." On the right is a big, bloated,
and hideous horned-toad, with a crested tail, which we are
informed is Henry VIII. To the left, another fat toad, not
charming by any means, stands for "Dutch William III."
Bishop Burnet, "The Rev." John Knox, Old Nick, Archbishop Cranmer, Titus Oates, and Queen Bess are represented by loathsome subterranean specimens of crawling ani-

mal life. There is a rumor that a temporary coolness sprang up between Waterton and Stonyhurst when the Rector of the college hesitated to manifest enthusiastic appreciation at the offer of this particular exhibit.

Norman Moore's account of Waterton's last days deserves reproduction.

After breakfast we went with a carpenter to finish some bridges at the far end of the park. The work was completed, and we were proceeding homewards when, in crossing a small bridge, a bramble caught the squire's foot, and he fell heavily upon a log. He was greatly shaken, and said he thought he was dying. He walked, notwithstanding, a little way, and was then compelled to lie down. He would not permit his sufferings to distract his mind, and he pointed out to the carpenter some trees that were to be felled. He presently continued his route, and managed to reach the spot where the boat was moored. Hitherto he had refused all assistance, but he could not step from the bank into the boat and he said, "I am afraid I must ask you to help me in." He walked from the landing place into the house, changed his clothes, and came and sat in the large room below. The pain increasing, he rose from his seat after he had seen his doctor, and though he had been bent double with anguish, he persisted in walking upstairs without help, and would have gone to his room in the top story, if, for the sake of saving trouble to others, he had not been induced to stop halfway in the sitting room of his sister-in-law. . . . The pain abated, and the next day he seemed better. In the afternoon he talked to me a good deal, chiefly about natural history. But he was well aware of his perilous condition, for he remarked to me, "This is a bad business," and later on he felt his pulse often, and said, "It is a bad case." He was more than self-possessed. A benignant cheerfulness beamed from his mind, and in spite of fits of pain he frequently looked up with a gentle smile, and made some little joke. Toward midnight he grew worse. The priest was summoned, and Waterton got ready to die. He pulled himself upright without help, sat in the middle of the sofa, and gave his blessing in turn to his grandson, Charles, to his granddaughter, Mary, to each of his sisters-in-law, to his niece, and to myself, and left a message for his son who was hastening back from Rome. He then received the last Sacraments, repeated all the responses, Saint Bernard's hymn in English, and the first two verses of *Dies Irae*. The end was now at hand, and he died at twenty-seven minutes past two in the morning of May 27, 1865.

The death of the squire was a calamity to his tenants and all the countryside, to Protestants and Catholics alike; for he was bountiful in his charity irrespective of creed. He disliked Protestantism thoroughly, but he could love those who practiced it in good faith. Englishmen who differed with him in religion, and suffered from his irony, were willing to accept Thackeray's judgment as final, that "he was a good man; his works were made to square with his faith, he dined on a crust, lived as chastely as a hermit, and gave his all to the poor."

The Thackeray episode in Rome, a touching evidence of Waterton's strong faith and his affection for his friends, ought to be coupled with another illustrating his love of dumb animals. It was his custom before going out on his afternoon walk to provide himself with a crust against chance meetings with some of his animal friends. One goose, especially, used to wait for him hopefully every evening at the end of the bridge over the moat. Norman Moore was with Waterton one day when the usual crust had been forgotten. On approaching the bridge, the squire hung back. He looked troubled. "How shall we ever get past that goose?" and there was worry in his voice. The lord of the manor thereupon adopted the Fabian strategy of skulking among distant trees on various pretexts, with much reconnoitering of the bridge, till Mariana at the most got tired waiting and waddled off. He could not bear, says Moore, "to give it nothing when it raised its bill."

Eminence in art and science does not often surpass itself in the most difficult art of all, that of life. And that is Charles Waterton's chief distinction. The sturdy Yorkshire squire was of a different type from that of the Oxford-bred Newman. But both men meet on a high plane of personal holiness, and in the grace of a Faith superior to all the challenges of the world, the flesh, and the devil. Excepting always the easy masters of fame, the student of literature is often at a loss to explain the survival of the chosen few in the deluge of oblivion which blots out the writers of every generation. If a guess be allowed on the survival of Waterton, it would be concerned more with his personality than with his literary qualities: though it cannot be a commonplace style which lets an interesting man shine through. In these pelagian days, so busy upon the old futility of making conduct keep an upright position without supernatural supports, the wholesome personality of Charles Waterton can raise the average of sanity and cheerfulness on the favorite bookshelf.

Chaucer's Nuns

BY

SISTER M. MADELEVA

THE NUNS IN the *Canterbury Tales* are characters around whom a proverbially romantic interest and an unproverbial set of difficulties gather. They are, like their twenty-seven companions on the pilgrimage, typical individuals of their class, seen through the fixating medium of Chaucer's personality; seen by us through the less luminous distance of five hundred years. Criticism seems to have followed methods of microscopic analysis of them out of their habitual environment rather than telescopic synthesis of them in their environment. The problems they present are acutely psychological and prosaically human. Let us come to the matter in this wise.

Before we can attempt an understanding either of Chaucer's Nuns or, indeed, of himself as artist in creating them, one must know in part the material on which he worked. A Nun, Religious, Sister—whichever name you wish—is not merely a woman in a "cloke ful fetis" and "ful semely pinched . . . wimple," nor even a woman upon whom the religious life has been superimposed, but a woman whose life has undergone a change more subtle and entirely spiritual than marriage but quite as real. The absolute proof of this statement is experience; the strongest ulterior proof is the word of one who has had this experience, corroborated by the whole world's recognition of the religious state. The forces by which this change is effected are two: the first, a mystical but most real relation between the soul and God; the second, the rules and customs and religious practices of the particular community in which the individual seeks to perfect that mystical relation. These determine almost entirely, apart from the personality of the individual, the manners, the deportment, the whole external aspect of the religious. So apparent are the effects that religious communities recognize among themselves their outstanding qualities and characterize one another by them. The point I wish to make clear is this: Chaucer in depicting the Nuns was not dealing merely with women wearing a particular and conspicuous costume, symbolic of religion, but women whose whole selves had undergone a subtle change by reason of the two influences just named. He was representing the visible effects of a spiritual life of which he had no experimental or vicarious knowledge. That fact should be italicized in considering critically his accomplished task. And—which is almost more important—the Nuns themselves, to be interpreted at all, must be interpreted in relation to their Rule, their customs, and the community prayers by which their entire lives were regulated. Such an interpretation of Chaucer's Nuns this paper proposes to make.

The Prioress and her chaplain were, according to Chaucer's allusion, members of the convent at Stratford at Bow, a Benedictine abbey of note and prominence in the fourteenth century. This means that they were living under the *Rule of St. Benedict,* that their exterior conduct was regulated by the norm and pattern laid down in it, and that their interior or spiritual life reflected its spirit as it fed and thrived upon the religious practices prescribed in it. Chief among these practices was the chanting of the Divine Office to which we shall come presently. What their exterior was we learn from the *Prologue;* what their interior life must have been we can guess from the spirituality of their own prologues and stories proper, unconscious as their breathing and quite as natural. Now for an interpretation of these through the *Rule of St. Benedict.*

Logically we begin with the Prioress as she appears in the *Prologue,* and we look to her holy rule rather than to any other source book for direction upon her smiling, her oath, her name, her singing, her table manners—well nigh threadbare with much quoting—her charity, her pets, her cloak and beads and brooch, her age—mind you—and her chaplain; everything in fact except her face, which is after Chaucer's best conventional pattern.

To interpret her "smyling . . . ful simple and coy" I would go sooner to the *Rule of St. Benedict,* with which Chaucer was easily familiar, than to the pastorelle of the fourteenth century where Professor Lowes hunts the phrase with such characteristic thoroughness.*

For in the Northern Verse version one reads:

> *A priores hir fast sal breke,*
> *And silence, when scho suld not speke,*
> *To myrth hir gestes in that scho may.***

The prose translated by D. Oswald Hunter Blair corresponds: "When, therefore, a guest is announced, let him be met by the Superior or the brethren, with all due charity. . . . When the guests have been received . . . let the Superior, or anyone he may appoint, sit with them. . . . The Superior may break his fast for the sake of the guest. . . . Let the Abbot pour water on the hands of the guests; and himself as well as the whole community, wash their feet." Chapter LIII.

Considering that this is the spirit of the rule under which the Prioress had enlisted, one feels that her smiling was the minimum of hospitality which she must have felt for strangers,

---

* J. L. Lowes, "Simple and Coy," *Anglia,* XXXIII, 440-451.
** *Three Middle English Versions of the Rule of St. Benedict,* Chap. li, 103.

at home, or abroad, and one understands her congeniality and cheer later remarked as a part of the same spirit.

Her lovely and romantic name is a sure target for remark. It is exactly what a little girl would be like to call her favorite doll. How did Chaucer hit upon it? By much the same process, I should think, as leads any author to prefer Anita to Hannah, or Eloise to Ella, as the name of his heroine. There is no written rule, so far as I know, for the giving of names in religious communities. It is a matter determined by custom, which is a form of written or unwritten practice in all communities, almost as binding as the rule and harder to depart from. In regard to names, three customs prevail. In some communities, the Sisters retain their family names, and Mary or Elizabeth or Susan Eglantine becomes in religion Madame Eglantine. This is not, I think, the practice of the Benedictines. Other communities, usually small ones, allow the prospective Sister to choose her own name. In most large communities the subject has no actual choice; she or her friends may express a wish in the matter, which may or may not be considered. However, the name given is either the whole or a part of a saint's name or bears traditions of sanctity. Magdalen is a familiar example, taken not from Mary, the sister of Martha and Lazarus, but from Magdala, her home. What clouds of sanctity trail from Madame Eglantine's name are lost in the mists of a hagiography more familiar to Chaucer than to me. At all events its chances of being "self-chosen" are two to one, and if self-chosen, the chooser was Chaucer. That his choice was a canny one, I admit, with the canniness of a journalist.

I have thought it unnecessary to speak of Madame Eglantine's negative oath, in view of Professor Hales' and Professor Lowes' articles on it.* The singing of the divine service contains two interesting bits of unexhausted inference. A word first in regard to the Office itself may be illuminating.

---

* Hales, J. W., "Chaucer's Prioress's 'Greatest Oath,'" *The Athenæum,* Jan. 10, 1891. 54. Lowes, J. L., "The Prioress's Oath," *Romanic Review,* V. No. 4.

Aside from the Mass, the Divine Office, or "service" as Chaucer calls it, is the most solemn liturgical prayer of the Church. It is composed chiefly of the psalms, arranged in seven parts with prose prayers and hymns appropriately introduced. The seven parts are: Matins and Lauds which are said late in the afternoon (by anticipation) or in cloistered orders, shortly after midnight; Prime, Tierce, Sext, and None recited during the morning hours, and Vespers in the afternoon or evening, followed by a postlude, so to say, called Compline. The Office is in Latin and is chanted and intoned, "entuned in the nose," in various keys. It is recited daily by all priests and chanted in choir in such monastic orders as the Benedictines, the Carthusians, the Carmelites. A shorter form of the same solemn prayer of the Church, known as the *Little Office, Little Hours of the Blessed Virgin,* or *Psalter,* was used during the Middle Ages by the laity and is still used by all religious orders that do not recite the Divine Office. The Office is chanted by the community together or "in choir," ordinarily, but when religious are on journeys they recite their office "privately"; that is, they read it to themselves. *The Rule of St. Benedict,* Chapter XIX, says on this subject: "Loke ye do yure seruise als ye stode by-fore god almihti. And lokis, when ye sing, that yure herte acorde wid yure voice; than sing ye riht." And, in truth, it is a matter of conscience with every religious to intone the Office "ful semely," as it is the most important of all vocal prayers.

Here are the bare facts; now for their two promised inferences. First, Chaucer must have been familiar with the Divine Office, so familiar that he knew how it should be said. That he knew even better the Little Office will appear in the discussion of the *Prioress's Prologue* later. Second, he must have been at some convent for only there could he have heard the "service divyne entuned." His statement regarding the Prioress in this connection evidently refers to her life in the cloister; no religious recites the Office aloud when traveling. One might go further and infer that through business or ties

of kinship * he must have been well acquainted with some
community; a stranger or a casual visitor does not ordinarily
hear the religious chanting the Office, or if he does, he is not
able to interpret it as Chaucer does. This inference reinforces
a theory offered later as to the possible unwritten source of the
Nun's stories.

One comes rather resentfully to the table manners of the
Prioress upon which so much trivial comment has been expended. I will connect her "cloke . . . ful fetis" with her conduct at table, as having no slight bearing upon it. The *Rule*,
Chapter LVI, makes this provision for clothing:

> *In comun places for alkins note*
> *Sufficis a kirtil and a cote;*
> *And mantels sal thai haue certayn,*
> *In winter dubil, in some playne. . . .*
>
> *And when thai sal went in cuntre, (i.e. on a journey)*
> *Thair clething sal mor honest be; . . .*
>
> *And home agayn when thai cum eft,*
> *Then sal thai were slik os thai left.*

Here is explicit provision for the "fetis" cloak, and a homely,
human reason for the Prioress's carefulness at table. She was
wearing not only a clean, but a new habit, which she would be
expected to give up on her return to her convent. Is it any
wonder that she was so effectively solicitous "that no drope
ne fille up-on her brest." I can well understand how Chaucer
might have misinterpreted such apparent over-daintiness, and
how critics have found it affected, even "a little ridiculous." **
But none of them ever wore a religious habit, nor had the
least idea of what real distress a Sister feels at getting a spot
on her habit, especially at table. Her habit is holy to her: "a
spot without is a spot within" is among the most venerable
of community proverbs, and St. Bernard's "I love poverty
always but dirt never" is applied to clothing almost more than

* Lounsbury, *Studies in Chaucer*, I, 100.
** Root, R. K., *The Poetry of Chaucer*, 190.

to anything else in religious life. This highly cultivated antipathy for dirt accounts more reasonably for the dainty details of Madame Eglantine's conduct at table than affectation or an aping of the manners of the world, the "chere of court," two things that are anathema in the spirit of every religious community.

One other determining element in the Prioress's character that even Chaucer might not have been able to account exactly for but which would manifest itself surely at table was her spirit of mortification. The veriest novice knows that mortification is the mainspring of religious life and bodily mortification is practiced in some measure by all religious at table. St. Benedict says: "Let two dishes, then, suffice for all the brethren. . . . For there is nothing so adverse to a Christian as gluttony, according to the words of our Lord: 'See that your hearts be not overcharged with surfeiting.'" Chapter XXXIX. This may suggest a new meaning to the line, "ful semely after hir mete she raughte."

The "rosted flesh, and milk and wastel-breed" for the "smale hondes" is an open extravagance except that these were gathered from the table after the meal was over. And this custom is as old as St. Francis and his brother Wolf, I suspect. Personally, I see every day of my life a Sister with as "tendre a herte" as the Prioress—an old Sister, by the way—gathering choice bits of meat and creamy milk for our excellent mouser, Fluff, and scattering "wastel breed" to the little warblers and finches around our door. I should say that this good Sister's heart goes out to the canine world to such degree that more than one "hounde" greets her with barks of joy. One would have to live in a convent to appreciate fully what Chaucer has really done in these sixty lines of the *Prologue*.

The well-pinched wimple is one of the most interesting details of the Prioress's dress. No one who has ever seen a Benedictine habit can miss its significance. The wimple or collar of this habit is as typical as the coronet of the Sister of Charity, if not quite so architectural. It is of white linen, accordion plaited or "pinched" to fit closely around the neck and over the shoulders in such manner that each plait forms a circle and the whole is a series of concentric circles. The mystery of its achievement might well defy the feminine mind; its neat and supple tidiness would scarce escape even the masculine eye. Small wonder, then, that Chaucer directs the attention of five hundred years to the well-pinched wimple. It was a feature of the Nun's habit to elicit admiration from the least observant. Suggestions of vanity on the Nun's part arise, it seems to me, from a lack of understanding of a Sister's attitude toward her habit. It is a matter not of vanity but of duty to her to wear it modestly and becomingly as the uniform of her high vocation. Here, again, a secular point of view fails to catch the chief significance of things that may have deceived even Chaucer.

On the subject of the "smal coral . . . peire of bedes" one might expand into a brief history of the origin and use of prayer beads. Let it suffice here to say that since the thirteenth century such beads have been in common use among religious and lay persons alike. At that time they were called Paternosters, from the prayer most often said on them. Their manufacturers, Paternosterers, were a recognized craft guild. Stephen Boyleau in his *Livres des Métiers* gives full details of the four guilds of "Patenotriers" in Paris in 1268. Paternoster Row in London commemorates the gathering place of a group of these same craftsmen. The prayer beads that the Prioress carried were the work of medieval handicraft rather than twentieth-century machines, an explanation quite sufficient to account for their exquisite beauty. Only one who has seen the large variety of beads in common use among Catholics can appreciate how lovely this particular pair must have been. The spirit of poverty would forbid a Sister today to use anything so elaborate, but in the days when things were not merely useful but beautiful, this pair of beads may not have been such an extravagance.

The suggestion that even Chaucer had in mind an ambiguous meaning for the motto, "Amor vincit omnia" or an eye to its cheaper journalistic value seems to me unworthy and inconsistent with his attitude of pronounced respect toward the Prioress. As a matter of fact, this is one of the commonest of epigrams among religious, and I know that one could find it worked in cross stitch, or painted in all the varying forms of realistic and conventional art and framed as a motto in dozens of our convents in our very unmystical and unmedieval United States today. I have no doubt that Chaucer himself had seen it so in some convent parlor, possibly in Norfolk where a ring bearing the same inscription has been unearthed and where there was a large Benedictine convent in Chaucer's time.* It is, in three words, the most typical motto that could have been engraved upon the brooch.

The "broche" itself, hanging from the beads, was undoubtedly a medal, one of the commonest sacramentals in the Catholic Church. It is a small object, much like a locket, bearing engraving and inscriptions of a religious nature. In itself it has no virtue; its value lies in the fact that it reminds the owner or bearer of some truth of religion and so inspires him to virtue. Medals are of unlimited variety and number and purpose. They are made of gold, silver, plated or oxidized metals, cloisonné, bronze, or cheaper substances and range from simple crudeness to exquisite beauty in workmanship and design. The Prioress's "broche" is a good, but not an over-elaborate, medal.

So much for the accidents of Madame Eglantine's exterior. The discussion of them has been neither scholarly nor pretentious; it has regarded them simply in the light of the Prioress's Rule, under a modified form of which the writer herself lives, and in that light has indicated details that the most luminous of old manuscripts might not shed upon them.

One other matter remains before leaving the *Prologue:* the question of the gentle Madame's age. By what evidence or inference critics conclude that the Prioress was young I do not know. Professor Lowes, referring to the touches of artistry in the details of description, remarks on "the skill with which they suggest still youthful flesh and blood behind the

* *Life Records of Chaucer,* III (2nd series), 135.

well pinched wimple. Not only in his account of the amiable foibles of the Prioress," he continues, "but in his choice of words and phrases, Chaucer suggests the delightfully imperfect submergence of the woman in the nun." Which implies, if it does not state, that she was, more than probably, young. The emphasis, I understand, is upon the nice perfection of Chaucer's workmanship and art. But from that very point of view I believe that there is a failure to appreciate his greater perfection. He has given us some one much harder to paint with his brush of words than a young Nun in whom the young woman is as yet imperfectly submerged. That task might have tempted his immaturity. But here is his picture of a woman a decade or more beyond middle age (my opinion) sweetened and spiritually transformed by the rules and religious practices of her choice, who can be in the world without being of it, gracious without affectation, and friendly without boldness. That she combines the wisdom of the serpent with the simplicity of the dove one realizes from her exquisite rebuke to the shipman when, in telling her story, she has occasion to refer to an abbot, and remembering his "daun John" she puts in her artless aside, "a holy man, as monkes been, or elles oughten be." * Personally, I think that a younger Nun would have expressed open resentment or have kept silence on the subject; only a mature woman of experience and courage and tact could have made and used an opportunity for a well-earned reprimand with such casual sweetness. She is a woman, evidently, who has taken to heart the Pauline lesson of becoming all things to all men, and learned it well. It is one of the ideals of all religious life, and it seems more natural to think that her "greet disport" and "amiable port" are the outcome of it rather than "compounded" like "her character," as Professor Root says, "of many affections." ** The cheerful, dignified, kindly woman of fifty years, perhaps, is what the religious reads out of Chaucer's Prioress, and she is decidedly a more complex char-

---

* Bregy, K., "The Inclusiveness of Chaucer," *Catholic World,* June, 1922.
** Root, R. K., *The Poetry of Chaucer,* 190.

acter to penetrate and portray than a Sister with the natural
gayety and exuberance of youth still about her.

One turns to the *Rule of St. Benedict* for some stipulation
as to the age requirement for the office of Prioress. In the
Northern Prose Version, Chapter LI, one reads, "The yung
salle onur thalde, and the alde salle lufe the yunge. Nane sal
calle othir by thaire name, but the priures sal calle thaim hir
'sistirs.' The abesse, for shoes in godis stede, sal be callid
'dame.' " This might imply, from its context, seniority; but
in the Caxton abstract one finds: "Such (Superiors) owe not
to be chosen thereto by their age, but for their wertuous lyuing
and wysdom, chastyte and sobre dealying, and also for their
pyte and mercy, the whyche they muste vse in all their dedys."
Then follows a list of other qualities that are the very reverse
of youthful virtues; prudence, for example, compassion, patience, industry, great and all-embracing charity. We are not
to suppose that the Prioress or any other Superior ever embodied them all, but one looks for and finds more of these
requisites in an old than in a young person.

Other proofs of the Prioress's age are not difficult to find,
proofs almost absurd in their homeliness. Most religious
rules or customs even today forbid the keeping of pet animals.
One remembers the terse injunction in the *Ancren Riwle*, "Ye
shall not possess any beast, my dear Sisters, except only a cat."
That abuses to this regulation grew up Grosseteste's comments leave no small doubt; a fact of more significance to us,
however, is that when an exception to the rule is made, it is
ordinarily in favor of an older religious. A Sister of fifty or
sixty can have a bird or a dog or a cat with propriety; a Sister
of thirty would scarcely think of such a thing. So do the
"smale houndes" betray the age of their gentle mistress.

This point may be too trivial to be of value; if it will serve
no other purpose we may "use it for our mirth, yea, for our
laughter." Chaucer says the Prioress

> *was so charitable and so pitous,*
> *She wolde wepe, if that she sawe a mous*
> *Caught in a trappe.*

Human nature in respect to mice has not changed since those days. No young Nuns that I have ever met, and they are many, would have been moved to tears at such a sight; most of them would certainly have screamed or have wanted to.

So the age of the Prioress rests, like Chaucer's own, an unknown quantity of continued speculation. For the unchivalry of exposing these evidences of her advanced age, we offer the high security of the maiden on the Grecian urn, "she cannot fade."

The presence of the Prioress's companion is in strict accord with apostolic tradition and is followed closely in most religious communities. One is startled to hear her spoken of as a chaplain, a name ordinarily applied to priests. An article published by Dr. Furnivall in the *Academy* some years ago clears up the difficulty by explaining that the nun-chaplain is a regular office in Benedictine convents.* And so the last difficulty in the *Prologue* disappears.

One quotation more from the Benedictine Rule will be of service in completing what I have pompously called a telescopic synthesis of Chaucer's Nuns in their environment. It is the rule on journeys. "Let the brethren who are about to be sent on a journey commend themselves to the prayers of all the brethren and of the Abbot, and at the last prayer of the Work of God let a commemoration always be made of the absent. (A custom still practiced in communities.) Let the brethren that return from a journey, on the very day that they come back, lie prostrate on the floor of the Oratory at all the Canonical Hours . . . and beg the prayers of all on account of their transgression, in case they should perchance upon the way have seen or heard anything harmful, or fallen into idle talk. And let no one presume to relate to another what he may have seen or heard outside the Monastery; for thence arise manifold evils." Chapter LXVII. This completes the portion of the Rule by which the Nuns in Chaucer and their conduct on the way to Canterbury should be judged. It is quoted to

* Furnivall, F. J., "Chaucer's Prioress's Nun-Chaplain," *Academy*, May 22, 1880, 385. Also in *Anglia*, IV, 238.

give some idea of the spirit in which a Prioress and her companion would undertake such a journey and what would be their responsibilities in regard to it. Nothing but a very urgent spiritual quest could have induced them to leave their cloister and join so worldly and public an excursion. It may be urged that the Rule was subject to many abuses, as no doubt it was, but nowhere does Chaucer give us any reason to think that his Nuns were of a tramp or derelict order; the reverence and courtesy of which he specifically says they were worthy is proof enough that he was depicting the typical "ninety-nine who need not penance" Sister rather than the well advertised one who does.

At the beginning of this study it was suggested that a fruitful and nearer-to-truth study of Chaucer's Nuns could be made by viewing them in the light of their rules, customs, and community prayers than by the measure of a social life that they had voluntarily abandoned. The Nuns as they appear in the *Prologue* are chiefly viewed from the outside; one sees them here as they have been molded and fashioned by their rule. That rule has been applied to every detail of their description and in most cases has yielded a more human, if not a different, understanding of them. Putting these parts together and viewing the united whole through the kindly telescope of our common human nature we get in the Nuns of Chaucer's *Prologue* more lovable characters and immeasurably finer creations than critical analysis shows us.

Hermann the Cripple

"PAIN IS NOT UNHAPPINESS"

1013–1054

BY

C. C. MARTINDALE

ST. AUGUSTINE DIED in 430, so that nearly six hundred years
went by before Hermann of Reichenau, of whom I am going
to speak, was born. Yet there is the queerest link between
them—a book, written before the birth of Christ, by the pagan
Roman Cicero, was read and re-read by St. Augustine, and was
a favourite of the little cripple Hermann. And now it is lost.
All *we* can do is to read scattered quotations from that book
Hortensius, written two thousand years ago, which lit visions
five hundred years later in the mind of the man who gave her
new soul to Europe, and that was so precious, on his death-bed,
to Hermann after another five hundred years.

On July 18th, 1013, a son was born to Wolfrad, Count of
Altshausen in Swabia, and his wife Hiltrud. They belonged to
gorgeous families, and noblemen, crusaders, and great prelates
provide names that jostle one another in those pedigrees. Yet
none of them do we remember, save the little fellow who was
born most horribly deformed. He was afterwards nicknamed
"Contracted," so hideously distorted was he; he could not
stand, let alone walk; could hardly sit, even in the special chair
they made for him; even his fingers were all but too weak and
knotted for him to write; even his mouth and palate were deformed and he could hardly be understood when he spoke. In
a pagan world he would, without argument, have been exposed,
at birth, to perish; modern pagans, especially when they ob-

From *What Are Saints?* by C. C. Martindale. Reprinted by permission of
the publisher, Sheed and Ward, New York and London.

serve that he was one of fifteen children, would announce that
he never should have been born; when they become still more
logical, they will announce that such an abortion should be
painlessly put out of the way. And twice over would they say
so, when I tell you that he appeared, to the judges of nine
hundred years ago, to be what we would call Defective. What
did these people, skulking in the murk of those "Dark Ages"
(as we have the steely nerve to call them) do? They sent him
to a monastery, and they prayed.

If you remember what I said about St. Anthony you will
recall that it was monasteries that took over what they could
from the ancient culture, and developed it. Into Germany,
that culture came not only from the Latin south, but by way
of England (St. Boniface of Devon) and most certainly from
Ireland. But it was popular. The rather hard Latin culture
was softened by charming elements from Germany. German
translations of the gospels were appearing; German sermons
were being preached; hardly a great name in Latin or Greek
literature but became known in this way, and always, need I
say, through those monasteries—like St. Gall, Fulda,
Reichenau—that formed vast libraries, and also schools that
moved about along with Emperors; indeed, Duke Bruno,
brother of the Emperor Otto I, did not disdain to act as professor; and, you may say, every student also taught. Would
that they did so, or could do so, now! Let me just add that
this was not a merely masculine culture. The nun Hrotswitha
of Gaudesheim had Otto's niece for abbess and as instructress
in the classics. Hrotswitha proceeded to write all sorts of
literature, including comedies, one of which has been quite
recently acted before an intensely interested audience in England.

To one such monastery the defective freak was sent.
Reichenau was on a lovely little island in Lake Constance
where the Rhine runs strong towards its cataracts. It had
existed before Charlemagne—for some two hundred years,
that is—by the high road on the shore opposite. Italian and
Greek, Irish and Icelandic travellers passed to and fro. It

sheltered famous scholars; it had its school of painting; tenth century paintings as at Oberzell, eleventh as at Niederzell, exist, made by monks with the heart, if not yet the hand, of Fra Angelico. Here the boy grew up. Here the lad that could hardly stammer with his tongue, found his mind developing under who knows what manner of religious psycho-therapy? Not once in his life can he have been "comfortable" or out of pain; yet what are the adjectives that cluster round him? I translate them from the Latin biography. Pleasant, friendly, easy to talk to; always laughing; never criticising; eagerly cheerful; trying as hard as possible to be—ah! here is a word I find difficult—to be "thoroughly decent" would be, I think, our equivalent. And the result was, that *"everybody loved him."* And meanwhile the courageous lad—never, remember, at his ease in a chair nor so much as flat in bed—learnt mathematics, Greek, Latin, Arabic, astronomy and music. He wrote a whole treatise upon Astrolabes. I believe that you found the Equator, or measured the height of the stars with astrolables. . . . In his preface he says: "Hermann, the leastest of Christ's poor ones, and of amateur philosophers the follower more slow than any donkey, yes, than snail . . ." has been persuaded by the prayers of "numbers of my friends" (yes, "everybody" liked him) to write this scientific treatise. He'd keep wriggling out of doing so, making all sorts of excuses, but really through his "lumpish laziness"; but at long last he offered to the friend to whom he dedicated his booklet at any rate the *theory* of the thing, and said that if he liked it he would work it out in practical detail later on.

And, would you believe it, with those twisted fingers the indomitable lad *made* astrolabes, and also clocks and musical instruments. Never conquered; never idle! And as for music —would that our modern choirs could read him! He says that a competent musician ought to be able to compose a reasonable tune, or anyway to judge it, and *finally,* to sing it. Most singers, says he, attend to the third point only, and never *think.* They sing, or rather howl, not realising that no one can sing properly if his thought is out of harmony with his voice. To such songsters loud voice is everything. This is worse than donkeys, who after all *do* make much more noise, but never mix up braying with bellowing. No one tolerates, says he, grammatical mistakes; yet the rules of grammar are artificial, whereas "music springs straight from Nature," and therein not only do men fail to correct their faults, but they actually defend them. . . . The jolly little cripple could use, when he wanted to, a rather caustic tongue! Yet it is practically certain that it was he who wrote the glorious hymn, *Salve Regina*, with its plain-chant melody, still used today all over the Catholic world, the *Alma Redemptoris*, and others. But besides this the active, vigorous brain of Hermann, who was not only in touch with every important family-tradition of that time, but in possession of many an ancient book now lost to us owing to the destruction of so many monastery libraries later on, wrote a *Chronicon*, or world-history from Christ's day to his own. Experts say that it was amazingly accurate, retailing, of course, tradition, yet objective and original. Here, then, you have the crippled monk in his cell, alert, eyes wide open to the outside world, yet never cynical, never cruel (so many sufferers grow cruel), but making a complete perspective of the currents of life in Europe.

Well, the time came to die. I leave his friend and historian Berthold to relate that. "When at last the loving kindliness of God was deigning to free his holy soul from the tedious prison of this world, he was attacked by pleurisy, and for ten days was almost all the time in agony. At last, one day, very early in the morning, after Mass, I, whom he counted his closest friend, went and asked him if he felt a little better. 'Do not ask me about that,' he answered; 'not about *that!* . . . . Listen carefully. I shall certainly die very soon. I shall not live; I shall not recover.' " And then he went on to say how during the night he had felt as if he were re-reading that *Hortensius* of Cicero's, with its wise sayings upon right and wrong, and all that he had himself meant to write upon the subject. "And under the strong inspiration of that reading, the whole of this present world and all that belongs to it—

yes, this mortal life itself has become mean and wearisome, and on the other hand, the world to come, that shall not pass, and that eternal life, have become so unspeakably desirable and dear, that I hold all these passing things as light as thistle-down. I am tired of 'living.' " Berthold, when Hermann spoke thus, broke down completely, and, says he, "uttered agitated cries and kept no proper control of myself." Hermann, after a while, "quite indignantly upbraided me, trembling, and looking at me sideways with puzzled eyes. 'Heart's beloved,' said he; 'Do not weep, do not weep for me.' " And he made Berthold take his writing-tablets and put down a few last things. "And," he added, "by remembering daily that you too are to die, prepare yourself with all your energy for the self-same journey, for, on some day and hour, you know not when, you shall follow me forth—me, your dear, dear friend." And on these words, he ceased.

Hermann died, after receiving the Body and Blood of Christ in Holy Communion, among all his friends, on September 24th, and was buried—hidden little monk as he had been—amid "great lamentation," in his own estate of Altshausen that he had given up so long ago.

When I first came across this "life" in a crabbed old Latin book at Oxford, I felt as if a wave of sweetest air were turning a stuffy room into freshness and fragrance. For the written Life is so very much alive—Hermann *lives* so vividly! Not just because he could write on the theory of music or mathematics, could compile laborious histories and knew so many languages, but because of his *pluck,* his fineness of soul, his gaiety in pain, his readiness to chaff and answer back, the sweetness of mood that made him "loved by all." And I beg of you to stand no nonsense from those who suggest that a sickly body produces a sickly mind, that it is on physical heftiness, body-breeding, that we should concentrate if we would have good citizens, or that physical well-being, though desirable, is in any sense whatsoever necessary for happiness. Vulgarest confusion of mind with nerves! Hardly one of those pedigrees of sickly and criminal families is worth anything at all. Hardly ever have the effects of environment upon the child or descendant of, say, two criminals, been disentangled from what is assumed to be their heredity. You are safe in doubting whether mental or moral characteristics *ever* are inherited. Proper bodily upbringing plays certainly its great but perfectly subordinate part; proper training for the mind plays a primary and enormous one—and this, believe me, must include as paramount two things—love and religion—and the two are intertwined. And in this twisted little fellow from the Dark Ages shines out the triumph of the Faith that inspired love, of the love that acted loyally by Faith, and Hermann provides the proof of how Pain does not spell Misery, nor Pleasure, Happiness.

8

THE CHURCH AND THE MODERN WORLD

There Are No Atheists

BY

JAMES M. GILLIS

THERE ARE NO atheists. At least no thinkers are atheists. "Freethinkers" rise to that bait more surely than a trout to the fly and snap at it more viciously. But it is equally axiomatic that freethinkers do not think freely. Proof? Well, suppose a freethinker thinks himself into religion. *Ipso facto* he is rated a renegade and apostate. He is free to think atheism, but not free to think theism.

Sometimes a freethinker lets the cat out of the bag. For example, John Stuart Mill says in his autobiography, "It would have been wholly inconsistent with my father's ideas of duty to allow me to acquire impressions contrary to his convictions and feelings respecting religion." So! Papa is a freethinker and Sonny must not think otherwise than Papa. The same phenomenon vastly magnified so that all may see it with the naked eye is now on exhibition in Russia. There indeed we have a World's Exposition of Freethought. Irreligion may be taught but not religion. That statement too makes the freethinkers' gorge rise, for oddly enough the breed is predominantly pro-Bolshevik. "Religion," they declare, "is not banned in Russia. A man may be religious if he will." Yes, be re-

From *The Catholic World,* CXXIV (Sept. 1934). Reprinted by permission of the Editor.

ligious and starve. He is free to think but if he thinks the wrong way, he dies. This is Liberty Hall. Here a man does what he pleases. And if he doesn't we make him. Stalin and Co. now do the thinking for the Russian people more tyrannically than the Czar or the Patriarch in the old Orthodox days. Under the Church a professor or a general or a diplomat could be an avowed unbeliever and hold his job. Under the Soviets, no one in office may go to Mass, pay pew rent or even make the sign of the Cross—visibly. It is ever thus. There is no freedom under Freethought.

But let us get back to the primary proposition: no thinker is an atheist. Herbert Spencer said atheism is "unthinkable." True, he also said that theism is unthinkable. In particular he said God is unthinkable. But thereupon he proceeded to do a great deal of thinking about the Unthinkable. Before he finished thinking, he had enumerated the attributes of God as confidently and as completely as St. Thomas Aquinas. . . .

These remarks are by way of preliminary to the declaration that I have recently read a wise and eloquent volume that is to all intents and purposes a commentary upon the text, "No thinker is an atheist." It might be called an elaboration of the equally familiar statement of Lord Kelvin that he had investigated a great many ostensibly atheistic systems of thought and had always found a god of some sort concealed somewhere. *The Unknown God* by Alfred Noyes is packed with profound and searching thought beautifully and stirringly expressed. Its author, one of the leading poets of our time, turns out to have been a philosopher from his very teens. Indeed so successful is he in the role of the philosopher that I rather think his prose—a beautiful, sensitive, imaginative, virile prose—may surpass his poetry in survival value, as, conversely, Chesterton's poetry will probably outlive his prose.

In *The Unknown God* Mr. Noyes reveals and comments upon many startling passages from the works of recognized agnostics and reputed atheists in evidence of God—not merely "a god of some sort," as Lord Kelvin says, but substantially and essentially the orthodox God, the God of Catholic

theology, the God of St. Augustine and St. Thomas Aquinas.
Mr. Noyes was an agnostic and is a Catholic. He came
from Agnosticism to Catholicism not like Chesterton by revul-
sion from the inanities and absurdities of "liberal" thought,
but by following hints and clues that he found in his agnostic
authors. He has read widely and deeply—so deeply that he
has dug up many a passage that had been buried—perhaps
purposely buried—in Huxley, Darwin, Tyndall, Spencer,
Swinburne, Thomas Hardy, Spinoza, Helmholtz and a dozen
others generally thought to be anti-theological, anti-Christian
and anti-theistic. He read the agnostics as an agnostic,
sympathetically. One and all they had their part in leading
him to Catholicism. It is a novel and interesting narrative.

Take Darwin, who though himself no philosopher was the
inspiration of Huxley, Spencer and a hundred other more
recent evolutionistic thinkers. Mr. Noyes evidently has read
his Darwin. Of not many contemporaries can that be said.
The Origin of Species and *The Descent of Man* are, I suspect,
no more read than Newton's *Principia* or Calvin's *Institutes.*
Every one says, "Oh, yes, Darwin!" just as they say, "Oh, yes,
Don Quixote!" But who reads the one or the other? But
Alfred Noyes used Darwin's *Origin of Species* as an outdoor
book, a companion of his recreational rambles as an amateur
naturalist. I for one never knew there could be such a Darwinian in our day. Well, knowing Darwin intimately, Mr. Noyes
quotes from *The Descent of Man* a passage which he thinks
Darwin's "friends and enemies have both forgotten to read."
Darwin says of the evolutionistic process, "This grand se-
quence of events the mind refuses to accept as the result of
blind chance. The understanding revolts from such a conclusion." None the less atheistic evolution *must* accept blind
chance. The only thinkable substitute for blind chance is a
Superintending Intelligence. But once an Intelligent Directing
Power is admitted you have God. For as St. Thomas Aquinas
says, "We see that things which lack intelligence nevertheless
act for an end not fortuitously but designedly. Now whatever
lacks intelligence cannot move towards an end unless it be

directed by some being endowed with knowledge and intelligence. And this Being we call God."

There is many a hard nut for the professed atheist to crack.
And here is the first one on which he may sharpen his teeth—
or more likely break them: "the understanding revolts from
blind chance"; very well, if not blind chance, what? Any
alternative will be as Aquinas says "What we call God." It
is entertaining as well as enlightening to find Charles Darwin
and Thomas Aquinas expressing the same truth, one negatively
and by implication, the other positively and directly.

Darwin, as we have said, and as all the world admits, was
no philosopher. He was not even a logician, that is to say a
close and relentless reasoner. If he had been, he would have
followed his own lead. "If not blind chance, what then?"
Pursuing one "And then?" to another "And then?" he would
have come to "What we call God." Darwin with what he
thought intellectual humility, said "Into these questions we
cannot enter." But reason like *das ewige weiblich zieht uns
hinan,* or like the gadfly it bids us "nor sit nor stand but go."
When reason urges us on it is not humble to refuse to follow.
And if we follow reason we end with God. We need no theologian from the Middle Ages to return and tell us that.
Socrates was no Scholastic, nor Aristotle, nor Seneca, nor Mar-
cus Aurelius. For that matter neither was Francis Bacon who
is called—perhaps inaccurately—"the father of modern
science." He said he "would rather believe all the miracles
in the Koran than believe that this universal frame had no
Maker." Belief in the absurd yarns of the Koran is not more
superstitious than the acceptance of blind chance. Between
the devil of chance and the deep sea of God a true scientist
will not hesitate. He cannot choose chance, for chance means
accident, and the first article in the creed of the scientist is that
there is no accident in nature. So the horns of Darwin's
Dilemma were Blind Chance and God. His understanding
revolted from Blind Chance, but he could not bring Himself
to speak the Immemorial Word. . . .

In Alfred Noyes' youth (I am still following him, though

reserving my liberty to wander considerably), Spencer loomed large. Noyes, like every one else in those days read him, but unlike almost every one else, Noyes got out of Spencer much that he afterwards discovered had been said by St. Thomas Aquinas. The casual reader may be tempted to think that Noyes' discovery of the Catholic hidden away in the agnostic is a mistake or a trick. But in spite of Spencer's familiar declarations that God is the Great Unthinkable he has made an amazingly complete and accurate assemblage of the attributes of God. He reasons thus: first there must be a cause of impressions produced in what we see, hear, taste and smell: a possible cause may be matter, but matter on the other hand may be only a mode of manifestation of spirit: in that case not matter but spirit is the true cause of sensation. Or matter and spirit may both be only "proximate agencies." If so, some first cause must lie behind them. Spencer even uses capitals for the First Cause, says it is "impossible to consider it as finite" and therefore "it must be infinite." That would suffice for us. "Infinite First Cause" is a fairly complete designation for God—indeed surprisingly complete for an agnostic who professes to know nothing about God. But the Darwinian philosopher goes on. "The First Cause must be independent. It exists in the absence of all other existence. It must be in every sense perfect, including within itself all power and transcending all law." And he concludes, "To use the established word, it must be Absolute." Noyes adds with wit and point: "To use the even more firmly established word, it must be God."

Even yet, however, Spencer is not done with his amazing asseverations—amazing I mean from an agnostic. In his stilted way, he says that the existence of the transcendent Absolute is "a necessary datum of consciousness." More simply and more epigrammatically he might have said that the fact of our thinking proves God. That goes further of course than Descartes' *Cogito ergo sum*. It approaches Newman's "two luminously self-evident beings—God and my soul."

Finally, as if to give the lie to his own agnosticism, Spencer says "the belief which this datum constitutes has a higher warrant than any other whatever," and that in "this assertion of a Reality utterly inscrutable in its nature, Religion finds an assertion essentially coinciding with her own." If I may venture yet once again to take some of the starch out of these stiff sentences, I think he means, "Nothing else is so well warranted as the fact of God's existence" and "In supplying this warrant philosophy plays into the hands of religion." But that too had been said by the Scholastics, *Philosophia ancilla theologiae:* Philosophy is the handmaid of theology.

For those who don't see the immediate logical connection between the statements "I think" or "I am" and the statement "God exists," it might be well to ask Spencer's question, "Why should there have been anything at all?" [Without God there could have been nothing at all. I have sometimes amused myself by setting this little problem to over-militant atheists: explain the origin of the world without a World Maker. If you manage that, try another: Explain the origin of life without a Life Giver. A third stickler might well be the one suggested by Spencer, Descartes, Newman and Aquinas: "If there be no First Thinker, how could anyone think?" Talk about making bricks without straw—atheism tries to make bricks without straw or clay or a brickmaker.

And here, if you please, we may pause for a little paragraph on what Noyes calls "extracting plus from minus," or "explaining everything by something less than itself." He puts it in verse:

> But men still trace the greater to the less,
> Account for soul with flesh and dreams with dust.

The supreme example of this impossible mental legerdemain was the attempt to explain the universe and all in it by supposing the aboriginal existence of a Nebula. There we have one more preposterous substitute for God—Bias, Bathybius, Nebula. For if Nebula made Nebula, Nebula is God. But if something back of Nebula made Nebula, that Something back of Nebula is God. I may twist and turn and double on my track, I may, as Francis Thompson says, "Flee Him down the labyrinthine ways of my own mind," but if I think at all I cannot escape God. "Whither shall I go from Thy Spirit? or whither shall I flee from Thy presence? If I ascend up into heaven, Thou art there; if I make my bed in hell, behold, Thou art there. If I take the wings of the morning, and dwell in the uttermost parts of the sea, even there shall Thy hand lead me, and Thy right hand shall hold me." "Perhaps the darkness will cover me," but though I create a darkness with large heavy philosophical words, "The Unknowable," "The Ultimate," "The Absolute," "The Transcendent" even "The Hidden Synthesis of Contradictions," or the "Resolution of Antinomies," it is all God. I cannot escape Him. I cannot escape Him in heaven or hell, in the uttermost parts of the earth, or in the mystic maze of my own mind. And so, I cannot hide from Him even behind the smoke-screen of the Nebula. Of the Nebular Hypothesis, Tyndall (of the Evolutionistic trinity—Darwin, Huxley and Tyndall) declared with scorn, "Strip it naked and you stand face to face with the notion that not alone the more ignoble forms of animalcular or animal life, not alone the nobler forms of the horse and lion, not alone the exquisite and wonderful mechanism of the human body, but that the human mind itself, emotion, intellect, will and all their phenomena—were once latent in a fiery cloud. Surely the mere statement of such a notion is more than a refutation."

"It is nothing of the kind," says Noyes, defending Huxley against his teammate Tyndall! But Tyndall had at least apparently good reason for scorn. For Huxley had spoken with sympathy of the proposition "that the whole world, living and not living, is the result of the mutual interaction, according to definite laws, of the forces possessed by the molecules of which the primitive nebulosity of the universe was composed. If this be true, it is no less certain that the existing world lay, potentially, in the cosmic vapour; and that a sufficient intelligence could, from a knowledge of the properties of the molecules of that vapour, have predicted, say, the state of the fauna in Britain in 1869, with as much certainty as one can say what will happen to the vapour of the breath on a cold winter's day."

I confess I am malicious enough to enjoy seeing one leading agnostic scientist of the nineteenth century calling his *confrère* an ass, and it does seem almost a pity that a Catholic should intervene and explain that Huxley and Tyndall were not contradicting one another, but that their statements require coordination. Still I suppose we can afford to be generous. We can get fun enough watching them both squirm away from the main question—Whence comes these "definite laws" and these "forces possessed by molecules," this "primitive nebulosity" of which the universe is composed? Composed, did you say? And was it composed without a Composer?

Once more we fall back on the never-failing common sense of Thomas Aquinas, "Whatever lacks intelligence cannot move to an end unless it be directed by some Being endowed with intelligence." The *perennial philosophy* is perennial because it is the philosophy of all normal sensible persons. And no normal sensible person believes that the flora and fauna, to say nothing of the humana, of Britain in 1869 came out of a fiery cloud of incalculable æons ago, without a Superintending Intelligence. Only in Atheism does the spring rise higher than the source, the effect exist without the cause, life come from a stone, blood from a turnip, a silk purse from a sow's ear, a Beethoven Symphony or a Bach Fugue from a kitten's walking across the keys.

In comparison with these prodigies, the ridiculous miracles of the Koran would be reasonable. *O vous incrédules,* says Pascal, *les plus crédules!* Unbelievers believe more than believers, and on less evidence. "Skeptical as I am," said Voltaire, "I declare such to be evident madness," speaking of some silly theory broached in his day to explain plus by minus and produce something out of nothing. No wonder he couldn't be an Atheist. . . .

Christian Freedom

BY

CHRISTOPHER DAWSON

AMONG SO MANY fundamental things that are being called in question by the present world crisis none is more important than the issue of religious freedom. No one can doubt it is in danger today in many countries and from many causes, and it is an urgent necessity that all Christians should become fully conscious of the changed situation. In this country and in America it is, perhaps, exceptionally difficult to do so, because religious freedom has been accepted for so long as a matter of course that it has become commonplace. It may even be felt that we have had too much of it, as we have had too much economic freedom, so that it is responsible for the loss of a clear sense of objective spiritual truth. But religious freedom is not the same thing as spiritual disorder, and, as the Pope has said in his Jubilee address a few weeks ago, the danger to religious freedom is at the same time a call to Christian unity.

It is no longer possible to defend religious freedom on the basis of nineteenth-century individualism and spiritual *laissez-faire*—a basis which was, in fact, never acceptable to Catholic tradition. What is at stake is the very existence of Christianity in a world hostile to Christ. "The new conditions have nothing in common with the learned controversies of the past"; they are like those which the early Church had to face, so that "today Christians are being reproached for the same offences against the law as those for which Peter and Paul were reproached by the Cæsars of the first century.*

At first sight it seems as though the conditions under which

From *The Dublin Review*, CVI (July, 1942). Reprinted by permission of the author and the proprietors of *The Sword of the Spirit*.

* Broadcast of Pius XII on 12 May, 1942.

the Church existed at that period made any kind of religious freedom impossible. But in fact this was not so. By a spiritual law of compensation the external pressure of persecution and proscription strengthened the sense of interior liberation and spiritual freedom which was so characteristic of primitive Christianity. For freedom is not something exterior to religion—in a profound sense *Christianity is freedom,* and the words which have become canonized and set apart as the classical terms of Christian theology—redemption, salvation, ἀπολύίδωσις, ἐξαγοδίζειν, σωιηδία—possessed for their original hearers the simple and immediate sense of the delivery of a slave and the release of a captive.

It is difficult to exaggerate the importance of the concepts of freedom and slavery in the thought of the ancient world. The society of the ancient world was built on the institution of slavery, as that of the modern world is built on capital and labour, and the wars and confiscations of the first century B.C. had both increased its extent and destroyed its traditional character, so that men of education and culture, the very opposite of Aristotle's "natural slaves," might find themselves reduced by some accident of world politics to a state of subhuman rightlessness. And behind this condition of personal servitude, which was the framework of social life, there were the traditions of corporate national servitude which formed Jewish thought in a pattern of social dualism.

The two cities—Babylon and Jerusalem—were the archetypes of this spiritual tradition; on the one hand, the predatory world empire or slave state which was the embodiment of human pride and power, on the other the holy community which was the representative of God's purpose in the world and the guardian of the Divine Law. For centuries the holy community had been a captive and an exile under the hard yoke of successive world empires, and the whole spiritual energy of Israel was concentrated on the hope of deliverance, the return of the exiles from their captivity and the coming of the Kingdom of God and of His people.

The Gospel of Christ was essentially the good news of the

coming of the Kingdom, but at the same time it raised the whole idea of redemption and deliverance to a new plane. It was no longer a question of national deliverance by the establishment of a social or political theocracy. It was the reversal of a universal cosmic process which had reduced the whole human race to a state of slavery. It was a moral deliverance, but it was also much more than that. We are so accustomed to the traditional Christian terminology of sin and redemption that we are apt to forget what these words meant to the early Christians. For to them sin was not simply unethical behaviour, it was a real state of slavery to powers outside humanity and stronger than man, the spiritual forces of evil which were the rulers of this dark age.

Modern writers, like Schweitzer and Warneck, have described almost precisely the same conceptions and the same psychological attitude among converts from paganism in the world today. The latter writes: "The insurmountable wall that rises up between the heathen and God is not sin, as among ourselves; it is the kingdom of darkness in which they are bound. That bondage shows itself in the fear that surrounds them: fear of souls, fear of spirits, fear of human enemies and magicians. The Gospel comes to unloose these bonds. It stands forth before their eyes as a delivering power, a redemption."

Thus humanity left to its own resources has no freedom and no power to free itself. It is involved in a progressive state of disorder which is at once physical and metaphysical, moral, social and political. This is quite a different conception from the Calvinist doctrine of the total depravity and reprobation of human nature, though the latter, of course, based itself on the same literary tradition and made use of the same theological language. But the view of the New Testament is based on a vision of a cosmic situation, while that of the Reformers is a theological theory based on *a priori* reasoning. The solidarity of mankind under the reign of evil is not an abstraction, it is a fact of experience, which has been recognized by philosophers and religious thinkers of every age from the time of Buddha to our own days. To quote a modern example, Tolstoy writes: "People bound together by a delusion form as it were a collective cohesive mass. The cohesion of that mass is the evil of the world. All the spiritual activity of humanity is directed towards the destruction of this cohesion. All revolutions are attempts to break up that mass by violence. It seems to people that if they break up that mass, it will cease to be a mass; and therefore they strike at it; but by trying to break it, they only force it closer. The cohesion of the particles is not destroyed, until the inner form passes from the mass to the particles and obliges them to separate from it."

Now the Gospel is the record of the dramatic irruption of Divine power into this closed order. "Now is the judgement of the world; now shall the prince of this world be cast out" (John xii, 31). The prince of this world is like a strong man guarding his house by force of arms, until a stronger than he comes and conquers him and takes away the armaments in which he put his trust (John xi, 21-2). Thus the Redemption is the turning-point in the history of humanity and inaugurates a vital process of liberation which is destined to integrate humanity in a new spiritual solidarity. The old world remains, superficially its power and its cohesion are unaffected, but under the surface a new vital process is at work, and men have only to adhere to this new principle of life to be freed from the immense and complicated burden of hereditary evil and to be reborn. "Therefore if any man be in Christ, he is a new creature. Old things are passed away. Behold all things have become new" (2 Cor. v). "Awake thou that sleepest and arise from the dead and Christ shall shine upon thee."

It was from this total psychological point of view that the Christian of the first century conceived the idea of freedom. Freedom was inseparable from Redemption. It was something entirely independent of external circumstances, a divine gift which the powers of this world could not limit or destroy. "If the Son shall make you free, you are free indeed." "Where the Spirit of God is, there is freedom."

Yet, on the other hand, it was also power. It flowed forth into the world, creating a new bond of community and overcoming the physical and social barriers that stood in its way, so that even fundamental differences of race and class and personal status were transcended and appeared insignificant. It was, in fact, a new kind of freedom that was entirely different from the civic freedom of the Greek city state which had been the dominant social ideal of the ancient world, though it sometimes made use of the same terminology. Nevertheless it was undoubtedly an effective freedom, something which really delivered men from real evils and servitudes and which transformed man and society, more completely than any political revolution has ever done.

Christian freedom entered the world as something Divine and miraculous. "The blind see, the lepers are cleansed, the poor have the Gospel preached to them." It is essentially theocentric—God-given and in no way dependent on human rights or human powers. It is an emancipation from the servitudes that seem to be the natural condition of human nature and an admission into the glorious liberty of the children of God. Yet it does not mean a withdrawal from social and physical reality like Buddhist asceticism and Neoplatonic mysticism which were also conceived as ways of deliverance. It was essentially a world-transforming power, and it manifested this power from the beginning in the creation of a new community and new forms of social action. Never, in fact, have individual and social consciousness been more completely identified than in the early Church. Christian freedom was from the beginning embodied in the life of a community, and the individual could only possess it in fellowship as a member of the new society which was more than a society, since it was a true spiritual organism, the divine body of the new humanity.

Nevertheless in spite of its mystical and transcendental aspects this society was conceived as the continuation and fulfilment of the Jewish community. In the ancient Paschal liturgy, the Church prays that "all the nations of the world may become the children of Abraham and partakers of the dignity of Israel," and in fact the historic vicissitudes of this particular people became the archetypes of Christian spiritual experience. The consequence of this is that every Christian people possesses a double tradition and a double citizenship, and this duality is reflected in the Western conception of freedom, which even in its most secular form depends half-consciously on spiritual values that belong to the common inheritance of Israel and Christendom.

This inheritance of the tradition of Israel with its consciousness of social continuity and separateness was, however, combined with a sense of liberation from tradition which finds such a clear and even revolutionary expression in St. Paul's attitude to the Law. There has never been a more drastic indictment of religious traditionalism in its external negative and repressive aspects than that of St. Paul. Nothing that modern rationalists and humanists have said about religion as the enemy of freedom is stronger than St. Paul's picture of the miserable state of humanity labouring under the bondage of the Law. "The yoke which neither our fathers nor we were able to bear." Even the high spiritual vocation of Israel did not save the chosen people from this bondage. They were the children of Agar the slave woman who was the archetype of Jerusalem "that now is, and is in slavery with her children. But Jerusalem which is above is free, which is our mother. We are not the children of the slave, but of the free, by the freedom wherewith Christ has made us free."

But to St. Paul the Law was not merely the yoke that enslaves, it was also the barrier that divided the Jews from the rest of humanity. The Jews, though under the Law, had their privileged position as the people of God. The Gentiles were free from the Law, but they were left without God and without spiritual hope. The great fact of the redemption was the breaking down of this barrier and the uniting of the two peoples in the unity of spiritual freedom. "For Christ is our peace who made both one and broke down the middle wall of partition . . . in order to create in himself of the two One New Man." Therefore the Gentiles were no longer foreigners

and exiles, but fellow citizens with the saints and of the household of God. One living temple founded on Christ, and built
up by the apostles and prophets as a house for God in the
Spirit.

Christian freedom has its beginning and end in this creative
act of redemption and reconciliation. It is not the creation of
human power and will, but the birthright of the Christian as
child of God, reborn in Christ and vivified by the spirit. It is
therefore a much more fundamental thing than what we commonly understand by religious freedom. In modern times
Christian freedom has usually been considered in reference
either to the freedom of the individual conscience against external compulsion or to the freedom of the Christian community—the Church—against the state. But the first freedom
from which these are derivative and dependent is the freedom
of the Spirit—the new creation which changes man's nature
and liberates him from the state of psychological and moral
bondage to the world and the forces that rule the world.

Now this essential spiritual freedom can be expressed in two
ways—intellectually as the result of the enlightenment of
divine truth—"you shall hear the truth and the truth shall
make you free"—or vitally as the communication of divine
life—a new birth which transforms human nature by the in-
fusion of the Spirit.

This twofold relation is especially clearly marked in the
Johannine writings. Both the Gospel and the First Epistle of
St. John equally insist that the communication of Divine Life
is made at once by the hearing of a Word and by the society
of a Person, and Word and Person were substantially one.

That which was from the beginning, which we have heard, which
we have seen with our eyes, which we have looked upon and our hands
have handled of the Word of life. . . .

That which we have seen and have heard we declare unto you that
you also may have fellowship with us, and our fellowship may be with
the Father and with His Son Jesus Christ.

The true freedom of the world—the only freedom that can

free man in the depths of his personality—depends on keeping open the channel of revelation, preserving the Word of Truth and communicating the Spirit of Life. These are the essential Christian freedoms, and it for this that the Christian Church as a visible institution exists. If the channel becomes choked or the bridge broken, the world falls back into darkness and chaos and humanity once more becomes bound in that state of slavery which the ancient world saw as an impersonal chain of necessity but which Christian tradition conceived in terms of active personal evil as the Kingdom of Satan.

It is this wholesale loss of spiritual freedom that is the real danger that faces the world today. The plain fact which we see displayed before our eyes is that the power of man has grown so great that it has denied and shut out the power of the Spirit and that consequently it is destroying the world. We have seen how the new totalitarian orders all tend to become closed orders—spiritual as well as economic autarchies which leave no room for true Christian freedom. And we have no reason to suppose that a new democratic order which bases itself on the ideals of technocracy and economic planning would be fundamentally different in this respect, even though it avoids the grosser evils of the existing totalitarian systems. In so far as this is so, all these new orders are orders of death.

In face of this great danger Christianity still stands as the hope of the world. It is true that Christendom is weakened and divided. At first sight it seems like a valley of dry bones, the dry bones of dead controversies and moribund traditions, since Christians are more tied to the dead past, more dependent on antiquated modes of thought, more wedded to the old social and political order than the rest of the world. There is hardly a social abuse or an intellectual fallacy that has not found its stoutest defenders in the ranks of Christian orthodoxy. Nevertheless, in spite of all this, Christianity is still a living force in the modern world. It has still the promise of new life and spiritual freedom as at the beginning. It may be difficult to see how this promise is to be realized under modern conditions. In fact if we could foresee the future of Christendom and plan out exactly what was to be done, we should be missing the essential nature of Christian freedom. What we can say, however, is that the nature of the new forces that threaten to enslave humanity will inevitably tend to make both Christians and non-Christians conscious of the essential truths of faith and spiritual reality on which the Church stands. The rise of the new totalitarian systems and ideologies is a religious as well as a political revolution. It destroys the traditional division of life into separate secular and religious spheres. It attempts to unify human life and to organize the total psychic and material energies of the community for common ends. And consequently it marks the end of the four centuries of religious development which followed the Reformation—a a period that was characterized by the progressive individualization of consciousness, by religious separation and division and by the identification of spiritual freedom with religious individualism. The totalitarian revolution reverses this tendency and leaves no room for any kind of individualism, either secular or religious.

But it goes further than that and attacks spiritual freedom itself. It is therefore vital that Christians should not allow themselves to become confused and divided on this fundamental issue. Christians are agreed that the spiritual anarchy of unbridled individualism is contrary to the whole Christian tradition of faith and order, however much they may differ in their definitions. But on the other hand they must be still more united in defending the vital principles of Christian freedom which is the fundamental law of spiritual action. For what we are defending are not only man's rights but the rights of God. If the channels are closed by which the word of Christ and the power of the Spirit are communicated to man corporately and individually, the world must fall back into the state of darkness and slavery which Christ came to destroy. It is, of course, true that the opposition and conflict between the Two Cities runs through the whole of human history, but hitherto a limit has been set to it by the limitation of human power and knowledge. But today the scientific development of the techniques of social control have created a new situation in which for the first time in history it has become possible to make the human soul itself a cog in the mechanism of planned organization. This is the challenge that Christians have to face today, and they can do so only by returning to the foundations—the organic principles of spiritual life and spiritual freedom which are the laws of the Church's life.

War and Loyalty

BY

ORESTES BROWNSON

. . . IN ASSERTING THAT war is not necessarily unlawful, we are far from pretending that all wars are just, or that war may ever be waged for slight and trivial offences. The nation is bound studiously to avoid it, to forbear till forbearance ceases to be a virtue, and appeal to arms only as the last resort, after all other appeals have failed, or it is morally certain that they must fail. But when its rights are seriously invaded, when the offender will not listen to reason, and continues his injustice, the nation may appeal to arms, and commit its cause to the God of battles. The responsibility of the appeal rests on the offender whose injustice has provoked it.

It may be said that war is unjustifiable, because, if all would practise justice, there could be no war. Undoubtedly, if all men and nations were wise and just, wars would cease. We might then, in very deed, "beat our swords into ploughshares and our spears into pruning-hooks," and learn war no more. We should, not in vision only, but in reality, possess universal peace. So, if all individuals understood and practised the

From *Essays and Reviews*.

moral and Christian virtues in their perfection, there would be no need for penal codes, and a police to enforce them. If no wrongs or outrages were committed, there would be none to be repressed or punished. If there were no diseases, there would be none to cure. If the world would be quite another world than it is, it—would be. But so long as the world is what it is, so long as man fails to respect the rights of man, the penal code and police will be necessary; so long as diseases obtain, the physician and his drugs, nauseous as they are, will be indispensable; and so long as nation continues to encroach on nation, the aggrieved party will have the right and be compelled to defend and avenge itself by an appeal to arms, terrible as that appeal may be, and deplorable as may be the necessity which demands it.

The evils of war are great, but not the greatest. It is a greater evil to lose national freedom, to become the tributaries or the slaves of the foreigner, to see the sanctity of our homes invaded, our altars desecrated, and our wives and children made the prey of the ruthless oppressor. These are evils which do not die with us, but may descend upon our posterity through all coming generations. The man who will look tamely on and see altars and homes defiled, all that is sacred and dear wrested from him, and his country stricken from the roll of nations, has as little reason to applaud himself for his morals as for his manhood. No doubt, philanthropy may weep over the wounded and the dying; but it is no great evil to die. It is appointed unto all men to die, and, so far as the death itself is concerned, it matters not whether it comes a few months earlier or a few months later, on the battlefield or in our own bed-chambers. The evil is not in dying, but in dying unprepared. If prepared—and the soldier, fighting by command of his country in her cause, *may* be prepared—it is of little consequence whether the death come in the shape of sabre-cut or leaden bullet, or in that of disease or old age. The tears of the sentimentalist are lost upon him who is conscious of his responsibilities, that he is commanded to place duty before death, and to weigh no danger against fidelity to his God and his country. Physical pain is not worth counting. Accumulate all that you can imagine, the Christian greets it with joy when it lies in the pathway of his duty. He who cannot take his life in his hand, and, pausing not for an instant before the accumulated tortures of years, rush in, at the call of duty, where "blows fall thickest, and blows fall heaviest," deserves rebuke for his moral weakness, rather than commendation for his "peaceable dispositions."

Wars, we have been told, cost money; and we have among us men piquing themselves on their lofty spiritual views, accusing the age of being low and utilitarian, and setting themselves up as moral and religious reformers, who can sit calmly down and cast up in dollars and cents the expense of war, and point to the amount as an unanswerable argument against its lawfulness. War unquestionably costs money, and so do food and clothing. But the sums expended in war would, if applied to that purpose, found so many schools and universities, and educate so many children! The amount expended for food and clothing would found a larger number of schools and universities, and educate a larger number of children. You should ask, not, Will it cost money? but, Is it necessary, is it just? Would you weigh gold in the balance with duty, justice, patriotism, heroism? If so, slink back to your tribe, and never aspire to the dignity of being contemptible.

The Conspiracy Against Life

BY

FULTON J. SHEEN

THE CHRISTIAN ORDER demands the restoration of those areas of life which are life-growing, life-sustaining, and life-forwarding, *viz.*: the family. As from the impoverishment of cells in the body there flows the tragedy of death, so from the disintegration of the family there springs and spreads the dry-rot of the body-politic, the nation and the world. As the family is the school of sacrifice wherein we first learn to bear each other's burdens, so the decay of the family is the unlearning of those sacrifices which bring on the decay of a nation as it faces the miseries and horrors of life.

That the family is disintegrating in our national life, no one will deny. The modern husband and wife, like isolated atoms, resent the suggestions that they should lose their identity in the family molecule. It is each for himself as against all for one and one for all. And when there is an offspring, never before have children been so distant and so separated from their parents. The family hardly ever meets. The family that once had permanent headquarters, now has none, as the mother assumes she contributes more to the nation by making bullets than by raising babies. About the only time the family meets is after midnight, when the home becomes a hotel, and the more money they have the less they meet. Less time is passed together than is spent at a motion picture, or a beauty parlor. Courtship takes place outside the home, generally in a crowded room with a low ceiling, amidst suffocating smoke, while listening to a tom-tom orchestra glamoured by a girl who invariably

From *Philosophies at War,* by Fulton J. Sheen. Reprinted by arrangement with the publishers, Charles Scribner's Sons, New York, and Blandford Press, Ltd., London.

cannot sing. The wife listens to radio serials with their moans, groans and commercials, wherein triangles are more common than in a geometry book. She reads magazine articles by women who never stay at home, saying that a woman's place is in the home. The family Bible recording dates of birth and baptism is no longer existent because few read the Bible, few give birth, and few are ever baptised. The intelligentsia love to read George Bernard Shaw on the family: "Unless woman repudiates her womanliness, her duty to her husband, to her children, to everyone but herself, she cannot emancipate herself." And as for Catholics there is hardly a Catholic man or woman in the United States today over fifty years of age who cannot remember that in the days of his or her youth the rosary was said every evening in the family circle and everyone was there. How many do it now?

The two most evident symptoms of the breakdown of the family are: divorce and voluntary or deliberate sterility, *i.e.,* broken contracts and frustrated loves. Divorce destroys the stability of the family; voluntary sterility destroys its continuity. Divorce makes the right of living souls hang up the caprice of the senses and the terminable pact of selfish fancy; while voluntary sterility makes a covenant with death, extracting from love its most ephemeral gift while disclaiming all its responsibilities. It is a great conspiracy against life in which science, which should minister to life, is used as it is in war —to frustrate and destroy; it is a selfishness which is directed neither to saving nor to earning, but only to spending; it is an egotism, which because it admits of no self-control, seeks to control even the gifts of God; it sees sex not as something to solder life, but to scorch the flesh; it is a denial that life is a loan from the great bank of life and must be paid back again with the interest of life, and not with death.

It is a world wherein musicians are always picking up their bows and violins, but never making music; a world wherein chisel is touched to marble, but a statue is never created; a world where brush is lifted to canvas, but a portrait is never born; a world wherein talents are buried in a napkin as life plays recreant to its sacred messiahship. It is therefore a world wherein the thirst for love is never satisfied for never will they who break the lute snare the music.

We as Christians have argued with those who believe in divorce and the mechanical frustration of love, but our arguments convinced no one. Not because the arguments were not sound. That is the trouble. They are too good! Good reasons are powerless against emotions. Like two women arguing over back fences, we are arguing from different premises. The majority of people who are opposed to the stability and continuity of family life, for the most part do not believe in the moral law of God. They may say they believe in God, but it is not the God of Justice. Few believe in a future life, entailing Divine Judgment, with the possible sanction of eternal punishment. Even professed Christians among them when confronted with the text: "What therefore God hath joined together, let no man put asunder" (Mark 10:9), will retort that God never intended that it should be so.

They argue from the need of pleasure, the necessity of avoiding sacrifice, and the primacy of the economic. We argue from the Eternal Reason of God rooted in nature, the teachings of His Incarnate Son, Jesus Christ the Redeemer of the world.

There is absolutely no common denominator between us. It is like trying to convince a blind man that there are seven colors in a spectrum, or like arguing with a snob that a ditch-digger is his equal.

Instead then of arguing against the modern pagan who believes in the disruption of the family, let us assume that his premises are right, namely, man is only an animal; that morality is self-interest; that if there is a God, he never intended that we should not do as we please, that every individual is his own standard of right and wrong; that the amount of wealth one has must be the determinant of the incarnations of mutual love; that when we die that is the end of us, or if there be a heaven we all go there independently of how we conduct ourselves in life.

Now, once you start with these principles, then certainly divorces are right; then certainly avoid children; then certainly shirk sacrifices. If we are only beasts, and love is sex, then there is no reason why anyone should assume responsibility.

But why not go all the way? By the same principle anything is right if I can get away with it. If the bonds between husband and wife are revocable at will and for the advantage of self-love, why should not the treaties between nation and nation be revocable at the will of either partner? If a husband may steal the wife of another man, why should not Germany steal Poland? If the possession of a series of lust-satisfying partners is the right of man, why should not the possession of a series of slave colonies be the right of a nation? If John Smith can break his treaty to take Mary Jones until death, who shall say Italy is wrong in breaking its treaties with Ethiopia, or that Japan is wrong in seizing Manchuria? If this life is all, if there is no Moral Order dependent on God, then any man is a fool for being true to his contract.

Why not do away with all business credit? Why should the government pay us for the bonds we buy? Why should we not repudiate our loyalty and trust? What guarantee have we of credit, when the most vital of all compacts can be "sworn" with reservations? Why should not international treaties be like marriage treaties: "not worth the paper they are written on?"

If divorces from marital contracts, why not divorces from international contracts? If in domestic society moderns sneer at marital fidelity as "bourgeois virtue," what right have they to ask that "bourgeois virtue" should be recognized in world society? "If the trumpet give forth an uncertain sound who shall prepare for battle?"

If the economic is primary to the human, then why should not the capitalist be more interested in profits, than in the right of subsistence of his workers; then why not artificially limit children for the sake of the economic and the financial? If a man outgrows his clothes why should he not starve himself;

if he lacks bread, why should he not pull out his teeth; if there is not enough room on a ship, why not like mutineers at sea throw sleeping comrades to the sharks? In each case it is the same principle: the primacy of the economic over the human.

We are at war with Hitler because he makes the human secondary to the racial. What is so different to making the human secondary to the economic? If Marxist Socialism says that only those belonging to a certain class shall live, and Fascism that only those belonging to a certain nation shall live, and, if we say that only those who have a certain bank account shall live or have the right to live, we are emptying our cause of all morality. Universalize this principle and in the end no one will be permitted to play a piano unless he does it in a grand salon, nor shall anyone have the right to drink cocktails unless he is in evening clothes. Such snobbishness is anti-democratic. It is wicked, because it exalts the economic over the human.

Some time ago a Nazi soldier in occupied France took his French wife into a hospital. Seeing a crucifix on the wall, he ordered the nun to take it down. She refused! He ordered her again saying that he did not want his child ever to look upon the image of a crucified Jew. The nun took it down under threats. The father's wish was fulfilled to the letter. The child was born—blind. Now shall we say only those of an economic status have the right to bring children into the world, as the Nazi said that only those of a certain race had a right?

And so we go back to the beginning. If we are only animals and not moral creatures of God, then certainly act like animals; then certainly permit divorces, and a pharmacopœia of devices, prophylactic and eugenic, to cultivate the animal that man is; make it a universe where the ethics of man are no different from the ethics of the barnyard and the stud.

Some day because of the refusal to live for others, to the full extent of our capacity, there will be the haunting conscience. As John Davidson puts it:

Your cruellest pain is when you think of all
The honied treasure of your bodies spent
And no new life to show. O then you feel
How people lift their hands against themselves,
And taste the bitterest of the punishment
Of those whom pleasure isolates. Sometimes
When darkness, silence, and the sleeping world
Give vision scope, you lie awake and see
The pale sad faces of the little ones
Who should have been your children, as they press
Their cheeks against your windows, looking in
With piteous wonder, homeless, famished babes,
Denied your wombs and bosoms.*

In contrast to this pagan view of life, the Christian principles governing the family are these:

Marriage, naturally and supernaturally, is one, unbreakable unto death: Naturally, because there are only two words in the vocabulary of love: "You" and "Always." "You," because love is unique; "Always," because love is eternal. Supernaturally, because the union of husband and wife is modeled upon the union of Christ and His Church, which endures through the agelessness of eternity.

The foundation of marriage is love, not sex. Sex is physiological and of the body: love is spiritual and therefore of the will. Since the contract is rooted not in the emotions, but in the will, it follows that when the emotion ceases, the contract is not dissolvable, for the love of the will is not subject to the vicissitudes of passion. A life-time is not too long for two beings to become acquainted with each other, for marriage should be a series of perpetual and successive revelations, the sounding of new depths, and the manifestation of new mysteries. At one time, it is the mystery of the other's incompleteness which can be known but once, because capable of being completed but once; at another time, the mystery is of the other's mind; at another the mystery is of fatherhood and motherhood which before never existed; and finally there is

* "Testament of John Davidson."

mystery of being shepherds for little sheep ushering them into the Christ Who is the door of the sheepfold.

Love by its nature is not exclusively mutual self-giving, otherwise love would end in mutual exhaustion, consuming its own useless fire. Rather it is mutual self-giving which ends in self-recovery. As in heaven, the mutual love of a Father for Son recovers itself in the Holy Ghost, the Bond of Unity, so too the mutual love of spouse for spouse recovers itself in the child who is the incarnation of their lasting affection. All love ends in an Incarnation, even God's.

Procreation then is not in imitation of the beasts of the field, but of the Divine God where the love that vies to give is eternally defeated in the love that receives and perpetuates. All earthly love therefore is but a spark caught from the Eternal Flame of God.

Every child is a potential nobleman for the Kingdom of God. Parents are to take that living stone from the quarry of humanity, cut and chisel it by loving discipline, sacrifice, mold it on the pattern of the Christ-Truth until it becomes a fit stone for the Temple of God, whose architect is Love. To watch a garden grow from day to day, especially if one has dropped the seed himself and cared for it, deepens the joy of living. But it is nothing compared to the joy of watching other eyes grow, conscious of another image in their depths.

At a time when the first wild ecstasies begin to fade, when the husband might be tempted to believe that another woman is more beautiful than his wife, and the wife might be tempted to believe that another husband would be more chivalrous— it is at that moment that God in His Providence sends children. Then it is, that in each boy, the wife sees the husband reborn in all his chivalry and promises; and in each girl, the husband sees his wife reborn in all her sweetness and beauty. The natural impulse of pride that comes with begetting, the new love that overblooms the memory of a mother's pain as she swings open the portals of flesh, and the joy of linked creatures in each other's fruit, are as so many links in the rosary of love binding them together in an ineffable and unbreakable union of love. Deliberately frustrate these incarnations of mutual love and you weaken the tie, as love dies by its own "too much."

Since nature has associated private property in a very special manner with the existence and development of the family, it follows that the State should diffuse private property through the family that its functions may be preserved and perfected.

If the bringing of children into the world is today an economic burden, it is because the social system is inadequate; and not because God's law is wrong. Therefore the State should remove the causes of that burden. The human must not be limited and controlled to fit the economic, but the economic must be expanded to fit the human.

Since the family by nature is prior to the State, and more sacred than the State, it is the duty of the State to establish such external conditions of life as will not hamper a Christian home life.

The head of the family should be paid a wage sufficient for the family and which will make possible an assured, even if modest, acquisition of private property.

The State should defend the indissolubility of the marriage ties rather than weaken the sancity of contracts, for divorces are in the highest degree hostile to the prosperity of families and of States, springing as they do from the depraved morals of the people.

Such is the Christian position concerning marriage, and one that is, outside of the Church, almost universally misunderstood. It is so often said: "They can divorce and remarry, because they are not Catholics," or "the Catholic Church says that deliberate frustration of the fruits of love is wrong." No! No! No! Divorce and voluntary sterility are not wrong because the Church says they are wrong. Why does the Church say they are wrong? The Church says they are wrong because they are violations of the natural law, which binds all men. There is not one God for Catholics and another God for Hottentots. And all who violate the natural law will be punished by God. A modern pagan is no more free to break God's law than a Catholic.

But why does almost everyone outside of the Church associate the objection to divorce and voluntary sterility with the Church? Because the Church is today alone defending the natural law. If a time ever came when the Church alone defended that natural truth that two and two make four, the world would say: "It is a Catholic doctrine." As the natural law continues to be defended only by the Church, a day will come when Catholics will have to be prepared to die for the truth that it is wrong to poison mothers-in-law and that apples are green in the springtime.

Sometimes nations and people learn through experience that a violation of the natural law is wrong. Such expressions as "crime does not pay," or "you cannot get away with it," or "it pays to live right," mean that, having burned our fingers, we learn that it is in obedience to law, and not in rebellion against it, that we find peace.

No country better illustrates this than Russia. In the first flush of its atheistic Marxian Socialism, it denied the necessity of marriage, established abortion centers, ridiculed fidelity and chastity as a "bourgeois virtue," compared lust and adultery to drinking a glass of water, after which you could forget the glass in one instance, and the person in the other; introduced postcard divorces, which required only that you send a notice that you were no longer living with a certain party, and all obligations thereby ceased.

Now, like a man who violates the natural law by overdrinking and then learns to respect the law through ruined health, so too Russia, by violating the natural law of marriage, has learned through its tragic effects to respect it. In 1934, without even cracking a smile, the Russians repudiated their Communistic immorality by a complete somersault, as the government declared "divorces and remarriage were a petty bourgeois deviation from Communist ideals." Divorces were made more difficult; fees for divorces were increased, so that, "silly girls would think twice before marrying a man with twenty or thirty records." Postcard divorces were abolished. Frequent remarriage after divorce was legally identified with rape and punished as such. Abortion clinics were eliminated; desertion was considered "bourgeois." On November 29, 1941, a tax was imposed on single persons and childless married couples, and a Decree of June 27, 1936, which sought to increase the size of the family, set up a system of payment to parents on the basis of the number of their children. Premiums were paid to mothers for every child after the sixth, and payments increased with the eleventh and subsequent children. Under this law a billion and a quarter million rubles were paid out by the government in the first nine months of 1941.

In 1919, Russia regarded the Christian concept of purity, chastity, and marriage with its unbreakable union, its forbidding of divorce and deliberate control of the number of children in a family, abortion and the like, as "bourgeois virtues." But the Russia of today we find looking on divorce, voluntary sterility, desertion, abortion, and the breakdown of family life as "bourgeois vices." Such change reveals not only the inner inconsistency of Marxian Socialism, but more than that, how Russia has apparently learned something that we in America have not yet learned, namely, that you cannot build a strong nation by disintegrating the family. It is conceivable that, in this respect, Russian family life may stand higher in the eyes of God, than America's.

If some of our "pinks," intelligentsia, fellow travelers, and Reds, who are under orders to bore into Civilian Defense to disrupt this country, would keep up-to-date, they might learn that they are trying to impose upon America the very scum which Russia rejected. History testifies that the prosperity of the State and the temporal happiness of its citizens cannot remain safe and sound where the foundation on which they are established, namely, the moral order, is weakened and where the very fountainhead from which the State draws its life, namely, wedlock and the family, is obstructed by the vices of its citizens.

A downward step in the stability of the family was taken on December 21, 1942, when the Supreme Court of the United States held that a divorce granted in Nevada must be accepted by every other state. There were only two dissenting votes, one by Mr. Justice Murphy, the other by Mr. Justice Jackson. The latter wrote the dissenting opinion, calling the Court's decision "demoralizing."

A few of his many objections against the majority opinion may be cited: (*a*) "The Court's decision . . . nullifies the power of each state to protect its own citizens against the dissolution of their marriages by other states." (*b*) "To declare that a state is powerless to protect either its own policy or the family rights of its people . . . repeals the divorce laws of all the states and substitutes the law of Nevada to all marriages, one of the parties of which can afford a short trip there." (*c*) "Settled family relationships may be destroyed by a procedure that we would not recognize if the suit were one to collect a grocery bill."

The universalizing of easy divorce means that the institution of marriage is slowly degenerating into State-licensed free love.

Legalized polygamy and polyandry are recognized now on condition that husbands or wives, as the case may be, do not harness other wives or husbands together to the coach of their egotism, but that they hitch them up in tandem fashion, or single file. To the extent that the courts disrupt this natural unity of a nation, they will incapacitate themselves for international fellowship. For if we destroy this inner circle of loyalty through disloyalty, how shall we build up the larger international circles of loyalty from which world peace is derived?

Without realizing it we may be getting back to a condition which shocked Cæsar. Plutarch tells us that one day Julius Cæsar saw some wealthy foreign women in Rome carrying dogs in their arms and he said: "Do the women in their country never bear children?" Apparently, even in those days, maternal instincts which should have been directed to children were perverted, in certain cases, to pomeranians.

Men and women of America, raise altars to Life and Love while there is time! If the citadel of married happiness has not been found it is because some have failed to lay siege to the outer walls of their own selfishness. The purpose of war is not for the loot of the private soldier, neither is the purpose of marriage for the loot of life. Like Apostles husband and wife have been sent out two by two, not that they might only eat and drink, buy and sell, but that they might enrich the Kingdom of God with life and love and not with death.

The soil that takes the seed in the springtime is not unfaithful to its messiahship of harvest, so neither may husband and wife play recreant to the responsibilities of love. The fires of heaven which have been handed down to them as an altar have not been given for their own burning, but that they may pass on the torch that other fires may climb back into the heavens from which they came.

Marital love is happiest when it becomes an earthly Trinity: father, mother and offspring, for by filling up the lacking measure of each in the store of the other, there is built up that natural complement wherein their love is immortalized in the offspring. If love were merely a quest or a romance, it would be incomplete; on the other hand, if it were only a capture and an attainment, it would cease to rise. Only in heaven can there be combined perfectly the joy of the chase and the thrill of the capture, for once having attained God, we will have captured something so Infinitely Beautiful it will take an eternity of chase to sound the depths. But here on earth, God has given to those who are faithful in the Sacrament, a dim sharing in those joys, wherein two hearts in their capture conspire against their mutual impotence and recover the thrill of chase in following their young down the roads that lead to the Kingdom of God. It was a family in the beginning that drew a world of Wise Men and Shepherds, Jews and Gentiles to the Secret of Eternal Peace. It will be through the family too that America will be reborn. When the day comes when mothers will consider it their greatest glory to be the sacristans of love's fruit, and when fathers will regard it their noblest achievement to be stewards of love's anointed ones, and when children realize that nature sets no limit on the number of uncles one might have, but that a man can have one mother—then America will be great with the greatness of its Founding Fathers and the greatness of a nation blessed by God.

The Everlasting Man

BY

BERTRAM C. A. WINDLE

PERHAPS MEDICAL MEN do not talk much about "alternatives" today, but not many years ago they were much concerned with this breed of drugs. The name sufficiently defines their supposed action in "altering" the ways of some forward organ and bringing it back to normal paths. Mr. Chesterton's book is a powerful "alternative," and the drug which is its most active ingredient is the reductio ad absurdum. How many mental constitutions will be benefited by partaking of the medicine exhibited, none can say, but no one can study this book without feeling that its powerful argument and close reasoning, as well as its brilliant flashes of wit, ought to be effective in the case of intelligent and impartial persons. "What is the disease?" may be asked after this exordium. An example will explain, and it shall not be one given by Mr. Chesterton, but one taken from a book written by a man who has contributed largely to the advancement of prehistoric studies. It gives his idea of early man.

Man's voice at that time was probably not an articulate voice, but a jabber, a shout, a roar. A shriek or groan of pain is heard—a shout of

From *The Commonweal,* III (Dec. 2, 1925). Reprinted by permission of the Editor.

alarm or a roar of fury. Loud hilarious sounds as of strange laughing are heard; and quick, jabbering, threatening sounds of quarreling. Coughing is heard, but no sound of fear, or hate, or love is expressed in articulate words.

Further on he says a great deal about the hairy individuals who cannot talk; in fact their color, their contours and their entire life story are detailed as if they were a living race of savages on some Pacific isle. Will it be believed that all this story is built upon a few bones and a few stones shaped by the hand of man? That is the kind of fancy set down as fact which Mr. Chesterton attacks in the first part of his book. His sample quotation is from some worthy who tells the world that prehistoric man "wore no clothes"—a strange fancy to draw from the same sources—stones and bones—and regardless of the fact that clothes can hardly have been expected to survive for thousands of years as these harder substances have. What is really known about these earliest men is that they had skulls at least as large as, and often larger than our own; that they could and did make admirably shaped implements out of flint, which proves that they had the hands of trained artisans, and that they believed in a future life since they buried their dead with food, implements and red ochre, all for use in the future life—the last probably that the deceased might parade there sufficiently adorned. Mr. Chesterton declares that the kind of rubbish which he attacks arises from the habit of thinking that early man was a recently evolved animal and reading into his remains what might be imagined to be the activities of such a being. His "alternative" is to say—"Come, let us think of him as an animal and see how what we know of him tallies with that idea."

Let us first of all abstract from disjecta membra, like the Trinil skull whose one-time possessor has received the resounding name of Pithecanthropus erectus. That fragment boldly described by most writers in the English language as belonging to a man, is equally boldly declared to be no more than that of an ape by most writers in the German language; and

as something betwixt and between by most writers in the
French language. Since all these cohorts consist of men of
real fame it must be obvious to any impartial observer that
the bone of contention in question is not one upon which should
be built—as have been built—towers of pretentious information nor "reconstructions," in which, as Mr. Chesterton remarks, "every hair of his head is numbered."

Setting aside such things and coming to what is known as
occurring in sufficient masses to justify a legitimate opinion,
the facts mentioned above appear. Animals, were they? Well,
as the author asks, were monkeys ever known to inter their
dead—still more, to inter them ceremonially—still more, to
bury nuts with them for their use in the forests of the hereafter?

Where again is a monkey, or any other animal, found making the faintest attempt at delineating his fellow creatures?
Nowhere of course, yet the successors of the early men under
discussion adorned the caves of Spain and of South France
with pictures of the animals of their period which excite the
admiration of modern artists; and their envy, when they consider the very inadequate outfit with which these early craftsmen were provided. And as Mr. Chesterton well says, art is
"the signature of man," his hallmark and nothing else.

To talk of an animal in this connection is ridiculous non-
sense; or to suppose that people capable of such ideas as the
immortality of the soul, and of such works as those of the
cave artists, were half beasts, incapable of talking to one another, is so preposterous that one cannot imagine such an idea
occurring to any instructed mind. When one adopts the author's
plan and looks at man as an animal, all the picture is out of
drawing, for man is always man, "and there's an end on't."

I must leave the consideration of the greater part of the first
section of the book merely by saying that in the description
and analysis of so-called primitive religions, philosophies,
devil-worships—the pantheons of Greece and Rome and the
later "mystery" religions, which hung like clouds round the
dawn and early light of Christianity—the reader will find mat-

ter so interesting and so admirably dealt with as to captivate
the mind and fill the imagination. Throughout this and the
second part of the book there is constant evidence of what
someone has said about the author—that he has an unrivaled
power of seeing the obvious. To the superficial reader that
may seem to be anything but a compliment, but it is about as
high as one can well be paid, since it should be clear to all who
think that a very large proportion of writers wholly fail to
see the simple explanations which lie right beneath their noses
in their frantic search for the unusual.

The author's piercing obviousness is displayed in his treat-
ment of the mystery of the Holy Trinity; the Oxford Movement; and comparative anatomy—surely diverse subjects.

Little space is left to speak of part two, incomparably the
more important, since it deals with the second Man. The first
man, of the earth earthy, was a cave-dweller as we know. One
often forgets that the second Man, of the heavens heavenly,
began His career on earth in a cave and that is the striking
thought with which Mr. Chesterton commences his study. I
am sure that no one who reads this study, especially the chapter entitled The Strangest Story, will quarrel with the statement that no more arresting account in brief of the Gospel
has ever been set down in print.

The truth is that it is the image of Christ in the churches that is
almost entirely mild and merciful. It is the image of Christ in the Gospels that is a good many other things as well. The figure in the Gospels does indeed utter in words of almost heart-breaking beauty His pity
for our broken hearts. But they are very far from being the only sort
of words which He utters. . . . The popular imagery carries a great
deal to excess the sentiment of "gentle Jesus meek and mild." . . . While
the art may be insufficient, I am not sure that the instinct is unsound.
In any case there is something appalling, something that makes the blood
run cold, in the idea of having a statue of Christ in wrath. There is
something insupportable even to the imagination in the idea of turning
the corner of a street or coming out into the spaces of a market-place,

to meet the petrifying petrifaction of that figure as it turned upon a generation of vipers, or that face as it looked at the face of a hypocrite.

Mr. Chesterton has, it seems to this reviewer, who is tolerably familiar with his writings, given us the best thing that he has yet produced—for his reception into the Church seems to have implanted in him a new assurance, and in his sayings, a new pungency. It is a book which no thinking man can afford to neglect. It will undoubtedly run into further editions and the opportunity of the next should be taken to correct the over-numerous misprints and omissions of short words which disfigure the present one, and to add an index.

Catholicism and the Future

BY

ROBERT HUGH BENSON

THERE ARE TWO sharply defined views as to the significance of what is called "modern religious thought." The first—that of the thinkers in question—is that it marks the beginning of an epoch, that it has immense promises for the future, that it is about to transform, little by little, all religious opinion, and especially such opinions as are called "orthodox." The second view is that it marks the end of an epoch, that it is of the nature of a melancholy process at last discredited, that it is about to be re-absorbed in the organism from which it takes its origin, or lost in the sands of time. Let us examine these two points of view.

The modern thinkers take their rise, practically, from the

From *The Atlantic Monthly,* CCVI (1910). Reprinted by permission of the Editor.

religious upheaval of the sixteenth century. At that period of Christendom the establishment of the principle of Nationalism in religion struck the first blow against the idea of a final revelation guaranteed by an infallible authority; for the substitution, as a court of appeal, of a written Book for a living voice could only be a transitional step towards the acceptance by each individual, in whose hands the Book is placed, of himself as interpreter of it. Congregationalism followed Nationalism, and Individualism (or pure Protestantism) Congregationalism; and since both the Nation and the Congregation disclaimed absolute authority, little by little there came into existence the view that "true religion" was that system of belief which each individual thought out for himself; and, since these individuals were not found to agree together, "Truth" finally became more and more subjective; until there was established the most characteristically modern form of thought— namely that Truth was not absolute at all, and that what was true and imperative for one was not true nor imperative for another. Further, the original acceptance of the Bible as containing Divine Revelation became itself modified by internal criticism until at the present day we find "modern religion" practically to consist in an attitude of mind, more or less Christian in sentiment, though often indignantly claiming the name; in an ethical system and a belief in progress toward an undefined and only gradually realizable goal, rather than in an acceptance of a series of historical events and of dogmas built upon them.

On the other side stands that body of opinion represented by the Catholic Church, whose tenets are as they have always been—involving, and indeed founded upon, the idea that theology is not, as the other sciences, merely progressive and inductive, but is rather the working out, under Divine guarantees, of a body of truth revealed by God two thousand years ago.

We find then at the present day two mutually exclusive views of the future of religion. To the "modern thinker" it appears certain that the process begun almost instinctively in the sixteenth century, justified as it seems to be by the advance of science and criticism, will continue indefinitely, to the final destruction of the other view. To the Catholic it appears equally certain that the crumbling of all systematic authority down to that of the individual, and the impossibility of discovering any final court in Protestantism to which the individual will bow, is the death sentence of every attempt to find religious Truth outside that infallible authority to whose charge, he believes, truth has been committed. The view of the writer of this paper is emphatically the second of these two.

That the "modern system" has accomplished great things and made important contributions to thought, is of course obvious. Much of the useful work that has been done recently, especially in the direction of popularizing science, as well as of correlating discoveries and compiling statistics, particularly in the sphere of comparative religion, has been done by these independent thinkers. But they have injured their own usefulness by assuming an authority which, by their own profession, they repudiate; and by displaying an almost amazing ignorance of the significance of certain enormous facts, and even of the existence of the facts themselves. Let us enumerate a few.

It is usually assumed by the members of this school that the Catholic Church is the discredited church of the uneducated. It appears to be their opinion that Catholics consist of a few Irish in America and a small percentage of debased Latins in Europe. They seem to be entirely unaware that a movement is going forward amongst some of the shrewdest and most independent minds in all civilized countries, which, if precedent means anything, implies as absolutely sound the prediction of Mr. H. G. Wells that we are on the verge of one of the greatest Catholic revivals the world has ever seen.

When men in France like Brunetière, Coppée, Huysmans, Retté, and Paul Bourget, come forward from agnosticism or infidelity; when Pasteur, perhaps the most widely known scientist of his day, declares that his researches have left him with the faith of the Breton peasant, and that further researches, he doubts not, would leave him with the faith of the Breton peasant's wife; when, in Great Britain, an Irish Protestant professor of biology, a professor of Greek at Glasgow, and perhaps the greatest judge on the bench, in the very height of maturity and of their reputation, deliberately make their submission to Rome; when, within the last few months, the Lutheran professor of history at Halle follows their example; when two of those who are called "the three cleverest men in London," not only defend Catholicism, but defend it with the ardor of preaching friars; when, in spite of three centuries of Protestantism, enforced until recently by the law of the land, the Catholic party in the English Parliament once more has the balance of power, as also it holds it in Germany; when, as is notorious, the "man-in-the-street" publicly declares that if he had any religion at all, it would be the Catholic religion; when a papal legate elicits in the streets of Protestant London a devotion and an hostility that are alike the envy of all modern "leaders of religious thought," and sails up the Rhine into Cologne to the thunder of guns and the pealing of bells; when this kind of thing is happening everywhere; when the only successful missions in the East are the Catholic missions, the only teachers who can meet the Oriental ascetics, the Catholic ascetics—surely it is a very strange moment at which to assume that the religion of the future is to be some kind of ethical Pantheism!

Of course, all these phenomena are not for one moment advanced in support of the truth of the Catholic claim (beyond the fact that they do exhibit a power of recuperation in the Catholic Church which no other religious society has ever displayed in the history of the world), but they are at least a very grave indictment of the extraordinary and fantastic visionariness of the academic mind which professes to deal with facts rather than *a priori* assumptions. Certainly arm-chair thinking is one essential in the pursuit of knowledge, but at least facts must be taken to the arm-chair. Certainly there is in Individualism the truth that each man has a mind of his own, but unless that mind is exercised on objective phenomena as well as on its own inner consciousness, it will end in hopeless limitation, senility, and dreams. As Mr. Chesterton points out, the man who believes in himself most consistently, to the exclusion of cold facts, must be sought in a lunatic asylum.

A second criticism of "modern religious thought" is that it attempts to restrict to terms of a part of human nature that which is the affair of the whole of human nature; it tends to reject all evidence which is not the direct object of the intellect in its narrowest sense. Mr. Arthur Balfour, in his *Foundations of Belief,* put the truth about the matter in a single sentence, to the effect that any system of religion which was small enough for our intellectual capacity could not be large enough for our spiritual needs. Professor Romanes traces the beginning of his return from materialism to Christianity to the discovery of that same truth. He had always rejected, he tells us, the evidence of the heart in his search for religious truth, until he reflected that without the evidence of the heart no truth worth knowing can be discovered at all. The historian cannot interpret events rightly unless he is keenly and emotionally interested in them; the sociologist cannot interpret events adequately unless he personally knows something of passion; and more than all this, the very finest instincts of the human race, by which the greatest truths are arrived at—the principle of the sacrifice of the strong in the cause of the weak, for instance, all art, all poetry (and these are as objective as anything else), chivalry, and the rest—all these things, with their exceedingly solid results in a thousand directions, could never have come into existence, much less have been formulated and classified, unless the heart had followed, not only as well as the head, but sometimes even in apparent and transient contradiction to the head.

Now, modern religious thinkers are undoubtedly acute, but

an acute point is more limited than a blunt one. They are acute, in that they dissect with astonishing subtlety that which they can reach; but they do not touch so many data as can a broader surface; and to seek to test all religion by a purely intellectual test, to refuse to treat as important such evidences as do not come within the range of pure intellect, is as foolishly limited and narrow-minded as to seek to deal with Raphael's Madonnas by a process of chemical analysis. I am not now defending mere emotionalism in attacking mere intellectualism; I am but arguing that man has a heart as well as a head; that his heart continually puts him in touch with facts which transcend, though they need not contradict, mere reason; and, with Romanes, that to neglect the evidence of the heart is to rule an eye-witness out of court because he happens not to be a philosopher or a trained detective. Man is a complex being whose complexity we name Personality; and any system which, like religion, claims to deal with his personality must be judged by his personality, and not by a single department of it. If religion must be brought to the bar and judged, it is the sociologist, rather than the psychologist or the philosopher, who ought to wear the ermine; for the sociologist, at any rate in theory, deals with the whole of man *en masse* and not merely with a selection of him. Our "modern thinkers" are not usually sociologists.

This, then, is the terrible and almost inevitable drawback of the specialistic or academic mind. It has studied so long one particular department of truth, that it becomes imbued with an *idée fixe* that there is no truth obtainable except in that particular department. Certainly these modern critics of supernatural religion are often learned men, and their names accordingly carry weight; yet, in nine cases out of ten, just because of their special knowledge—or rather because of the specialization of their knowledge, and their consequent loss of touch with life and thought as a whole—they are far less competent judges of the claims of religion than are those men with half their knowledge but twice their general experience.

"I have searched the universe with my telescope," cries the astronomer, "and I have not found God." "I have searched the human body with my microscope," cries the biologist, "and I have not found the soul." But did they really expect it? "I have smelt Botticelli's Primavera, and I have detected no odor of beauty; I have licked a violin all over, but I can find in it no passion or harmony."

So far we have glanced at a couple of very serious defects in the modern method; but undoubtedly there are a great many more. For instance, these "modern thinkers" are perpetually assuming the attitude of standing alone in the world as independent and impartial observers; and there is nothing more disastrous than this for a searcher after truth. For none of us is independent or impartial for one instant, ever, anywhere. Each of us begins with a bias, partly temperamental, partly educative, partly circumstantial. Possibly we may succeed in changing our point of view altogether, certainly we all modify it; but we all do, always, occupy some position from which we view the universe. You cannot observe a mountain unless you stand still; and to stand still in one place implies the impossibility of standing still simultaneously in another place.

To take one example of the unhappy effect of not being aware of this very fundamental fact, it is only necessary to glance at biblical criticism. It is notorious that biblical critics who have renounced Christianity's claim, above all others, to approach the Scriptures impartially; but that is exactly what they do not do. They have already decided that the Christian interpretation of the Bible is untrue, that the Scriptures are merely the work of more or less acute or imaginative human minds; and they therefore are obliged—of course unconsciously —to find evidence for their position. They discover, let us say, that in certain points there are apparent discrepancies in the accounts of Christ's resurrection. "You see," they say, "we told you so. The stories do not even agree." A little further on they discover minute and accurate agreement in the various accounts. "You see" they repeat, "it is just as we said. Obviously Matthew has copied from Mark."

Now, I do not desire to blame these critics for taking a biased and prejudiced view of the Scriptures, for I have no doubt that I do myself; but they do deserve blame for pretending that it is not so; and what is worse, their ignorance of their own prejudice is an absolute bar to their making allowance for that prejudice. To use an unpunctual watch is not necessarily to be an unpunctual man; he only is unpunctual who is unaware that his watch is so. And further, in the particular example that we have considered, the "impartial" thinker suffers under a yet further disadvantage, in that he is not vitally interested in what he studies—(how can he be?) And not to be vitally interested is to be short-sighted. Only a lover can understand a love-letter; a father who watches his child drowning, or being rescued, sees more of what is happening, *ceteris paribus,* than another man who chances to be passing by. Love is not always blind; it is in nine cases out of ten far more clear-sighted than indifference, or even than philosophical interest.

To pass on, however, from mere criticism to more positive statement, it is necessary first to glance at the contributions of psychology to the controversy.

These "modern thinkers" rely to a large extent for their conclusions upon this very important and rapidly developing branch of science; and say, quite rightly, that no religious system can stand for the future which does not take into account the new discoveries in this direction. They further add that an enormous number of phenomena hitherto considered as sanctions and evidences of supernatural religion have at last been accounted for by a greater knowledge of man's own inner nature, and that the miracles hitherto advanced by Catholics in support of their claims can no longer bear the weight rested upon them.

There is of course a very solid argument underlying these assertions, but an argument which it would be impossible to discuss within the limits of this paper. There are one or two observations to make, however, which affect the weight of the argument very considerably.

Up to fifty years ago it was commonly asserted by thinkers who were at that particular date "modern," that the phenomena alleged by Catholics to have been manifested at certain holy places, or in the lives of holy people, simply did not take place and never had taken place, because miracles were, obviously, impossible. It was a magnificent and beautiful act of faith to make—an act of faith since it rested upon an unproved negative principle, and a universal principle at that— but it was not science. For within the last fifty years it has gradually been discovered that the events did take place, and still take place, in every corner of the world. For example, the Church has observed for about two thousand years that every now and then a certain human being manifested every sign of being two persons in one, two characters within one organism; further she observed that the use of very forcible and dramatic language administered by authority, if persevered in long enough, frequently, but not infallibly, had the effect of banishing one of these apparent personalities. She called the first phenomenon "Possession," and the second "Exorcism." I suppose that there was no detail of the Church's belief more uniformly mocked than was this. Yet at present there is hardly a single modern psychologist of repute who is not familiar with these phenomena, and who does not fully acknowledge the facts. It is true that "modern thinkers" give other names to the phenomena—"alternating personalities" to the one, and "suggestion" to the other—but at least the facts are acknowledged.

It would be possible to multiply parallels almost indefinitely. Communications made at a distance by other than physical means; phantasms of the living (called by the Church "bilocation"), and of the dead; faith-healing; the psychical effect of monotonous repetition; the value of what the Church calls "sacramentals," that is, of suggestive articles (such as water) in which there is no intrinsic spiritual value; even the levitation of heavy bodies; even the capacity of inanimate objects to retain a kind of emotional or spiritual aroma of the person who was once in close relation to them (as in the case of relics)—all these things, or most of them, are allowed today, by the most materialistic of modern thinkers, if not actually to be established facts, as least to be worthy of very serious and reverent consideration. When men like Sir Oliver Lodge, Professors Richet, Sidgwick, and Lombroso are willing to devote the chief energies of their lives to the investigation of these things, it is hardly possible even for other scientists to dismiss them as nonsense.

Now, I am not concerned here with the discussion of the two main explanations given to these facts by Catholics on the one side, and "modern thinkers" on the other; for each explanation rests on a theory of the entire cosmos. The Catholic who is quite certain that a supernatural world, peopled by personalities, lies in the closest possible relation with this, is perfectly reasonable in attributing phenomena of this kind to those relations. The "modern thinker" who either does not believe in that supernatural world, or who thinks it indefinitely distant (whether in time or space), and is simultaneously absolutely certain that all the phenomena of this world arise from the powers of this world, is equally reasonable in his own superb act of faith. But it is surely very significant and suggestive to find that, whatever the theories may be, at least on the actual facts (professedly the particular province of the "modern thinker"), the Church has been perfectly right and the "modern thinkers" perfectly wrong; and that the Church has not only enjoyed through her "Tradition" (which is another word for continuous consciousness) wider and longer experience, but has actually been more accurate in her observation.

Is it so entirely unreasonable to think that, since she has been right in her facts, she is at least entitled to some consideration with regard to her interpretation of them? For, after all, the Church is not so absolutely idiotic as some of her critics appear to think. She too is really quite aware of the failings of human evidence, of the possibilities of deception, fraud, and error. Her theologians, too, perfectly realize that it is often extremely hard to discriminate between objective and subjective energy, as her rules for the testing of alleged miraculous events show quite plainly. Yet I would venture to assert that not one out of every ten of her psychologist opponents has ever heard of, much less read, the very sensible and shrewd directions on these very points, laid down by Benedict XIV.

And if, finally, it could possibly be shown that the modern psychological theories are correct, and that these abnormal phenomena were, after all, produced by hitherto unknown powers in human nature, there would still remain for discussion the very grave question as to why it was that religion managed to control these powers when every scientific attempt to do so lamentably failed; why it is that even today "religious suggestion" can accomplish what ordinary suggestion, even under hypnotism, cannot; and how it is that certain undisputed facts brought about at Lourdes can only partly be paralleled, certainly not equaled, by all the psychological experimenters in the world. Allow, even, for the sake of argument, that the childlike and pathetic faith in nature, shown by so many infidel doctors in the face of these problems, will one day be justified, and that all the cures of Lourdes will be capable of classification under the convenient term of "law"; yet, even so, how is it that these doctors cannot, even now, reproduce the conditions of that "law" and the consequent cures? It is surely very remarkable that in this instance, as in so many others, things hidden from the "wise and prudent" are revealed to "babes"; and that the rulers and representatives of the "dark ages" managed, and manage, somehow or another, to control and use forces of which the present century of light and learning has only just discovered the existence.

Now, the facts mentioned are surely suggestive, not necessarily of the truth of the Catholic religion, but of the extreme likelihood that that religion, and not a benevolent Pantheism or Immanentism, is to form the faith of the future. Here is a religious society which is not only up to the present the one single religious force that can really control and unite the masses, but also the one single religious body with clear dogmatic principles which can attract at any rate a considerable selection of the most advanced and cultivated thinkers of the age. It is the easiest thing in the world to become an Individualist; it is always easy to believe in the practical infallibility of one's self; one only requires the simple equipment of a sufficiently resolute contempt of one's neighbor; but it is not very easy to believe in the infallibility of someone else. That requires humility, at least intellectual. The craving for an external authority is not, in spite of a popular and shallow opinion to the contrary, nearly so natural to man as a firm reliance upon his own. Yet here the fact remains of this continuous stream of converts into the most practically and theoretically dogmatic society in the world, of converts who through their education and attainments surely should be tempted, if any were tempted, to remain in the pleasant Paradise of Individualism and Personal Popery.

Next, there is the consideration of the undoubted tendency of academic minds to be blind to all data except those which fall under the particular science to which they have devoted themselves; faced by the very sensible and Catholic way of treating man as a feeling as well as a thinking animal, and of taking into account in the study of truth, not only matters of dry intellect, but those departments of knowledge to which access can only be gained by the heart. Thirdly, we glanced at the extraordinary vindication that Catholic experience has received, at least with regard to facts, from the most modern of all modern sciences.

There remain, however, several other signs of the future which must not be disregarded.

Mr. Charles Devas, in his brilliant book, *The Key to the*

World's Progress, points out by an argument too long to reproduce here that, so far as the word progress means anything, it denotes that kind of development and civilization which only makes its appearance, and only is sustained, under the influence of Catholicism. He traces with great sociological learning the state of comparative coma in which "ante-Christian" nations seem always involved; the exuberance of life, for both good and evil, that bursts up so soon as Catholicism reaches them (whether directly, as in the case of Africa and Spain, or indirectly, by imitation, as in the case of Japan); and the activities of corruption that, together with the dying impetus of the old faith, keep things moving, so soon as Catholicism is once more abandoned, as in the case of France. In regard to both virtues and vices, the ante-Christian, the Christian, and the post-Christian nations are clearly and generically distinguished. The object of his book is to indicate the strong probability of the truth of a religion which exhibits these effects; but it is also of service in indicating the probability that that same religion should accompany and inspire progress in the future as it has in the past.

A large and very significant detail in this process lies in the effect of Catholicism on the family. Not only are Catholics more prolific than other nations (directly in virtue of Catholic teaching on the subjects of divorce and race-suicide), but the Church also is the one body that resolutely regards the family, and not the state or the individual, as the unit of growth. And it is simply notorious that where the family is overshadowed by the state, as in the case of Sparta, or by the individual, as in the case of every really autocratic despotism, no virtues of patriotism or courage can avail to save the country from destruction. It seems astonishing that our modern arm-chair philosophers seem unaware of the significance of all this with regard to the future of religion.

Another sign of the times surely lies in the province of Comparative Religion. Our more recent researches have taught us, what the Church has consistently known and maintained, that there are great elements of truth common to all religions. Once more our modern theorists have leaped forward enthusiastically, and acclaimed the discovery of this very ancient fact as a proof that Catholicism is but one among many faiths, and no truer than the rest. "Here," they say, "are contemplation and asceticism in Buddhism; a reverence for the departed among the Confucians; the idea of a Divine Redeemer in Mithraic worship; and sacramentalism among the American Indians." Very prudently they do not lay stress upon the eternal despair of Buddhism, the puerilities of the Confucians, or the religious brutality and materialism of the Indians. They select those elements of sanity and truth that are distributed among the various faiths of the world, those elements which appeal to *all men,* in some degree, and find in their diffusion an argument against the one faith that holds them all!

"Comparative Religion" has done, in fact, an enormous service to the claims of Catholicism. It has revealed to the world exactly that phenomenon which should be looked for, *ex hypothesi,* in a Divine Revelation, namely, that the creed which embodied that Revelation should contain, correlated and organized into a whole, all those points of faith of which each merely human system of belief can catch and reflect but one or two. For it is inconceivable that, if there is to be at any period of history a revelation from God, many points in that revelation should not have been anticipated, at least partly and fragmentarily, by groups of human minds for which, later, that revelation was intended. In rejecting Catholicism, then, our "modern thinkers" are rejecting not merely one Western creed, but a creed that finds an echo of nearly every clause, under some form or another (from the doctrine of the Blessed Trinity down to the use of holy water), in one or another of all the great world-religions that have ever controlled the eternal hopes of men. And yet our "modern thinkers" seriously maintain that the religion of the future is to be one which contains none of these articles of what is, diffusedly, practically universal belief!

One last indication of the future of Catholicism lies in its power of recuperation. Not only is it the sole religion which has arisen in the East and has dominated the West, and now once more is reconquering the East; but it is also the one religion that has been proclaimed as dead, over and over again, and yet somehow has always reappeared. Once "the world groaned to find itself Arian"; now Arius is enshrined in the text-books, and the Creed of Athanasius is repeated by living men. Once Gnosticism trampled on the ancient faith everywhere; now not one man in a hundred could write five lines on what it was that the Gnostics believed. Once the Turks overran Africa and Spain and threatened Christendom itself; now the nations trained by Christianity are wondering how they can best dispose of Constantinople. Nero thought he had crucified Christianity in Peter; now Peter sits on Nero's seat. Once Elizabeth disemboweled every seminary priest she could lay hands on, and established Protestantism in Ireland. Now Westminster Cathedral draws immeasurably larger congregations than Westminster Abbey, where Elizabeth lies buried; and Catholic Irishmen are dictating in an English Parliament how the children in English schools are to be educated.

At every crisis in the history of Christendom—at the captivity of Avignon, the appearance of Luther, and the capture of Rome in 1870—it was declared by "modern thinkers" that Catholicism was discredited forever. And yet, somehow or other, the Church is as much alive today as ever she was; and that, in spite of the fact that she is, in her faith, committed to the past and to doctrines formulated centuries before modern science was dreamed of.

Is there any other society in the world, secular or sacred, that has passed through such vicissitudes with such a burden on its shoulders, and survived? For it is a burden which she cannot shift. She cannot, at least, "recast her theology" and drop unpopular or unfashionable dogmas (as can all sects which claim merely human authority), and yet live. Yet who can doubt that she is more of a force today than all the most accommodating denominations around her. She has lived, too, in the tumultuous rush of Western life, not in the patient lethargy of the East. She has struggled, not only with enemies in her gate, but with her own children in her own house. She has been betrayed over and over again by the treachery or wickedness or cowardice of her own rulers; she has been exiled from nearly every country which she had nursed into maturity; she has been stripped in nearly everyone of her lands of all her treasures; she has finally seen her supreme sovereign on earth driven to take refuge in his own house by the children of the men whom she raised to honor. And yet on her secular side she has seen every kingdom of Europe rise and fall and rise again; she has seen a republic give birth to a monarchy or an empire, and an empire yield to a republic; she has seen every dynasty fall except her own; she has seen, in religious affairs, every "modern" sect—whose one claim to efficiency lies in its modernity—fail to keep pace with herself who has the centuries on her shoulders; and she remains today the one single sacred and secular commonwealth which has faced the revolutions and the whirling religions of the West and has survived, with a continuity so unshaken that not one of her enemies can dispute it, and an authority which they can only resent; she reigns even in this day of her "discredit" over more hearts than any other earthly sovereign, and more heads than any philosopher of the schools; she arouses more love and obedience on the one side and more hatred or contempt on the other than the most romantic, the most brutal, or the most constitutional sovereign, sage, or thinker ever seen.

I called this characteristic of her Recuperation. I call it now Resurrection, for this is the "sign of the Prophet Jonas" to which her Divine Founder appealed. And yet our "modern religious thinkers" are dreaming in their arm-chairs of another "creed"!

BIOGRAPHICAL NOTES

BARING

Maurice Baring (1874-1945), fourth son of the first Lord Ravelstoke, was born in London. He served in the diplomatic service, was a news correspondent in the Russo-Japanese and Balkan wars, and served in World War I as a Major in the Royal Air Force. One of England's well-known converts, he is a member of the Chesterton-Baring-Belloc trio, made famous by Gunn's Royal Academy picture, "A Conversation Piece." As a writer Baring is most placid, with little of the belligerent Catholicism of his partners. His immense erudition made him an eminent authority on Russia; his versatility produced such books as *Cat's Cradle, Daphne Adeane, The Coat Without Seam, Diminutive Dramas, Selected Poems, The Russian People, The Puppet Show of Memory, Dead Letters,* and *Lost Lectures.*

BELLOC

Hilaire Belloc (1870-   ), a stalwart leader of the Catholic Revival, excels as an historian, controversialist, essayist, poet, and novelist. This pupil of Cardinal Newman is irrevocably linked with G. K. Chesterton: together they form what Shaw has called "that four-legged animal, The Chesterbelloc." As militant Catholics, they shared a hatred of many modern isms and an energy to write prolifically in varied fields. Belloc is an essayist of genius, writing endlessly in a masterly Anglo-Saxon style. His published works fill several shelves; of his essays, *On Nothing, Essays of a Catholic, A Conversation with a Cat and Other Essays, This, That and the Other, On Everything,* and simply *On* are typical.

BENSON

Robert Hugh Benson (1871-1914) came of a family noteworthy in both clerical and literary quarters. His father was the Anglican Archbishop of Canterbury; A. C. Benson and E. F. Benson, his brothers, were distinguished writers. Educated at Eton and Cambridge, he took Anglican Orders, but entered the Catholic Church in 1903 and was ordained at Rome in 1904. During the following ten years he literally "burned himself out" in preaching, lecturing, and writing. His literary

342 A Century of the Catholic Essay

works became channels of his missionary zeal. Of his novels, *Lords of the World, Come Rack! Come Rope!, By What Authority?* and *The Necromancers* are justly popular. *The Friendship of Christ* and *Christ in His Church,* both theological works, are filled with the same vitality.

BROWNSON

Orestes Brownson (1803-1876), controversialist, essayist, and philosopher, was born in Stockbridge, Vermont, and reared on a neighbor's farm. Except for elementary schooling, his education consisted of wide reading. His early career was marked by much shifting, but like John Dryden's, each step was progressively toward orthodoxy. Brownson, in 1826, was ordained a Universalist minister; later he became a Unitarian; was associated with the Brook Farm experiment; and finally became a Catholic in 1844. His magazine, *Brownson's Quarterly Review,* was the first American periodical to attain wide circulation in England. His dynamic, noisy prose—exemplified even in *The Convert, Essays and Reviews* and *The American Republic*—has, with some warrant, earned for him the label of "a vociferous and truculent propagandist." In very recent years, however, the truly imposing stature of Brownson is being recognized, the latest study being Theodore Maynard's *Orestes Brownson: Yankee, Radical and Catholic.*

CHESTERTON

Gilbert K. Chesterton (1874-1936), "the last knight of modern Christendom," was, like his collaborator, Hilaire Belloc, a leader of unforgettable gusto and versatility. Born in London, he was educated at St. Paul's School, the Slade School of Art, and King's College. Journalist, critic, story-teller, biographer, dramatist, poet, and illustrator—he was a giant intellectually as well as physically. G. K., always a crusader, entered the Church in 1922 and wrote vigorously in defense of Christian teachings. In all his uncountable writings he is an inimitable stylist: a brilliant ironist, a master of surprise and paradox, and the creator of dazzling newness for the oldest orthodox ideas.

COLUM

Padraic Colum (1881-   ) was born in Ireland, but has lived a large part of his life in the United States. He is married to Mary (Maguire) Colum, one of America's best women critics. Along with James Stephens and Thomas MacDonagh he founded the *Irish Review,* and with Yeats and Lady Gregory he helped establish the Irish National Theater. His stories, dramas, and poems deal in the main with Irish legend; his essays, with Irish life and with literary criticism. *Wild Earth, The Road Round Ireland, Three Plays* and *The Legend of St. Columba* are among his more popular works.

CONRAD

Joseph Conrad—Theodor Jozef Konrad Korzeniowski (1857-1924)— was the son of a Polish political exile. In 1886 he became a British subject, learned English, and joined the merchant service. Never ostensibly Catholic in his writings, he is one of the world's supreme novelists of the sea and a consummate realistic artist. The whole world knows his *Lord Jim, Nostromo, The Nigger of the Narcissus, Chance,* and *Victory.*

DALY

James J. Daly (1872-   ), educator and author, received his education at St. Ignatius College in his native Chicago and at St. Louis University. When only eighteen he was already a Jesuit, and was ordained to the priesthood in 1905. For some time he served as literary editor of both *America* and *Thought,* and, since 1931, as professor of English in the University of Detroit. *Boscobel and Other Rimes* appeared in 1934. His essays in *A Cheerful Ascetic and Other Essays* and in *The Road to Peace* are noteworthy for their scholarly finesse.

DAWSON

Christopher Dawson (1889-   ) is unquestionably one of the greatest living philosophers of history. Receiving his M.A. at Trinity College, Oxford, he studied as a private pupil of the Swedish economist Gustave Cassel, before returning to Oxford for postgraduate work in history and sociology. He was received into the Church in 1914. The central idea of his work is that "the creative element in human culture is spiritual." Not all of his writing makes easy reading, for Dawson is a synthesist with a reticent style. Two volumes of his proposed "History of Culture" have thus far appeared: *The Age of the Gods* and *The Making of Europe.* Other important books are *Progress and Religion, The Modern Dilemma, Enquiries into Religion and Culture,* and *Judgment of the Nations.*

DE VERE

Aubrey De Vere (1814-1902), son of the poet Sir Aubrey De Vere, was born in County Limerick, Ireland. At Trinity College, Dublin, he gave himself chiefly to the study of metaphysics. In 1838 he entered Oxford. Both Wordsworth and Newman, with whom he was intimate, left their marks on his work and character. In 1851 he followed Newman into the Church. De Vere was throughout his life active in the Celtic revival. At the special request of Pope Pius IX, he wrote *May Carols,* in honor of the newly-defined doctrine of the Immaculate Conception. As a letter writer and as a critical essayist, he ranks high. His important prose is found in *Essays, Chiefly on Poetry* and *Essays, Chiefly Literary and Ethical.*

DUNNE

Finley Peter Dunne (1867-1936) is throughout America known as "Mr. Dooley." After doing newspaper work in Chicago, his birthplace, he went to New York where he eventually became editor of *Collier's Weekly.* The "Dooley" sketches (says one authority) have made Dunne our greatest humorist after Mark Twain. He is associated in spirit with the Petroleum V. Nasby–Artemus Ward–Bill Nye group of writers. Despite the fact that their Irish dialect makes them a bit difficult for modern readers, many of his pieces are most appropriate to present-day problems. The choice sketches have been edited by Elmer Ellis in *Mr. Dooley at His Best.*

EDEN

Helen Parry Eden (1885-   ), English poet, critic and story-teller, was educated at Roedean School and studied painting under Bryan Shaw and Rex Cole at King's College, London. She won the history scholarship of Manchester University and the Vice-Chancellor's prize for verse. In 1909 she, with her husband, embraced Catholicism. Both her poems and essays have rightfully merited for her the title, "a modern medievalist": her poems on children and on Christmas have all the simplicity and faith of Merry England; her stories and sketches, likewise, have the color and quaintness of an age long gone. *Bread and Circuses, Whistles of Silver,* and *Poems and Verses* are representative of her best work.

FAIRBANKS

Charles Bullard Fairbanks (1827-1859) "belongs to the high manner of a century agone." Born in Boston, he found his way through Unitarianism and Episcopalianism into the Catholic Church. Ill health kept him from attaining his goal of the priesthood; he died while a seminarian. The identity of the author of the delightfully urbane *My Unknown Chum* was long hidden under his *nom de plume,* "Aguecheek." In his *Manuscripts and Memories* Father Michael Earls, S.J., has clearly established the identity of Fairbanks and Aguecheek.

FEENEY

Leonard Feeney (1897-   ), poet and essayist, was born in Lynn, Massachusetts. In 1914 he entered the Jesuit Novitiate and after his ordination in 1928 spent two years studying at Oxford, England, and the Sorbonne, Paris. He is at present the literary editor of *America*. Father Feeney's volumes of poetry—*In Towns and Little Towns, Riddle and Reverie, Boundaries,* and *Song for a Listener*—reveal his whimsical and daring ideas as well as his flare for distinctive versification. His essays and sketches, whether light and humorous as in *Fish on Friday,* or profound and simple as in *You'd Better Come Quietly,* are charmingly informal. Father Feeney has written one biography, *An American Woman,* the life of Elizabeth Seton.

GILL

Eric Gill (1882-1942), English sculptor, engraver, and philosopher of art, was educated privately and at Chichester Art School. Some of his best artistic work is seen in the Stations of the Cross at Westminster Cathedral, in the grave monuments of Francis Thompson and G. K. Chesterton, and in the war memorial at Leeds University. In 1913 Gill was received into the Church, together with his wife and family. His writings on art, economics, and culture are replete with challenging Catholic ideas presented in an equally challenging style. Among his books are numbered *Songs without Clothes, Money and Morals, Beauty Looks after Herself,* and his inimitable *Autobiography.*

GILLIS

James M. Gillis (1876-   ), popular editor, author, and lecturer, was reared in Boston and received his early training in the famed Latin School of that city. After attending St. Charles College, Baltimore, and St. Paul's College, Washington, he secured his doctorate in theology from the Catholic University of America in 1903. Previously, in 1898, he had joined the Paulist Fathers and was ordained three years later. For twelve years Father Gillis was a member of the Paulist mission band. Since 1922, armed with a vast store of literary and historical acumen, he has been editor of *The Catholic World.* Direct, concise and pungent, his editorials have been termed the pièce de résistance of each issue of that cultural magazine. One of Father Gillis' most influential books is *False Prophets.*

GUINEY

Louise Imogen Guiney (1861-1920), daughter of the Civil War soldier-patriot, General Patrick Guiney, was born in Boston. Despite early recognition by the Boston literati, her work bulks comparatively small, for the death of her father demanded that she support her mother and an aunt. She served as postmistress in suburban Auburndale and later as cataloger in the Boston Public Library. After 1901 she worked in the Bodleian Library, Oxford, and began there a large anthology of the work of the Recusant Poets. Christopher Morley has justly called her "one the rarest poets and most delicately poised essayists this country has reared." Among her works are found *Happy Ending* (poems), *Lovers' St. Ruth's and Other Tales, Hurrell Froude,* and two volumes of essays, *The Goose Quill Papers* and *Patrins.*

HARRIS

Joel Chandler Harris (1848-1908), the universally beloved "Uncle Remus," was born near Eatonton, Georgia. Already while serving as a typesetter's apprentice, he began to immerse himself in Negro folklore. For many years he did invaluable editorial work on the Atlanta *Constitution,* and later founded his own *Uncle Remus's Magazine.* A few weeks before his death, Harris embraced the Catholic faith of his wife and children. Unfortunately, perhaps, his essays have been overshadowed by the Uncle Remus stories, yet they abound with the same noted gaiety and common sense.

JOHNSON

Lionel Johnson (1867-1902), British critic and poet, was educated at his beloved Winchester and at New College, Oxford. In his early twenties he became a convert to the Catholic Church. His powers as a critic were quickly recognized on publication of *The Art of Thomas Hardy.* His poetry reveals his love for his newly-found Faith and for the Irish cause. Indeed, his early efforts presaged a great career for young Johnson, but his frail physique cut his life brief. Both his poetry and prose have a classic quality that place him permanently among England's best minor authors.

KILMER

Joyce Kilmer (1886-1918), author of the popular poem "Trees," was born in New Brunswick, New Jersey. Through reading Patmore, Thompson, and Chesterton, he found his way into the Church in November, 1913. His zeal led him to attempt, not an English Catholic revival, but an American one. When World War I broke out, he immediately enlisted and as a member of the famed Fighting 69th was killed in the summer offensive of 1918. His death was a great loss to American Catholic letters. Robert Holliday, his biographer, has edited his essays, poems, and letters.

KNOX
Ronald Knox (1888-   ), England's modern Dean Swift, was educated at Eton and Balliol where he won the Hertford and Ireland scholarships. For five years he served as Anglican chaplain at Trinity College, Oxford; converted to Catholicism in 1917 and ordained priest in 1919, he became in 1925 Catholic Chaplain at Oxford. Here he soon was regarded as one of England's eminent apologists. His essays and sermons (and even his detective stories) are marked by "his urbanity, his exuberance, and his ability for satire." To these achievements he has added that of translating the New Testament into splendid idiomatic English. *Reunion all Around, A Spiritual Aeneid, Essays in Satire, Broadcast Minds,* and *Barchester Pilgrimage* are but a few of his works.

LEWIS
Dominic Bevan Wyndham Lewis (1894-   ) must not be confused with the radical novelist-painter, Wyndham Lewis, to whom "D.B." is unrelated. While yet a student at Oxford, "D.B." enlisted in the infantry and saw action in World War I. Shortly after the war, he entered the Church. He is acclaimed as one of Britain's foremost humorists. Along with his friend, J. B. Morton, he conducted for many years a popular column, first in the London *Daily Express* and later in the *Daily Mail,* under the pseudonym of "Beachcomber." His warm, scintillating wit fills his historico-biographical studies of Villon, Louis IX, Charles V, and Ronsard. A rich cultural background is required to appreciate the now pungent and sophisticated, now bizarre and whimsical humor of such volumes as *A London Farrago, On Straw,* and *Welcome to All This.*

MacMANUS
Seumas MacManus (1869-   ), Irish-American scholar and novelist, is a leader of the Celtic revival. Practically his only formal education was obtained in a mountain school of his own County Donegal, Ireland, which he has glorified with his folk-tales and with his original sketches of Irish life and history. In 1901 he married the Irish poet, Ethna Carbery. He has for years been a resident of the United States, lecturing here annually in many cities. His voluminous writings include *The Donegal Wonder Book, Story of the Irish Race, Lad of the O'Friels* and *Bold Blades of Donegal.*

MADELEVA

Sister Mary Madeleva (1887-   ) is beyond dispute the finest poet-nun in contemporary literature. Born in Cumberland, Wisconsin, the daughter of Frederick and Lucy Wolff, she graduated from St. Mary's College, Notre Dame, Indiana, in 1909. After joining the Holy Cross Sisters she obtained her M.A. from Notre Dame University and, in 1925, her doctorate from the University of California. All her life she has been an educator and since 1934, President of her Alma Mater, St. Mary's. Her poetry, alive with religious mysticism, is vivid, personal, and often passionate. Her essays are never pedantic, but are models for all scholars who wish to avoid a dry-as-bone approach. *Chaucer's Nuns and Other Essays* and *Pearl: A Study in Spiritual Dryness* represent her best prose studies.

MARTINDALE

Cyril C. Martindale (1879-   ) became a Catholic on leaving Harrow and entered the Society of Jesus. Later, at Oxford, he took the highest classical honors. He was ordained priest in 1911. He has written ceaselessly, even while a prisoner of the Nazis in Denmark. Few English writers have done so much as he in rebuilding Catholic apologetics around the doctrine of the Mystical Body. His position as a lecturer and hagiographer is likewise a most enviable one. *The Vocation of Aloysius Gonzaga, Toward Loving the Psalms, The Life of Robert Hugh Benson,* and *What are Saints?* are part of the long list of his writings.

MEYNELL

Alice Meynell (1850-1922) was the mother of the English Catholic literary revival as truly as Newman was its father. She it was who, in her literary salon, gave direction to the movement with her saying, "Let us be of the center, not of the province." She was educated at home, but spent a large part of her girlhood in Italy. As a young lady she found her way into the Church. With her husband, Wilfred Meynell, she was the saviour of Francis Thompson. Such poems as *Renouncement* rank, says Alfred Noyes, among the supreme sonnets ever written by a woman. Her essays, distinctive like her poems in their intellectuality and restraint, are cherished pieces. All of her work is permeated with a high degree of mysticism and religious emotion.

NEWMAN

John Henry, Cardinal Newman (1801-1890), mainspring of the Catholic Revival, was born the son of a London banker. Always studious, he entered Oxford and later took Orders in the Anglican Church. His preaching at St. Mary's, Oxford, revitalized religion at the University and led to the Oxford Movement, of which he was the guiding spirit. In October, 1845, he embraced Catholicism and was ordained a priest less than two years later. The rest of his life was occupied with educating, writing, preaching, and conducting controversy. In 1879 Pope Leo XIII elevated him to the cardinalate. Misunderstood, he failed in his attempt to establish a Catholic University of Dublin, but this failure led to the composition of that classic statement of a liberal education, *The Idea of a University*. His *Apologia* remains, alongside St. Augustine's *Confessions,* the world's greatest autobiography. Newman, one of the most courageous religious leaders of all time, is hardly equaled as a literary master. Perfection of form, intellectuality, and superb psychological insight grace all he wrote or spoke.

NOYES

Alfred Noyes (1880-   ), English poet and essayist, was educated at Oxford. In 1913 he gave the Lowell Lectures at Harvard; from 1914-1923 he taught modern English literature at Princeton. Two years later he entered the Church. Noyes is unrivalled in modern literature as a writer of stirring ballads. His national epic, *Drake,* and his epic of science, *The Torch-bearers,* merit for him the title of the "twentieth-century Homer." As an essayist he has given contemporary prose a rare poetic touch and an even rarer balanced critical judgment. Some of his finest prose is found in *The Opalescent Parrot, The Unknown God,* and *Pageant of Letters.*

O'FAOLÁIN

Séan O'Faoláin (1900-   ), Irish novelist and biographer, was born in Cork and as a young lad participated in the Irish Revolution. After graduating from the National University of Ireland, he became a Commonwealth Fellow at Harvard in 1926 and a John Harvard Fellow in 1929. His first writing was done in Gaelic. His novels— *A Nest of Simple Folk* and *Bird Alone*—and his biographies—*The King of Beggars* and *The Great O'Neill*—are distinguished by his "gift for sharp characterization and atmosphere." He is a member of the Irish Academy of Letters.

PATMORE

Coventry Patmore (1823-1896), "the laureate of wedded love," was born in Essex and privately educated. His family's financial reverses constrained him to seek employment in the library of the British

Museum. Not until his marriage to a well-to-do lady was he able to cultivate the life of scholarly leisure he had been seeking. Identified with the Pre-Raphaelites, he counted among his best friends Browning, Tennyson, Ruskin, and Alice Meynell. In 1854 he published *The Angel in the House;* after his entry into the Church in 1864, his poetry took on a deep spirituality. His theme, developed in *The Unknown Eros,* and very likely completed in the lost *Sponsa Dei,* is married love as a symbol of the divine. His essays, brilliant discourses on his philosophy of love, are collected under the titles *Religio Poetae, The Rod, the Root, and the Flower,* and *Principle in Art.*

REPPLIER

Agnes Repplier (1858-   ), "the dean of American essayists," did not learn to read until she was sent to Sacred Heart Convent in her native Philadelphia, at the age of ten. Here she received her only formal training, though she holds honorary doctorates from the universities of Pennsylvania, Yale, Columbia, and Princeton. In 1911 she won the Laetare Medal of Notre Dame and in 1935 the gold medal of the National Institute of Arts and Letters. Miss Repplier is master of that fine literary form, the genuine familiar essay, and belongs to the genteel tradition of Lamb and his *Elia.* Her *Books and Men, The Fireside Sphinx, Americans and Others* include some of the most polished essays in English. She has likewise written several biographies—*Père Marquette, Mère Marie of the Ursulines,* and *Junípero Serra*—and an autobiography, *In Our Convent Days.*

SHEED

Francis J. Sheed (1897-   ), translator, publisher, and author, was born in Sydney, Australia. Preparing for the bar, he studied at Sydney University. Here he won many medals and scholarships, including the Coutts Scholarship for Literature, the Harris Scholarship for Jurisprudence, and the Wentworth Medal twice. For a number of years he was Master of the Catholic Evidence Guild, both in London and in Sydney. He is married to Maisie Ward, daughter of the late Wilfrid Ward. Together the Sheeds founded the publishing house of Sheed and Ward. No one has done more than they in popularizing the Catholic Revival and in attempting to unify it as an international movement. Two of Mr. Sheed's most widely read books are *A Map of Life* and *Communism and Man.*

SHEEHAN

Canon Patrick A. Sheehan (1852-1913), Irish priest-novelist and essayist, was pastor of Doneraile. He graduated from Maynooth Col-

lege and was ordained in 1875. His considerable leisure time he
devoted to writing essays—scholarly and practical—and novels—pronounced by Tolstoy the greatest of the early twentieth century. The
range of thought and the spiritual insight so admired in the novels
My New Curate, The Triumph of Failure, Luke Delmege, and *The
Blindness of Dr. Gray,* likewise distinguish his essays in *Parerga* and
Under the Cedars and Stars.

SHEEN

Fulton J. Sheen (1895-   ), philosopher and orator, was born near
Peoria, Illinois, in the heart of America's great Midwest. After
completing studies at St. Viator's College, at St. Paul (Minn.)
Seminary, and at Catholic University, he won the Cardinal Mercier
Prize for International Philosophy—the first time Louvain had given
it to an American. Leaving Louvain, Monsignor Sheen joined the
faculty of St. Edmund's College, Ware, England; in 1926 he returned
to Catholic University as professor of scholastic philosophy. Though
his books, *God and Intelligence in Modern Philosophy, The Life of
All Living, Religion without God,* etc., are widely read, his influence
as the greatest of the Catholic Hour speakers is immeasurable. His
sermons—whether read or listened to—are vital, possessing striking
imagery, poetic fancy, and sound thought.

SPALDING

John Lancaster Spalding (1840-1916), first bishop of Peoria, Illinois,
was born at Lebanon, Kentucky, of one of the oldest Catholic families
in America. He studied at Louvain and Rome, and was ordained
priest in 1863. Consecrated bishop of Peoria in 1877, he soon revealed
his unusual powers both as an administrator and as a spiritual and
cultural leader. Interested especially in Catholic higher education, he
was largely instrumental in establishing the Catholic University of
America. Though known for his verse and lectures, Bishop Spalding
is best remembered for his inspirational essays *Means and Ends in
Education, Opportunity and Other Essays,* and *Education and the
Higher Life.*

STODDARD

Charles Warren Stoddard (1843-1900), poet and traveler, was born
in Rochester, New York, and as a boy moved with his family to
California. There he contributed verse to *The Golden Era,* the
magazine edited by Mark Twain and Bret Harte. In 1867 Harte
edited a volume of Stoddard's poems. That same year Stoddard embraced Catholicism. For some years he taught at the University of

Notre Dame and at the Catholic University of America. Always physically weak, he traveled widely in order to sustain his health. His journeyings to the South Seas supplied material for the delightful *South-Sea Idyls.*

TALBOT

Francis X. Talbot (1889-   ), editor, historian, and scholar, attended St. Joseph's College in his home city of Philadelphia. In 1906 he entered the Society of Jesus and was ordained to the priesthood in 1921. For thirteen years he was literary editor of *America,* and in that position organized The Catholic Book Club and the Spiritual Book Associates. From 1936 to 1944 he was editor of *The Catholic Mind*; from 1936 to 1939, editor of *Thought*; and until recently editor-in-chief of *America.* Most of his essays are uncollected, having appeared in various periodicals and in the *Encyclopedia Britannica.* His masterpiece to date is *Saint Among Savages,* a life of St. Isaac Jogues.

THOMPSON

Francis Thompson (1859-1907), "the poet of the return to God," is one of the most authentically religious poets in English literature. Born of convert parents, he studied at Ushaw and at Owens College, Manchester. Despondent because of his unfitness for either the priesthood or the medical profession, he went to London to launch himself in a literary career. His tragic existence there and his rescue by the Meynells constitute one of the great stories of literary history. *The Hound of Heaven, Sister Songs,* and other poems are loved by believer and unbeliever alike. Undoubtedly one of the finest pieces of subjective criticism in modern letters is his monograph on Shelley. Thompson the poet is visible in nearly all his prose.

WINDLE

Sir Bertram Windle (1858-1929) studied medicine at Dublin University. For some years he was dean of the Medical Faculty of Birmingham University, where he held the Chair of Anatomy and Anthropology. From 1904-1919 he was President of Queen's College (now University), Cork, Ireland. In the nineteen-twenties he was professor of anthropology at St. Michael's College and special lecturer on ethnology in the University of Toronto. Sir Bertram became a Catholic in 1883. In *The Church and Science* he did pioneer work in the field of philosophy-science. This book was awarded the Gunning Prize by the Victoria Institute in 1917. For his labors in education and science Sir Bertram was given many high honors, academic and papal.